Adversity and Challenge in Life
in the New Germany and in England

Anglo-German Foundation for the Study of Industrial Society

The Anglo-German Foundation for the Study of Industrial Society was established by an agreement between the British and German governments after a state visit to Britain by the late President Heinemann, and incorporated by Royal Charter in 1973. Funds were initially provided by the German government; since 1979 both governments have been contributing.

The Foundation aims to contribute to the knowledge and understanding of industrial society in the two countries and to promote contacts between them. It funds selected research projects and conferences in the industrial, economic and social policy areas designed to be of practical use to policymakers.

Titles include:

Bernhard Blanke and Randall Smith (*editors*)
CITIES IN TRANSITION
New Challenges, New Responsibilities

John Bynner and Rainer K. Silbereisen (*editors*)
ADVERSITY AND CHALLENGE IN LIFE IN THE NEW GERMANY AND IN ENGLAND

Maurie J. Cohen (*editor*)
RISK IN THE MODERN AGE
Social Theory, Science and Environmental Decision-Making

Stephen Frowen and Jens Hölscher (*editors*)
THE GERMAN CURRENCY UNION OF 1990
A Critical Assessment

Eva Kolinsky (*editor*)
SOCIAL TRANSFORMATION AND THE FAMILY IN POST-COMMUNIST GERMANY

Howard Williams, Colin Wight and Norbert Kapferer (*editors*)
POLITICAL THOUGHT AND GERMAN REUNIFICATION
The New German Ideology?

Anglo-German Foundation
Series Standing Order ISBN 0–333–71459–8
(*outside North America only*)

You can receive future titles in this series as they are published by placing a standing order. Please contact your bookseller or, in case of difficulty, write to us at the address below with your name and address, the title of the series and the ISBN quoted above.

Customer Services Department, Macmillan Distribution Ltd
Houndmills, Basingstoke, Hampshire RG21 6XS, England

Adversity and Challenge in Life in the New Germany and in England

Edited by

John Bynner
Centre for Longitudinal Studies
Institute of Education
London

and

Rainer K. Silbereisen
Friedrich Schiller University of Jena
Jena
Germany

in association with
ANGLO-GERMAN FOUNDATION
FOR THE STUDY OF INDUSTRIAL SOCIETY

First published in Great Britain 2000 by
MACMILLAN PRESS LTD
Houndmills, Basingstoke, Hampshire RG21 6XS and London
Companies and representatives throughout the world

A catalogue record for this book is available from the British Library.

ISBN 0–333–73375–4

First published in the United States of America 2000 by
ST. MARTIN'S PRESS, INC.,
Scholarly and Reference Division,
175 Fifth Avenue, New York, N.Y. 10010

ISBN 0–312–22427–3

Library of Congress Cataloging-in-Publication Data
Adversity and challenge in life in the new Germany and in England / edited by John Bynner and Rainer K. Silbereisen.
p. cm.
Includes bibliographical references.
ISBN 0–312–22427–3 (cloth)
1. Social change—Germany. 2. Germany—Social conditions—1990– 3. Social change—England. I. Bynner, J. M. II. Silbereisen, R. K. (Rainer K.), 1944– .
HN445.5.A63 1999
306'.0943—dc21 99–25943
CIP

This book is printed on paper suitable for recycling and made from fully managed and sustained forest sources.

10 9 8 7 6 5 4 3 2 1
09 08 07 06 05 04 03 02 01 00

Printed and bound in Great Britain by
Antony Rowe Ltd, Chippenham, Wiltshire

Contents

PART 3 Social change and social exclusion

Postscript

Preface

Before the end of communism, England and what was then West Germany had similar capitalist political systems and demand economies, in contrast to East Germany with its communist political system and command economy. On the other hand, West and East Germany shared common cultural traditions, underpinning similar social institutions, and distinct from those of England. All three countries have been subjected, over the last forty years to the same globalization processes arising from technological change and international media expansion, and all have local variations reflecting different cultural traditions. Against this backcloth, the unification of East and West Germany offers what has been described as a 'quasi-experimental' opportunity to investigate the effects of social change, with England serving as a non-German comparator.

Although much research has been carried out in Germany on the effects of German re-unification, with few exceptions the results are published only in German. This book also sets out to increase knowledge of this work among English-speaking audiences. The workshops on which it is based provided the opportunity for German and English social scientists with an interest in factors affecting the human life course to exchange ideas and information on the effects of social change, with particular focus on the effects of German re-unification. The workshops took place in London in December 1995 and in Jena in July 1996. Jena, with its mixture of Prussian and Weimar historical roots, immediate communist past, and post-communist economic expansion, was a particularly appropriate setting for the second workshop, exhibiting the effects of transformation close-up.

The workshops were supported by grants from the Anglo-German Foundation, the United Kingdom Economic & Social Research Council and the German Research Council. City University in London and the University of Jena gave support in the form of meeting facilities and administrative backup. John Bynner and Sheila Young of the Social Statistics Research Unit, City University organized the London workshop and Matthias Reitzle, Annette Weise and Kathrin Mueller of the Department of Developmental Psychology, University of Jena, organized the Jena workshop. Verona Christmas managed Anglo-German liaison and contributed to the editing of the German papers. Jane Horne typed the final version of the manuscript.

The workshops brought together over twenty social and behavioural scientists, thirteen of whom, besides the editors, have written the chapters (sometimes with co-authors) for this book: Karen Evans, Ken Roberts, Nick Emler, Gisela Trommsdorff, Matthias Reitzle, Klaus Boehnke, Ingrid Schoon, Hans Bertram, Bob Coles, Martin Diewald, Bernhard Nauck, Nick Emler and Fred Vondracek. Other contributors to the workshops, who were unable to take part in both of them, or, through circumstances beyond their control, were prevented from completing all stages of the writing were: Stefan Hormuth, Sabine Walper, Uta Meier, Simone Kreher, Frank Coffield and Claire Wallace.

The book is an edited collection of papers providing theoretical analysis and empirical results of research conducted primarily in Germany. The papers were presented first in preliminary form at the London workshop with the aim of defining a research agenda for the study of the effects of German re-unification. They were then developed further for a final examination of research issues and findings in Jena. Following the Jena workshop, revised papers were produced, in some cases following further analysis of new and existing data sources. Peer review was then conducted with each author reading at least one other author's chapter. Consolidated comments, with guidelines for rewriting, were then supplied by the editors. Following further detailed revisions, final drafts were produced by the authors and edited for the book.

JOHN BYNNER
RAINER K. SILBEREISEN

Notes on the contributors

Hans Bertram is Professor of Micro-Sociology, Humbolt University, Berlin. His research interests are in family development and the life course. He has previously directed the Deutsches Jugendinstitut (Youth Research Institute). Together with Gil Noam he directed the Summer Institute on Family Development, Life Styles and Life Events at Humbolt University, Berlin (1994), at Harvard University, Cambridge, MA and Craigville, MA (1995), funded by the German American Academic Council.

Klaus Boehnke, has been Professor of Socialization Research and Methodology in the Department of Sociology of Chemnitz University of Technology since 1993. He has previously held positions as Assistant and Associate Professor in the Department of Education of the Free University of Berlin. His research interests are in youth research and its methods, especially political socialization and youth and the media.

Petra Butz is a research scientist at the Free University of Berlin and at Chemnitz University of Technology. Her main research interest is youth development in the context of societal change.

John Bynner is Professor of Social Sciences in Education and Director of the Centre for Longitudinal Studies at the Institute of Education, London University, where he directs the National Child Development Study and the 1970 British Cohort Study. He has previously held positions at City University, the Open University and the Office of Population Censuses and Surveys. He directed the ESRC 16–19 Initiative research programme, which included the Anglo-German comparative study, Youth and Work in England and Germany. His research interests are in the field of transition to adulthood, basic skills, social exclusion and longitudinal research methodology.

Bob Coles is Senior Lecturer in Social Policy at the University of York. He has a long-standing interest in youth studies and the impact of social policies on youth transitions, as developed in his recent book, *Youth and Social Policy: Youth Citizenship and Young Careers*. His recent work has focused on youth policy and vulnerable groups, including research on the spatial concentration of vulnerability. With the Barnado's charity he has recently been evaluating a range of youth intervention projects.

Martin Diewald is a researcher at the Centre of Sociology and the Life Course of the Max Planck Institute for Human Development, Berlin, where he heads the project East German Life Courses after Unification. His main research interests lie in life course research, social stratification and career mobility, living arrangements, family development and social networks and the transformation of the former GDR.

Nicholas Emler is Professor of Social Psychology at the Department of Experimental Psychology, Oxford University. He was previously Professor of Social Psychology at Dundee University and has visiting positions at Johns Hopkin's the University of Tulsa, Baltimore, USA, the Ecole des Hautes Etudes en Sciences Sociales in Paris, Bologna University and Geneva University. His main research interest is in youth and adolescence in which he has focused on questions about delinquency, patterns of social participation, the development of political identity and economic socialization.

Karen Evans is Professor of Post-Compulsory Education in the University of Surrey's School of Educational Studies. She has directed numerous research studies on aspects of youth transition, learning and work in Britain, the European Union and Canada. Her interest in international and comparative studies is reflected in her recent books, *Technical Training Mastery in the Workplace* and *Shaping Futures: Learning for Competence and Citizenship*.

Klara Foti is Senior Research Fellow at the Institute for World Economics of the Hungarian Academy of Sciences, in Budapest, Hungary. She has been a Visiting Fellow in the Institute of Development Studies at the University of Sussex, and has a special interest in labour market issues, defending her 'Kandidatura' thesis on labour markets in the '*Visegrad*' countries (Czech Republic, Hungary, Poland, Sovakia) in 1994. Recently she has participated in international projects, comparing employment situations in East European countries.

Bernhard Nauck holds the Founding Chair of Sociology at Chemnitz University of Technology. Previously he has been a professor of Sociology in the Universities of Wuppertal, Cologne, the Paedagogishe Hochschule in Weingarten and, until 1988, was Head of the Department for Family Research at the State Institute for Early Education and Family Research, Munich. Since 1992 his research interests have been in family, life-span, demography, social indicators, migration, inter-ethnic relations, cross-cultural and international comparisons.

Matthias Reitzle is Associate Professor in the Department of Developmental Psychology at the Friedrich Schiller University of Jena, Germany. His research interests concern individual development and social change, personality development and problem behaviour in adolescence, and the school-to-work transition.

Ken Roberts is Professor of Sociology at the University of Liverpool. His recent books include *Poland's First Post-Communist Generation* and *Surviving Communism: Young People in Armenia, Georgia and the Ukraine.* He took part in the Anglo German Foundation sponsored comparative study on Youth and Work, co-editing one of the books reporting the study: *Transition to Work in England and Germany*. Since 1992 he has directed a series of studies of young people in former communist countries. His main current projects are based in Russia and Kazakhstan.

Ingrid Schoon is Senior Lecturer in Psychology at City University, London. Her research interests lie in the study of human potential, psychological, social and physiological development across the life-span. Her study of creativity and talent includes her book, *Creative Achievement in Architecture*. Recent projects have been funded by the Leverhulme Trust, INTAS and the UK Economic and Social Research Council (ESRC). She is a visiting Research Fellow at the Bartlett School of Architecture, University College London, and is a research associate in the Centre for Longitudinal Studies, Institute of Education, London University.

Rainer K. Silbereisen holds the Chair of Developmental Psychology at the Friedrich Schiller University of Jena, Germany, and is Adjunct Professor of Human Development and Family Studies at the Pennsylvania State University, USA. His main research interests concern human development across the life-span. He had conducted longitudinal studies on such topics as problem behaviour in adolescence, effects of early adversities on the timing of psychosocial transitions, the impact of social change on adolescent development, acculturation among immigrants, and bio-behavioural aspects of adolescent development. He is editor of the *International Journal of Behavioral Development.*

Gisela Trommsdorff has held the Chair of Developmental Psychology at Konstanz University since 1987. She has held visiting professorships at Keio University, Tokyo; Kansai University, Institute for Statistical Mathematics, Tokyo and has been invited to be a research fellow by the Japanese Society for the Promotion of Science. Her present research is on socio-emotional development in cultural context, and on subjective theories and values of children in different cultures. She is presently a member of several scientific and advisory committees – Scientific Council of the Remiers-Stiftung, Scientific Council of the Socio-economic Panel and Scientific Council for Science and Research for the Minister of Culture and Science of the Federal State of Bavaria.

Fred W. Vondracek is Professor of Human Development at the Pennsylvania State University, where he has been since 1969. His main research interest is career development seen as an integral component of life-span human development, and, with Richard Lerner and John Schulenberg, he has written a book on this subject: *Career Development: A Life-Span Developmental Approach*. He serves on the editorial boards of the *Career Development Quarterly*, the *International Journal of Behavioral Development*, the *Journal of Adolescent Research* and the *Journal of Vocational Behavior*.

Introduction

The life course and social change

John Bynner and *Rainer K. Silbereisen*

The latter part of the twentieth century has been characterized by rapid social change, exemplified by the social, economic and political restructuring of the former communist countries of Eastern and Western Europe. In the case of the reunification of Germany, transition from communism occurred largely through the transfer of West German institutions of government and business to East Germany. This may have seemed a relatively straightforward basis for re-union because of the common language and culture. In reality, for East Germans the speed of change constituted a dramatic rupture with the assumptions and expectations of the immediate past. For West Germans the cost of the whole enterprise soon converted some of the initial enthusiasm for re-unification into concern about the economic and social consequences of the change.

The central theme of this book is that one of the main effects of radical social change of the kind that took place in Germany is its impact on life course trajectories. We are especially interested in the ways in which new conditions impacting early on, and later in life, affect the life course subsequently. In Glen Elder's terms (Elder, 1987), the life course trajectory represents the pattern of an individual's life from birth to old age. It comprises the succession of key developmental transitions, such as the move from school to work or having the first child, on which external influences arising from social change may be expected to have an impact. Life courses encompass the socializing influences on individuals stemming from family, school, the peer group and the workplace. They also embrace the 'developmental timetable' – first kiss, first job – whereby individual differences in biological make-up and acquired characteristics, dictate the timing and form of transitions (Silbereisen, in press).

Adverse conditions affecting the life course may be identified with disadvantaged social and family backgrounds and disruptions in developmental processes, which impinge on the acquisition of skills and values. They may both precede and arise from the response to social change. Thus the growth of unemployment following economic restructuring – accentuated in East Germany after re-unification – brings adversity of various forms in its wake: income is reduced, expectations and aspirations may be dashed and the family put under strain. Yet at the same time, the likelihood of losing a job will be affected by adversity in life as it was before the change, including disadvantaged family circumstances and poor skills. Challenges reside in the ability of individuals to resist the adverse features of social change in achieving desired social roles – qualified worker, spouse – and personal fulfilment in all the domains of life, or to gain advantages from them. New opportunities may be offered through education, training and the labour market for individuals to move their lives in more rewarding directions. The issue for social science is what determines the ability to adapt to, be defeated or be unaffected by the challenge of social change. Is it founded in the individual's position in the social and institutional structure, in individual aptitudes, in the particular social contexts (at work or at home) in which the challenge arises, or in a combination of all three?

Radical social change of the kind experienced through German re-unification also needs to be contextualized in terms of the cultural traditions prevailing in the places where it is experienced. Cultural differences are often confused with the effects of change itself. Thus on many indicators East Germany, before and after re-unification, shared more culturally with Northern Germany than with Southern Germany and communism merely produced variations in, or sometimes reinforced, the values that were already there. Thus geography is an important factor to set against social change. The effects of re-unification also need to be separated from those arising from social change more generally. Thus all societies are evolving on a near continuing basis in response to political and economic movements, with periodic upheavals brought about by rapid transformation of the kind that the collapse of communism produced. To analyse the specific effects of unification, we therefore need to take account of longer-term societal trends. This introduces questions about the differential effects of social change on cohorts and generations in different places and in different periods, i.e. we need to take account of its location in socio-historical time (Alwin, 1994).

Social change in Germany and England

Transition to employment

The end of the 1980s was a period of considerable economic and social change for all industrialized countries. The new technology revolution, which began in the 1970s, reached its culmination in a massive restructuring of Western European industry, with large numbers of people losing their jobs or having to retrain for new ones. Under such globalization pressures, the job market for 16-year-olds in Britain collapsed and apprenticeship places in Germany were much reduced. Some countries were able to use their educational and training institutions to buffer (particularly young) people against these effects. The corporatist approach to training, for example, as embodied in West Germany's dual system (mirrored in certain respects in the apprenticeship schools attached to the state enterprises of East Germany) offered an extended period when young people could be prepared for occupations and employment opportunities. A critical element of the system was the role of the 'social partners' (politicians, employers and trade unions) in taking responsibility for ensuring that every young person was properly prepared for employment. East Germany's greater economic instability, following unification, meant that the protection for young people available in West Germany was not so prominent there. In many respects the experiences of East German youth mirrored those of young people in England, particularly in the old industrial areas of the North and Midlands, where traditional industries associated with coal and steel collapsed (Bynner and Roberts, 1991; Evans and Heinz, 1994).

Adaptation of the life course to social change typically lags behind its occurrence. It took fifteen years for British young people leaving school at 16 (the minimum leaving age) to realize the advantages of extended education and vocational preparation. By the end of the 1980s staying on rates, which in the middle of the 1970s had been one-third of the age cohort, had risen to over two-thirds. Similar lags can be seen in East Germany's adjustment to re-unification, with each new generation getting more like its Western counterparts.

In West Germany, of course, all young people were required to stay in touch with education, either through apprenticeship or through various kinds of alternative training up to the age of 18. Unemployment as such, without any education and training, was not therefore a real option. Young West German's experience of it tended to come later. However, much of the remedial training available as an alternative to apprenticeship carried a liability. In Germany there was something of a stigma attached to young people who had not gained occupational qualifications through the conventional apprenticeship route, which could lead to problems in gaining acceptance from an employer later. It is perhaps not surprising that in an Anglo-German comparative study of young people in 1988, the most common aspiration one year from the time of interview for young people in Germany involved in a training scheme was to gain an apprenticeship place. For young people similarly engaged in England the desire was to get a job (Bynner and Roberts, 1991). In East Germany the lack of first apprenticeship places, and then jobs to follow them, put the whole transition system under strain, which raises questions of whether the unadulterated form of the 'dual system' imposed on East Germany was appropriate for the young people's needs.

Apart from the effects on immediate employment prospects and the looming problem of 'social exclusion' of those young people without qualifications, which became increasingly evident through the 1990s, there were other trends accompanying the new technology revolution. The traditional routes to adult identity, from particular socio-economic (social class) backgrounds, to post-16 routes through training or into employment direct, gave way to more complex developmental patterns. Young people were increasingly having to 'negotiate their way' through education, training and employment, until they were able to find their niche in the new labour market (Evans and Heinz, 1994; Evans and Furlong, 1998). Such developments, characteristic of risk societies (Beck, 1986), passing through late modernity (Beck, Giddens and Lash, 1994), challenge particularly the German notion of identity based on occupation, 'I am what I am trained to be'.

Problems in gaining entry to the adult labour market in risk societies not only damage economic prospects, but impact on the quality of life in other ways. Effective communities depend on common purpose and high levels of trust. Their absence hinders the accumulation of social capital on which education and the skills needed in employment build (Coleman, 1988).

The weakening of the ties associated with the structural determinants of class, location and gender on adult identity outcomes, placed much emphasis on ideas of risk and individualized responses to it. The young person, and to a certain extent his or her family, therefore needed to create their own opportunities in response to changing circumstances (Bynner, Chisholm and Furlong, 1997). On the other hand, structural determinants continued to play a part, but more in holding up certain kinds of movement, rather than inhibiting them completely, as had been the case in the past. Thus class, gender, race, locality, nation continue to have a role in shaping the individual life course. It is better, therefore, to see the trends displayed from the 1970s through the 1980s and now into the 1990s as representing a steady shift from one set of socio-cultural assumptions to another about the way the life course is shaped. Clearly, the world of the 1990s is radically different from the world of the 1960s, but not perhaps quite as much as some advocates of post-modernity argue (Furlong and Cartmel, 1997).

Family life

Besides the longer-term changes associated with employment, another characteristic of the 1970s and 1980s was the changing nature of family structure and family life. In all Western European countries (though with marked variation between them) there was a shift towards single-parent households, marriage break-up and reconstitution (Utting, 1995). This was accompanied by the development of a strongly independent single lifestyle, which included postponement of marriage and family commitment, especially among the more highly educated. Thus the age of marriage rose steadily through the 1980s in all countries, as did the age of having the first child.

This trend was not so obvious in Eastern Europe generally and in Eastern Germany in particular. Though in common with Northern European countries single parenthood was a frequent occurrence, by Western standards early marriage and childbearing was the norm. This was part of the quite different pattern of arrangements in communist countries whereby state-funded childcare at no cost to the user was available to enable both parents to work. In fact, there was positive encouragement to have children young, when the parents were still completing their vocational training. What childcare was not provided by the state was supplied by grandparents, who usually had a central role in bringing up the children. The assumption was that after a relatively short break for childbirth mothers would return to full-time employment. Consequently one of the most dramatic effects of the end of communism in East Germany was the breakdown in these arrangements and the expectations that went with them. Parents who wanted to work had to fund childcare privately, and those without the resources to do this – through unemployment for example – were forced increasingly into the traditional role of child carer (Trommsdorff and Chakkarath, 1996).

The family is one institution that has undergone change, yet at times of social change the family remains perhaps the strongest bastion of security and support, especially for children – providing the basis of 'intergenerational solidarity' against adversity. Such a finding has been demonstrated repeatedly in countries passing through the transformation from communism to market economies, in which every area of adult life and work, in leisure and parenting was placed under strain (Roberts and Jung, 1995).

On the other hand, the impact of post-communist transformation was sharply differentiated between different socially defined sections of East German society, which reflected those in Germany as a whole. Women with children, for example, found their roles and opportunities radically altered. Their expectations of paid employment and the automatic provision of state-funded childcare were confronted in the unified Germany by having to make more private choices between work and family and to accept personal responsibility for meeting the costs. The extension of adolescence through continued dependency of young people on their parents, as the demands for the extension of education and training increased, therefore placed new strains on the family. This was exacerbated by the increasing uncertainty about prospects in the labour market, and the widening experience of unemployment. The consequence was increased vulnerability to social exclusion of certain groups who in the past had been absorbed into adult society relatively easily.

Extended dependency was more easily accommodated in former communist countries, with comprehensive state provision, and consequently little need to defer having children. As we have noted earlier, generally by Western standards people in East Germany married and had children young and did so at much the same age. This contrasts with the considerable variability in these status changes in Western Germany, which are closely linked with education and occupation.

Generational shifts

Although many people of retirement age in East Germany fared reasonably well after the end of communism, those still seeking an active role in employment faced difficulties. In sharp contrast with other countries undergoing the transformation, the retired generation in East Germany gained the benefit of West Germany's generous pension provision. But apart from this favourable aspect of the change, adults generally had more difficulty in making the adjustments to new circumstances than young people. For adult cohorts the challenges to assumptions and expectations, the reduction in other forms of state provision – especially childcare – and the rising cost of maintaining a family were the most difficult to bear. As we move down the age-groups, resistance to change on the part of the older generation gives way to young people's more responsive approaches to the world as it is rather than the world as it was under communism.

Much of this value shift was underway in the younger generation well before the fall of communism. In consequence the younger cohorts were, in many respects, more in tune with the requirements of the market economy, especially in relation to the use of media and information technology. They had little desire for a return to the old institutions and statuses of East Germany, whereas for substantial elements of the adult population, 'rebuild the wall' was a not uncommon refrain. In the new open political systems of Eastern and Central Europe, support for political parties with a background in the Communist party that preceded them, is a significant consequence of the uncertainties, if not unhappiness, that the extremely radical nature of the post-communist changes produced (Roberts and Jung, 1995).

For the younger generations in all European countries life courses are changing so rapidly that there is far less continuity from the past to the present generations in the values and behaviour that underpin political affiliation, pointing to the possibility of a growing 'generation gap' (Inglehart, 1990). This provides another threat to the building of social capital, which requires community cohesion within and across the generations (Coleman, 1988). However, in analysing such effects we always need to be aware both of the diversity of forms in which social capital is generated in different communities – north–south, east–west, and the overriding significance of familial ties in resisting the potential for conflict. As some of our authors conclude, it is questionable whether social capital theory, which assumes that the generation of human capital depends on community-based social ties, has much application in Germany. This is because belief in the importance of such ties is a value common to all communities.

Life course processes and outcomes

In Glen Elder's terms the life course can be viewed as the product of sets of interactions between individual agency, biological predisposition, and the social structure – comprising the socially and culturally defined structural categories and institutions through which the individual passes. The process is in part linear but also to a degree cyclical in the sense that experience later in life can affect achievements earlier on: for example (a vicious circle) unemployment can lead to a loss of skill among those whose skills are poor to begin with (Bynner and Parsons, 1988). The process may also display, across cohorts, changes in the relative balance between the social structure and personal agency effects – individualization – and widening gaps between socially defined groups – polarization.

Life course outcomes at a particular stage in life are the values, behaviour, statuses that form the core of personal identity. They are the products of the influences that shape, and are shaped by, individual (and collective) agency. Broadly, a sequence can be identified whereby the individual, equipped with certain personal and family resources (human, social, cultural capital and individual biology), interacts with the social structure, at a given point in time and in a particular location. He or she passes through the various social institutions of society (family, education, employment and community), moving into the particular social roles, and statuses, which define adulthood. The mediating factor is the social relationships encountered in these different institutional settings. Again human agency dictates that we are both influenced by and influence these relationships in moving towards particular outcomes.

Characterizing the long-term processes involved is the idea of 'accumulated risk'. Adverse outcomes in adulthood can frequently be traced back to adverse conditions earlier on. Such conditions may accompany birth and the early years of life, but they will also arise from personal choices much later on. Failure to surmount them may effectively lead to marginalization in relation to employment, community, family life and citizenship, the main consequence of which is social exclusion.

Finally there are objective and subjective features of these processes, which need to be taken into account. For example, in relation to the impact of a social change (cohort comparison), such as German reunification, how the individual appraises the situation may be just as important as the objective features of the damage or improvement the change brings. Clearly the reduction in income produced by unemployment may impact in a direct sense on life quality, but as important is the subjective evaluation of this change, and how the individual internalizes it. A further set of factors here are control beliefs, which are the extent to which the individual believes they are in a position to control events rather than be controlled by them.

Such processes leading to particular life course outcomes were a major focus of the workshops. Outcomes included achieved labour market statuses, realization of talent, and attitudes and values. Labour market statuses can be conceived in terms of the products of 'human capital', which provide the best prospect of survival in a world of shifting opportunities (Becker, 1975). Attitudes and values are likely to exhibit more fluidity in response to changing contexts, e.g. changing political orientation and affiliation or growing xenophobia. They may also reflect the deeper and more lasting dispositional or 'personality' characteristics that supply the main means of adapting to or resisting social change. This emphasizes again the centrality of subjective appraisal in driving the ability to adapt: 'How is the change affecting me personally?'

Social change demands particular kinds of motivation and aspirations to meet its challenges. The personality attributes associated with success under communism were likely to be at just as much of a premium under capitalism. So even though party membership could be temporarily a liability under the new system – in the professions for example – in the longer term, such membership of elites could prove advantageous. The *nomenclatura* (government officials), of communist states, especially, provided the degree of continuity which was essential to the successful transformation of East German society. But such personal attributes as motivation, self-efficacy and resilience were also of course at a premium.

The book

In a variety of ways this book displays the main facets of the effects of social change on the life course processes and their outcomes. The comparative analysis between Germany – East and West – and England brings in the role of institutions and what happens to them under such transformations as German re-unification. The chapters are grouped under the following headings: *Systems, structures and social life; Social change and individual development; Social change and social exclusion.*

Systems, structures and social life

Karen Evans compares the systems of education and training in England and Germany before and after re-unification and the cultural assumptions lying behind them. Her analysis displays the huge differences that exist between Germany and England with respect to this part of their institutional structure, contrasting the relatively clear-cut *trajectories* characteristic of German transitions with the more varied and complex *pathways* to employment in Britain. However, ironically, following the breakdown of the East German system, and its inadequate replacement by the West German model, young East Germans shared much in common with their British counterparts at the beginning of the 1980s. This is when the traditional routes to employment were closed off to British young people, as the youth labour market effectively collapsed.

Ken Roberts and Klara Foti pick up some of the same themes, examining the question of regulation versus deregulation of young people's entry to employment, which in Germany reaches its most institutionalized form. They identify parallel experiences in a number of ex-communist countries to set against those of East Germany. The question arises as to whether the highly regulated German education and employment system is appropriate for the new market economies, or whether the *laisser-faire* polices of the British kind are inevitably going to replace them

Nick Emler's chapter on interpersonal relations of different groups in different settings demonstrates the consequences of such changes. He examines conversational and other forms of encounters in education, at home and at work, demonstrating the relative impoverishment in this respect of unemployed young people. University students had the most social interactions and consequently the best opportunities to accumulate the social capital on which successful entry to employment increasingly depends.

Social change and individual development

Papers under this heading turn to the topic of individual development under different circumstances and the effects of social change. Gisela Trommsdorff provides a detailed theoretical analysis of the life courses processes involved in re-unification particularly as they impacted on children. She stresses the centrality of subjective appraisal in driving the ability to adapt. Her chapter is followed by Matthias Reitzle and Rainer Silbereisen's account of findings from their follow-up study of East and West Germans' attitudes one year and six years after reunification. They demonstrate a faster move towards convergence of attitudes between East and West among the younger than the older age groups.

In Klaus Boehnke's paper we see the darker side of the attitude picture through his East and West German comparison of the effects of economic difficulties on 'xenophobia' in young people. Against expectation such attitudes were found to be strongest among the upwardly mobile working class – *hauptschule* students. Against prediction from Elder's theory, the quality of family relations provided no discernible buffer against the xenophobia. Rather it appears that the xenophobic young people saw foreigners as threatening their improving prospects.

Finally we move to England with Ingrid Schoon's account of the development of scientific talent in young people, using data from Britain's large-scale birth cohort studies. Scientific talent is revealed early, appearing to signify a distinctive type of personality, with strong roots in biological make-up. But its realization in terms of a scientific career is strongly conditioned by social structural factors and societal characteristics. Thus compared with boys, English girls with scientific talent are less likely to pursue a scientific career. In Germany, because of the greater commitment to technological education, both sexes are more likely to realize their scientific talents in scientific careers than in England.

Social change and social exclusion

The last four papers bring social structural factors back into the picture Hans Bertram uses large-scale surveys of family values, conducted across the whole of Germany, to test predictions that the take-up by young people of post-materialist ideology has changed fundamentally traditional solidarities within the family, especially obligations of parents toward their children and obligations of children towards their parents. He shows that the sense of responsibility remains as strong as ever, suggesting the family can be largely impervious to generational value shifts produced by social change.

Martin Diewald shows from his comprehensive cross cohort analysis of survey data from East and West Germany the centrality of 'control beliefs' in adaptation to the changes brought about through re-unification. These beliefs were much stronger in the more highly educated *Gymnasium* sections of East German youth, who as young adults also experienced the least unemployment after the fall of communism. He sees these findings as reflecting continuity of success under communism with success under the new market economy, based on the ability of certain privileged strata to adapt.

Bernard Nauck looks at the other end of the East German spectrum, using survey data from different areas to examine the effects of unification on the economic well-being of children. He demonstrates the increasing propensity to 'poverty risk' factors in such groups as single parents. In pursuing hypotheses from Coleman's social capital theory that the generation of human capital is community-based, he finds little evidence of their applicability in Germany. Rather he reveals cultural differences in family values broadly corresponding with the divide between southern, Catholic Europe and northern, Protestant Europe. In many areas these are more significant than the East–West distinctions associated with the presence or absence of communism.

Finally Bob Coles broadens the discussion on vulnerability to the adverse effects of social change, looking across Europe at groups who suffer particularly from them. He highlights such vulnerable groups as young people growing up in care, homeless young people, disabled young people and teenage parents. It is in these groups particularly that the protection young people need is missing. The intergenerational solidarity to be found in families serves both to mediate the effects of change and provides the essential buffer against its worst outcomes.

The new research agenda

In response to this scenario of challenges and threats to previous certainties in the life course, social and behavioural research is developing new perspectives. As Fred Vondracek points out in the concluding chapter, these stress the way in which biological maturation relates to the development of psychological functions and competencies and how both the latter interact with changing social environments. He argues the case for 'life-span career development theory', which explains careers in terms of the dynamic interactions between individual personality (temperament, motivations, goals and values), social context and social change.

Social change incorporates ideological, technological, and economic ecologies within societies, which exert their influence on individual development via a number of mechanisms in the family, in social life and in education and the workplace. This perspective, developed by such writers as Elder, Bronfenbrenner, Brooks-Gunn and many others (for example, see Moen, Elder and Luscher, 1994; Robins and Rutter, 1990; Reitzle, Vondracek and Silbereisen, 1998), offers a means of studying the processes and mechanisms involved within a single coherent research framework. Such a perspective needs to embrace the formation and function of social roles and statuses, social relations and the way they are mediated through the distinctive institutions, which each society has constructed to manage life course transitions. It is this final set of interactions which lies at the heart of the more comprehensive and integrated comparative analysis which is needed for the study of the effects of social change.

What are the key methodological components of such a strategy? The different studies reported in the book help to draw them out. First and most important is the need to capture the dynamics of the relationship between social change and development. This requires longitudinal data, i.e. data collected from the same individuals over an extended period of time. Second, there is the need to set the social change against the secular societal trends which are taking place. This requires the monitoring of successive cohorts and collecting data contemporaneously with the change itself.

Most important of all is to capture the variability within societies and across societies in the experience of response to change. This demands representative sampling and control groups for comparison either within a society or across two or more societies. Finally adaptation, as with any developmental or life course process, is difficult to model by the standard linear methods of multivariate analysis. We need to elaborate our approaches to embrace contextual factors through hierarchical modelling. We also need to use qualitative enquiry (social biographical methods) to help disentangle the complexity and different cultural origins and meanings of life course processes in different places, and the effects of social change upon them.

For a variety of reasons the research reported here on the effects of German re-unification could only match this model to a limited extent. The impossibility, with rare exceptions, of gaining access to comparable East German life course data before the Berlin Wall came down within a properly worked out research design meant that most data collection began after the event. There was a large investment of funds into research on the effects of re-unification, but the speed with which it had to be implemented inevitably reduced the chances of building in cross-national or other kinds of controls. However the large-scale databases comprising multiple cohorts that existed in West Germany, which have subsequently been extended to the East, provide an effective means of contextualizing many features of the change.

Taken as whole, therefore, the book provides rich insights into the effects of social change on the life course, as experienced particularly in Germany, and points the direction in which the social change research agenda of the future needs to go.

References

Alwin, D. F. (1994) 'Taking time seriously: studying social change, social structures and human lives', in P. Moen, G. H. Elder and K. Luscher (eds), *Linking Lives and Contexts: Perspectives on the Ecology of Human Development.* Washington DC: American Psychological Association.

Banks, M., Breakwell, G., Bynner, J., Emler, N., Jamieson, L. and Roberts, K. (1992) *Careers and Identities.* Buckingham: Open University Press.

Beck, U. (1992) *Risk Society*, London: Sage.

Beck, U., Giddens, A. and Lash, S. (1994) *Reflexive Modernization: Politics, Traditions and Aesthetics in the Modern Social Order.* Cambridge: Polity Press.

Becker, G. S. (1975) *Human Capital.* Washington, DC: National Bureau of Economic Research.

Bynner, J. and Parsons, S. (1998) *Use it or lose it: The impact of time out of work on literacy and numeracy skills.* London: Basic Skills Agency.

Bynner, J. and Roberts, K. (eds) (1991) *Youth and Work.* London: Anglo-German Foundation.

Bynner, J. Chisholm, L. and Furlong, A. (eds) (1997) *Youth, Citizenship and Social Change.* Aldershot: Ashgate.

Coleman, J. S. (1988) 'Social capital in the creation of human capital', *American Journal of Sociology*, **94** (supplement), S95–S120.

Elder, G. H. (1987) "'Lives and social change', in W. R. Heinz (ed.), *Theoretical Advances in Life Course Research.* Weinheim: Deutscher Studien.

Evans, K. and Furlong, A. (1997) 'Metaphors of youth transitions: niches, trajectories and pathways', in J. Bynner, L. Chisholm and A. Furlong (eds), *Youth, Citizenship and Social Change.* Aldershot: Ashgate.

Evans, K. and Heinz, W. R. (1994) *Becoming Adults in the 1990s.* London: Anglo-German Foundation.

Furlong, A. and Cartmel, F. (1997) *Young People and Social Change: Individualisation and Risk in Late Modernity.* Buckingham: Open University Press.

Ingelhart, R. (1990) *Culture Shift in Advanced Society.* Princeton: Princeton University Press.

Moen, P., Elder, G.H. and Luscher, K. (eds) (1994) *Linking Lives and Contexts: Perspectives on the Ecology of Human Development.* Washington, DC: American Psychological Association.

Reitzle, M., Vondracek, F.W. and Silbereisen, R.K. (1998) 'Timing of school to work transitions: a developmental contextual perspective', *International Journal of Behavioral Development*, **22**: 7–28.

Robins, L. and Rutter, M. (1990) *Straight and Devious Pathways from Childhood to Adulthood.* Cambridge: Cambridge University Press.

Roberts, K. and Jung, B. (1995) *Poland's First Post-Communist Generation.* Aldershot: Avebury.

Silbereisen, R. K. (in press) 'German unification and adolescents' developmental time tables: continuities and discontinuities', in C. Crockett and R. K. Silbereisen (eds.), *Negotiating Adolescence in Times of Social Change.* Cambridge, MA: Cambridge University Press.

Trommsdorff, G. and Chakkarath, P. (1996) 'Kindheit in transformations prozess' (Childhood during the political transformation), in S. E. Hormuth, W. R. Heinz, H. Kornadt, H. Sydons and G. Trommsdorff (eds), *Individuelle Entwicklung, Bildung und Berntsverlaeute* (pp 11–78). Opladen: Leske & Budrich.

Utting, D. (1995) *Family and Parenthood.* York: Joseph Rowntree Foundation.

Part 1

Systems, structures and social life

1
Educational systems and transition

Karen Evans

Comparisons between the vocational education and training systems at age 16 in the United Kingdom and Germany show how the German system is characterized by a combination of school and on-the-job training (the dual system), while the British system has been much more focused on specific skills which bear a direct relationship to the particular job. Against this background, the transition to work is accomplished in the UK about two years earlier than is common in Germany. Consequently, the main aim of young people in Germany is the accumulation of education and relatively general qualifications for the occupation. For British young people, however, what counts is specific experience at a work site. A major problem is that work values are quite often less well developed than is usual among German young people.

These differences in the school to work transition between the two countries can be captured by two particular metaphors. The term trajectory seems to be more adequate for the German system, since it implies direction fixed at the outset, whereas the term pathway presents a better representation of the British system, characterized by more options and freedom of choice. In spite of many advantages identified with the German system, such as the development of strong work values, various drawbacks cannot be overlooked. One is the scarcity of apprenticeships, mainly attributed to their high associated costs. Further, more and more young people try first to complete the highest school track (*Abitur*) and then start an apprenticeship. This has resulted in major problems in recruitment to the traditional lower tracks of the German school system (*Hauptschule*), because of the reduced opportunities these now provide for an apprenticeship.

Regional variations are also highly significant in both countries. In Britain, the relatively non-institutionalized nature of post-16 arrangements means that, at local level, the actual patterns of provision are very variable. In Germany, the highly institutionalized and regulated system is proving difficult to sustain, particularly under the economic conditions of the new *Länder*.

This chapter is based on findings from a series of Anglo-German Studies carried out by the author and colleagues in British and German universities over a decade.[1] The rationale for comparing England and Germany goes beyond recognition of the global impact that German approaches have had in the sphere of vocational education and training over much of the century. There is a deep historical affinity between England and Germany which has led England to evaluate its performance by looking in that direction. There is a shared history of mediaeval guilds from which an apprenticeship tradition evolved in both countries. In Germany, this tradition, when overlaid with German bureaucracy, developed into the huge institutionalized national system of apprenticeship, covering all occupational fields and absorbing well over half of school leavers. In Britain, the apprenticeship tradition, when overlaid with *laisser-faire* economic liberalism, all but disappeared, with regular calls for its return in one form or another in response to long-term difficulties in securing adequate participation levels and standards in British vocational education and training.

The transition of young people to economic independence is more strongly institutionalized in Germany than in Britain. The differences reflect the legacies of German bureaucratization, on the one hand, and British *laisser-faire* economic liberalism on the other. Centralised interventions in training have always been resisted in Britain and have eventually foundered or been replaced (see, for example, the Industrial Training Act (1964) and, more recently, the rise and fall of the Manpower Services Commission (Ainley and Corney, 1990)). Similarly, British interventions in the social support of youth stemmed largely from voluntary roots at the end of the last century as philanthropists and others responded to the 'moral panics' such as the creation of juvenile delinquency amongst working class youth (Gillis, 1975). These interventions eventually took the shape of a weak institutional 'youth service' operating as a loose partnership of statutory and voluntary organizations at the margins of educational and social welfare policy. In Germany, youth has historically been a target for intervention and protection. Centralizing and regularizing state interventions are characteristic of Germany, yet these co-exist with a decentralizing tendency reflected in the federal structure and the execution of state functions by a range of autonomous institutions. This results in greater devolution of power, in some respects, than we find in Britain. The *Länder* governments are responsible for school/college education. Training policy and standards are the responsibility of the federal government, through *Bundesinstitut für Berufsbildung* (BIBB) (Federal Institute of Vocational Training), which focuses on content rather than standards. Each Land has a tripartite vocational education committee and at local level chambers of commerce and craft guilds carry major responsibilities. Control comes through legislation in Germany, and through regulation of qualifications in Britain.

The dual system in Germany

Apprenticeship is highly developed in Germany. It covers all occupational sectors and is entered by the majority of young people leaving school before the age of 18/19. Employer-sponsored apprenticeship is entered at age 16/17 via the *Realschule* (Intermediate School) or *Hauptschule* (General High School). Training is undertaken for three years involving three or four days per week in firm-based training and the remaining one or two days in the *Berufsschule*. Acquisition of skills is certified by a diploma, which qualifies young workers for entry to skilled worker grades through mutual recognition by the social partners. Jallade (1989: 123) states that 'the involvement of the social partners in defining the contents of training and the weight given to firm-based training ensures a good match between certification and qualification', that is the certificate is recognized as qualifying its holder to practise in skilled occupations. More males than females enter employer-sponsored apprenticeships, with the training for female-typical occupations concentrated more in vocational schools.

This system contrasts radically with Britain's 'mixed model' in which a proliferation of post-16 provisions offering a variety of forms of vocational education and training sprang up in the 1970s and '80s. This was in response to the problems of youth unemployment which, at their peak, virtually eradicated the traditional 'route' of direct job entry for 16-year-olds in all but the most prosperous labour markets. While Germany has a 'dominant mode' of vocational education and training (VET) in relation to which other provision can be planned, Britain does not (Raffe, 1991). The greater uniformity and regulation of German vocational education reduces local labour market effects, in that systemic factors determine the forms of vocational preparation available, mediated by local labour market conditions. In Britain training arrangements in any particular locality are more closely tied to local labour market conditions than they are to anything resembling a national system (Evans and Heinz, 1991). A study of Swindon at a time of economic buoyancy showed that market-led vocational preparation under those conditions polarized into:

a) direct job entry reflecting high wages in youth jobs, and
b) 'traditional' VET courses offered through colleges, either full-time or by day release.

Skill formation leading towards skilled worker status is far less standardized than in Germany, taking place through YT Jobskills with training, or through traditional apprenticeships where these remain, through full-time vocational courses, and through some forms of firm-based YTS.

Young people on apprenticeships in Germany receive theoretical and practical training, which is usually well integrated. They are unlikely, however, to experience the degree of responsibility and remuneration given to their British peers (Bynner and Roberts, 1991; Evans and Heinz, 1994). Young adults experience slower progression to responsibility but greater depth of education and training, combined with the expectation of ongoing development through training into their early 20s. The last point is of great significance, in that culturally accepted and expected timescales for preparation and accession to adult roles and responsibilities differ between the two cultures. For German young people, the steps taken between 16 and 19 represent only the first stages in a transition process which continues to higher levels of training and qualification. Young people in Britain may well be employed with adult status and pay, but also with some supervisory responsibilities by age 19, particularly in the more buoyant labour markets. In general, British young people enter the labour market at least two years ahead of their German counterparts. These differences can be conceptualized as extended vs. accelerated transitions. Our initial Anglo-German studies concluded that 'Training as a preliminary to employment has still not penetrated very deeply into the British psyche. The prevailing view still seems to be that whatever you need to know in a job can be taught on the job itself; getting the job is what matters' (Bynner and Roberts, 1991:xxiii). In the 1990s, expansion of post-school participation in education has not removed this underlying tendency. High levels of dropout from vocational education programmes at 17 and beyond have continued to beset the system. These issues prompted, in part, the Dearing Report of 1996 on provision for 16–19 year olds, commissioned by the government to produce recommendations for improving the quality and consistency of provision, as well as retention of young people in the system, working towards recognized qualifications (Dearing, 1996).

There is an expectation in Germany among both young workers and employers that continuous training and upgrading of status in the workforce will take place subsequent to initial vocational education and training. The stronger base of academic *and* vocational training is seen as providing the potential to benefit from further education and training as adults. Three times as many Germans have a vocational qualification through apprenticeship, incorporating theory and practice and assessed by external examination. 'Half the British labour force has *either* a practically oriented vocational qualification *or* an academic qualification; in Germany half the labour force has both' (Rose, 1990:23).

German arrangements ensure that young people of lower ability are trained in order to make use of their potential. Where British young people do receive training it would be a mistake to assume that this has the same scope and standard as the German 'equivalent', particularly where there is a significant in-company component (Evans et al., 1997). In Britain this is still largely left to ad hoc training arrangements. The National Vocational Qualification development has tended to reduce the scope and content of training in some sectors, while introducing new forms of training in sectors which previously had little. There is nothing to parallel the *meister* system for training and recognition of trainers. Germany is engaged in a 'virtuous circle' in which an already strong manufacturing base requires higher skills levels from its workers and these are expected and sought by the workers themselves. There is a social consensus around the importance of training as an employment process that does not exist in England.

While German vocational education and training (VET) had been relatively stable over time, the UK VET changed substantially between the mid-1980s and mid-1990s. In the UK the change to a competence-led model of vocational qualifications can be traced to the New Training Initiative of 1981. This has been the subject of much controversy in which criticisms of its narrowly-based and bureaucratic nature, its reductionist approach to training and the inadequacies of control of standards have been set against claims about the utility and employer-relevance of the qualifications. In the 1990s, German VET, particularly the dual system, has itself come under considerable pressure to change. The Anglo-German studies which provided one of the starting points for this book (Bynner and Roberts, 1991; Evans and Heinz, 1994) highlighted the variability in quality of provision in the dual system. In Germany we had our attention drawn to the generally low status and poor facilities of many *Berufsschulen* compared to the *Gymnasien.* In England, it is common to imagine that German state institutions will be well funded and viewed favourably. The *Berufsschulen* were seen in much more negative terms. Young people saw the *Berufsschule* as continuing the schooling they had hoped to get away from, often in worse conditions. Employers questioned whether what went on in the *Berufsschule* had much vocational value. In the education system generally, as part of the poor status attached to vocational courses, the *Berufsschule* was poorly regarded, and morale was often low among the teachers. For boys undertaking apprenticeships, this negative perception was offset by satisfying work-based training. For girls, whose training was more heavily concentrated in vocational schools, or typically the *Berufsfachschule,* the poor quality suggested an inferior form of VET for them. One of the major challenges for Germany is to restore the *Berufsschule* to its rightful place as a core element of VET by improving funding and the co-operation with companies. This means better training for teachers and much more investment of resources.

But this is only part of a wider issue: the need to give vocational courses and qualifications full parity of esteem with academic (general) ones. The major criticism that German trade unions have continually made of the dual system (e.g. Schweitzer, 1989) is that it has inferior status, despite claims of parity. The increasing demand for places at *Gymnasien,* which have doubled in size relative to *Hauptschulen* since the Second World War, reflects parents' and young people's concern that they do genuinely get the best.

In contrast to the German *Berufsschule,* the English further education college was found to have a good reputation among young people who entered it. This finding has been further supported by evidence from a study carried out between 1993 and 1997 into student perspectives on vocational further education (Rudd and Evans, 1998). The evidence from the questionnaire surveys and the group interviews suggested that the students in the selected colleges were 'broadly satisfied' with their college experiences. The fact that many of the students were optimistic and felt in control, to some extent, of their transitions, was at least partly due to the efforts of the college tutors and to the way in which the college provided a supportive framework. In general in the colleges surveyed, the students were allowed a great deal of independence, but advice and support were generally available and there were well-developed counselling services. In Britain the whole world of 'technical' day-release schools, with methods not unlike that of the *Berufsschule,* gave way from the 1970s onwards to further education colleges in which a wide range of both academic and vocational courses were on offer. The problem in England was, as ever, a need to build up interest in further education for the still significant number of young people who found that trying their lot in the labour market was more attractive than the provision on offer.

This is the crucial issue for England: how to integrate further education and youth training provision with what is on offer in the local labour market to ensure that both students and employers see the two elements, VET and jobs, as inseparable. Britain's Training and Enterprise Councils (TECs) have been given the responsibility for bringing this about. The difficulty is that they represent only a tiny proportion of employers in their area. Most potential employers of young people, particularly small and medium-sized employers, need much more incentive from government, in the form of financial and other material support, to take trainees on under a voluntaristic system. The TECs' dominant concern has been to find ways of honouring the government's pledge to find a training place for every young person who wants one. In 1992, the shortage was running at 60,000 places, and concentration on 'finding places' undermined originally broad-based policy intentions. There is also evidence that training providers have become pressured to reduce the quality of their provision by outcome-related funding which emphasizes the benefits of cost-cutting and meeting short-term targets and there has been little systematic investment in 'training the trainers' (Brown et al., 1994; Hodkinson and Sparkes, 1994).

The regional dimension is of growing significance. The continuing poor labour market conditions in some areas inhibit the operation of any effective local VET policy in Britain. This problem is now also spotlighted in Germany, where the new *Länder* from the former East Germany face considerable problems in offering a VET provision which is anywhere near comparable to that which used to be taken for granted in the former West Germany.

In the former East, many apprenticeship routes led into the state industries. These routes no longer exist, many industrial plants having been closed for environmental and other reasons. With West German companies able to expand capacity to take up demand from the new *Länder,* local enterprises able to provide extended training and apprenticeships have reduced substantially. Growing youth unemployment is indicated in the statistics for numbers of applicants and vacant training places. In Saxony in 1997, the unplaced applicants outnumbered training places by 4,069 to 319. In 1994 there were 401 unplaced applicants for 568 training places.

Training places have dramatically reduced as companies struggling for existence in the early years of unification finally collapsed in 1995/6. High unemployment, together with casualization and falling skills and qualification levels in the adult workforce, has begun to create conditions somewhat similar to those faced in depressed economic regions of Britain. The ways in which these conditions impact on youth are different, however, since the relatively low-skilled and unregulated labour markets in Britain have always been more accommodating than the German labour markets to young people who attempt to enter them without training and qualification.

Differences between the German and English systems of vocational education and training

Historically, differences between the English (E) and German (G) systems have centred on depth and duration of VET, degree of institutionalization of a 'dominant mode' of VET and status of trainees and qualifications. To summarize some differences between English and German routes into work:

1. Accelerated (E) *v.* extended (G) transitions: E greater than two years ahead in labour market entry in all career tracks;
2. G: emphasis on general labour market utility of apprenticeship qualifications (followed by more than half of all school leavers).
3. G: surrounds young adults with strong institutional structures for education and training, at all levels, into their 20s

   E: non-institutionalized by comparison and surrounds young people with job- and work-related substitutes for education at a very early age; but
4. E: higher exposure to 'real' work experiences and responsibilities at earlier stage at all levels.

The difference in age of first labour market entry is most marked at graduate level, where average age of first entry to the labour market is 28 years in Germany compared with 22 years in Britain. The higher exposure to 'real' work experiences and responsibilities at earlier stage at all levels is indicated by the findings shown in Figure 1.1 which compare reported frequency of exposure to different kinds of experi-

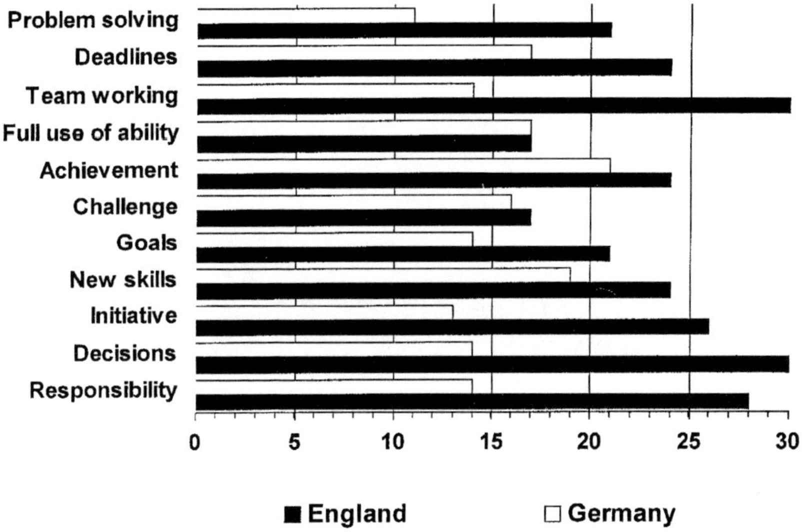

Figure 1.1 16–20-year-olds in England and Germany: general work skills

ences in work-related settings among samples of young adults in the two countries. For example, respondents recorded how often they had been able to take initiatives, work in teams, experience achievement and working towards goals in work-related settings.

In all categories, English respondents (N = 320) recorded greater frequency of these experiences than their German peers (N = 320) matched by age, gender and career trajectory.

We also asked about experience of testing and assessment. Given the image of the rigour of German vocational education, a heavy emphasis on skills testing and examinations might be expected in Germany. In fact, Germans also reported much lower frequency of written and practical tests. Whatever it is that is so successful about the German VET system it appears does not to rely on extensive testing and assessment of work-related tasks.

Does the key to German success lie in attitudes? How do young Germans differ from English counterparts in their attitudes to work and the wider world? What effects do cultural and systemic differences have in the formation of work identities?

Figure 1.2 shows that young Germans surveyed generally scored higher on a measure of work commitment comprising agreement with such attitude statements as: 'A person must have a job to feel a full

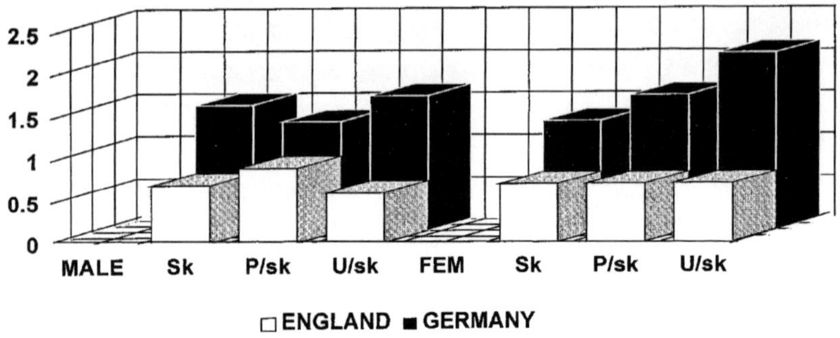

Sk = Skilled, P/Sk = Partly skilled, U/Sk = Unskilled, FEM = Female

Figure 1.2 16–20-year-olds in England and Germany: work commitment

member of society'; 'It is important to hang on to a job even if you do not like it'. This applied for both males and females and across all skills levels.

Political interest was also generally higher in Germany (Figure 1.3). The *Berufsschule* in Germany have citizenship and political education as an essential part of their curriculum, an approach first pioneered by Kerschensteiner in the early 1900s (Kerschensteiner, 1911). The contrast with Britain is marked in that these elements are practically non-existent in the institutional post-16 curriculum. They are most apparent in youth work, which was encouraged in these aims by the 1982 Thompson Report (Department of Education and Science, 1982),

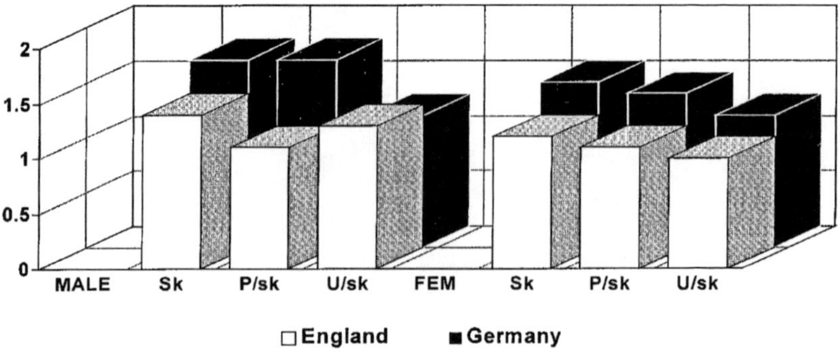

Sk = Skilled, P/Sk = Partly skilled, U/Sk = Unskilled, FEM = Female

Figure 1.3 16–20-year-olds in England and Germany: political interest

only to be later discouraged by the government in the 1990/91 review of the youth service (National Youth Bureau, 1990). The latter attempted to identify an outcomes-based 'core curriculum' for the youth service emphasizing the role of youth work in containing some of the problems of marginalized youth and downplaying the political and broader citizenship education aspects.

The only attitude measure which showed the opposite pattern with relatively higher scores in the English samples was, ironically, employment confidence, comprising such attitudes as 'In ten years' time I will have the kind of job I want'; 'I will be able to impress an employer in a job interview'; 'I will avoid unemployment'. This showed greater confidence among young people in all career routes in their ability to find and maintain a job in England, although actual prospects of doing so were lower than in the German labour markets from which the samples were drawn. Confidence was at its highest in Britain in lowest career routes: those least likely to secure stable employment (Figure 1.4).

This may be more evidence of British policies working in sustaining beliefs; it is, perhaps, also to do with lack of political education; and with the deregulated labour market. Getting a job which comes up by luck is much less likely in Germany. In depressed labour markets in England young people were kept going by the belief that something might be just around the corner, even for the least qualified.

Significantly more young German respondents expected to obtain further qualifications after starting work than English young people matched by age, sex and career trajectory; while more English expected

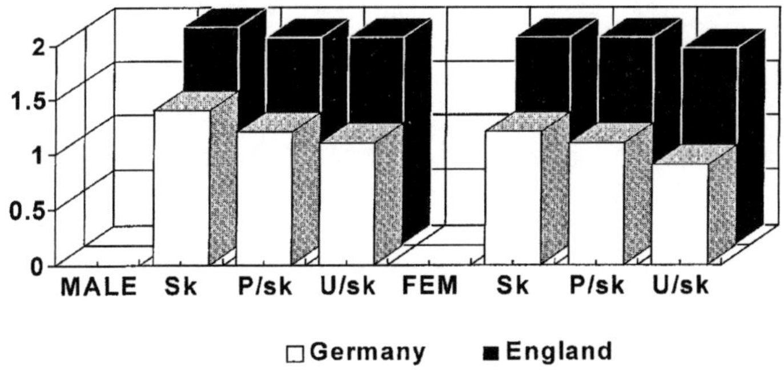

Sk = Skilled, P/Sk = Partly skilled, U/Sk = Unskilled, FEM = Female

Figure 1.4 16–20-year-olds in England and Germany: employment confidence

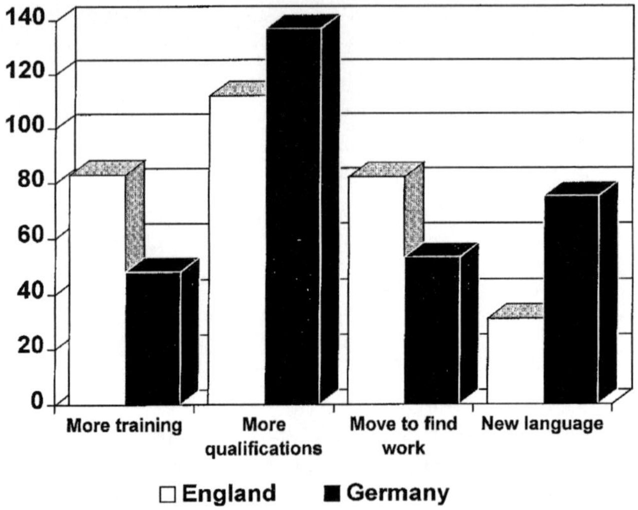

Figure 1.5 16–20-year-olds in England and Germany: expectations

to have to retrain for a different job and to have to move to find work (Figure 1.5). Unsurprisingly, many more Germans expected to learn a new language in adult life than did their English counterparts!

This suggested a 'short-termism' perspective among English trainees, which contrasted with the German disposition towards building up educational capital in the chosen '*Beruf*'.

Experiences in the 'new *Länder*'

While the findings suggest that the work ethic has not been substantially eroded by unemployment in Britain, and may have been sustained by vocationalism in education, culturally it is at much lower levels than in Germany, with which country comparisons have traditionally been made. Recent data from interviews carried out in labour markets in the former East indicate the extent of changes in motivational factors, both amongst trainers and young trainees, in that region of Germany.

In common with their counterparts in the western *Länder*, the passing of the examination at the end of training was a source of feelings of achievement, pride and 'relief' for all interviewees. For those who went on successfully into the workforce, their qualification as a skilled worker was all-important, as the following quotations from interviews with young East Germans show.

> (I was) full of energy: I then went to work. It would have been terribly problematic for me, if they had not taken me on..., I would have had terrible problems with myself, not to find work with such a successful qualification.

> Yes certainly. I didn't go through training for three and a half years merely for nothing. A profession that is not very easy and then to go though a retraining and do something else.

For those for whom the intended occupational field, as a result of political changes, had lost its attractiveness or disappeared, biographical breaks and disjunctions opened up. Young people who started an alternative such as retraining or returning to study could sometimes compensate. Self-doubt and negative self-evaluations were manifested in many of these interviews. Young people saw the fault as lying with themselves: if they were 'average people' or unqualified, what hope did they have in a highly competitive market?

> I think there are many like me. Well, I'm just an average person. I've got many wrong points – but then I'm not really good at anything.

> I think, there are thousands of other secretaries, who are better than me. If I had to start again, I would do the same again. Why should he take me when he had thousands who are qualified. It's always the same. It's just as well that I've got two years experience now. That's the only thing that I can build my hopes on.

Interviews with trainers who had been carrying out this role under the previous system and had retained their jobs after reunification showed and awareness that training cannot now exist 'removed from the companies (financial) balance and staffing'. A trainer who perceived the change in positive terms said:

> Yes, it's better. Most of the young people know what is important today. Their behaviour, attitudes, efforts and the way they act on their own initiative has much improved. Formerly they all felt safe and said: 'I'll just muddle my way through this, they'll push me through the examination and at the end I'll work in one of the

> nationally owned companies (VEB) until I retire.' Well, that's completely different today. The worries of not being taken on are enormous. So I try to help them somehow – give them fresh heart: if not here, then you have to try to somewhere else.

Motivation of some young people is increased by the 'worry'. It is reduced for others because they believe they will not find a job after training. Another trainer observed:

> While it was formerly possible to put pressure on the trainee to stimulate him, nowadays trainers are relatively helpless, concerning this process they can merely try to encourage or console.

Many young people who, for whatever reason, do not complete their training appear to have lost their main opportunity for stable employment, but some find a place somewhere in the labour market and non-traditional, unqualified routes into the labour market appear to be growing (Evans, Behrens and Kaluza, 1998).

Vocational qualifications and VET policy

Basic vocational preparation and the *Berufsfachschule* in Germany and further education college and YTS in England all offer opportunities for young people to move their careers in positive directions. They also play their part in undermining careers and allowing young people to stagnate or damage their prospects irrevocably. There is much to be said for more pro-active policies to help young people with difficulties and develop better means of protecting them within the VET system along German lines.

With regard to the curriculum and qualifications, there has historically been more certainty in Germany about the content of training and the meaning of certification that comes from it. Long-established systems of regulation and monitoring, both nationally through BIBB (*Bundesinstitut für Berufsbildung*) and locally through chambers of commerce, ensure that the content and standards of training can be properly communicated and recognition given to the vocational qualifications everywhere. In England, despite the existence now of the National Council for Vocational Qualifications (NCVQ) with the brief of developing nationally accredited standards for all vocational training (NVQs) there is still much further to go before these are universally accepted by employers or young people and their parents. Indeed, a range of surveys and studies (Beaumont, 1996; Dearing, 1996) have concluded that significant changes in the new system of NVQs are needed if they are to provide a credible answer to Britain's further education and training needs.

It was striking in Germany how important the goal of a vocational qualification in the form of a completed apprenticeship was to the young people in our study. In England, for the majority of early school-leavers, a vocational qualification still remained of minor importance. Work experience through employment was still the dominant goal.

These differences in the school to work transition between the two countries can be captured by the two particular metaphors introduced at the beginning of this chapter. *Pathways* place the emphasis on the individual finding the right way through the maze without too many dead ends and wrong turnings. *Trajectories* place the emphasis on a flight path determined by the social equivalent of angle of projection and velocity. The term trajectory seems to be more adequate for the German system, due to the fact that it implies direction, whereas the term pathway presents a better representation of the British system, characterized by more scope for 'choice' but enduring problems of a confused and confusing array of options of differing status, with a significant proportion of young people rejecting what is available, 'status zero youth' who effectively disappear from the official statistics.

Employer reluctance to invest in quality training and the lack of a real training tradition is offered as one explanation of the long-term failure of British training policy to secure high level of qualifications from participants. A second explanation, sometimes offered, blames the victim, arguing that the fault lies with young people who select jobs with no future training. This latter explanation is another search for a single variable, i.e. youth as the explanation for employers' failure to invest in their young employees. In order to understand why young adults do, or do not, develop their skills, it is necessary to explore the pull of the wage and the access it brings to adult pleasures and commodities. Why do young people leave school and pursue wages within restricted occupational sectors where a low premium is given to training? Why do young women and men enter jobs in gender segregated and segmented labour markets where a process of early closure reduces future occupational opportunities? A third explanation centres on 'fragmentation' and competing interests within and between agencies involved in various aspects of skills formation. The fact that all three are offered as explanations reflects the weak institutionalization of the processes of youth transition and skills formation in Britain and the ways through the 'maze' or 'jungle', presented as *pathways* too often turn out to be dead-ends, with real penalties and few ways back for those who have taken 'wrong' turnings.

The strongly institutionalized German system, by contrast, sets young people on their *trajectory* at an early stage through tripartite schooling. In spite of many advantages identified with the German system, such as the development of strong work values, the drawbacks of the system cannot be overlooked. The apprenticeship system reinforces structural inequalities, a process started in a stratified schooling system. Gender-based inequalities are particularly marked, with males outnumbering females by significant margins in the more advantaged academic and vocational routes into the labour market (Bynner and Evans, 1994). Apprenticeships for young women tend to be of poorer quality and prospects than those for boys, and many young women are channelled into vocational schools full-time with domestic orientation. More and more young people now try first to complete the higher school track (*Abitur*) and then start an apprenticeship. This has resulted in major problems in recruitment to the traditional lower track of the German school system (*Hauptschule*), where opportunities provided for apprenticeships are now much reduced.

There is, therefore, some displacement of trajectories, one by another, in terms of outcomes in the labour market, but social stratification remains intact. For those at the bottom of the heap, the labour market is hostile to those without qualifications and there are few openings for the flexible forms of work-based learning of the kind available in Britain. Special schemes all too often serve only to stigmatize and disadvantage further.

Young people in the *Länder* of the former East have been caught in a double bind: a hostile labour market which effectively excludes unqualified young people but which can no longer sustain the training routes and social support previously provided for the large majority. The striving for work identities, so strongly fostered by German culture and tradition, does not diminish, and there is evidence of growing frustration of marginalized and excluded youth. There is, at the same time, a growth in casualized work opportunities available for unqualified adults, producing a situation which begins to mirror that in Britain. Many young people in their early 20s are gaining their foothold in the labour market in these jobs.

With constraints on public funding and diversified demands on the system, neither the stratified trajectories of Germany nor flexible but confused (and often fore-shortened) British pathways are working well as routes into the labour market.

In Britain, student experiences reflect the considerable change and unrest in the FE sector. Group sizes have increased as colleges strive to recruit the necessary target numbers of students, and new funding arrangements have resulted in many colleges facing financial difficulties. Funding issues in FE were not a direct concern for the young people taking part in this research, though it has to be said that some did raise the topic and several showed at least an indirect awareness of how influences of 'the market' and 'competition' were having an effect on their college experiences. Interview respondents in the study carried out by Rudd and Evans (1998) expressed some dissatisfaction with levels of resources. Additionally, the fact that a large proportion of the questionnaire sample had part-time jobs (over 60 per cent) indicated that many felt that they needed to put in extra hours of paid work in order to fund their studies and their leisure activities. This seems to have become the norm for 16- to 19-year-old college students. Some of the students, along with a number of their tutors, could see the problems that might arise in their own college from a reliance on 'market forces' to shape FE provision. The data provided by the student samples supports the view that national VET policies need to take a longer-term perspective and need to be based on a more coherent qualifications and assessment framework. Colleges, students and employers are looking for a period of stability and consolidation, with clarity in the meanings and levels of post-16 qualifications.

For Britain, the need now is to:

- *establish broad-based education and training after 17 as the norm*, with the aim of improving both breadth and depth of achievement;
- *evolve a climbing frame structure*, encouraging an enlarging curriculum with flexible combinations of general, vocational and work-based elements, not age-tied.
- *restrict youth labour market*, which is one of the 'pull' factors: i.e. make it difficult to employ young people under 18 full-time without providing quality training;
- *maintain a work-based route to qualification*, building it on employers able to provide, individually or in partnership, quality careerships and traineeships to equivalent standards of breadth and depth;
- *emphasize entitlement to learn* as well as outcomes (partly addressed by Dearing, 1996);
- *invest in training culture:* train trainers and key workers

The need to establish breadth and depth has been embraced in policy, and the previous downplaying of knowledge in vocational qualifications has now been recognized as a grave policy error. The restriction of the youth labour market is not popular because it requires reforms in labour market and employment practices, but the evidence shows it to be necessary. Allowing a work-based route to qualification recognizes its importance as a route, but there must be better incentives and support for provision of educational breadth in work-based programmes, as well as giving priority to training trainers and key workers. Finally, targeted financial support must be provided to enable people to participate and withstand the difficulties of combining study with working life and life transitions.

For Germany, the challenge is to improve and re-orientate the *Berufsschule*, with more flexible partnerships between educational institutions and industry which enable the former to support those elements of VET which the latter are finding increasingly difficult to sustain within available resources. Probably for the first time, there are some signs that Germany is looking towards the flexibility of British further education as a model to be considered (Stach, 1997).

The answer in dual system critics' terms, which our research supports, is to break down the distinction between general and vocational education by, for example, opening up access to higher education via the vocational education route and encouraging a much greater mixture of academic and vocational experience for all young people. The more conservative response, in keeping with the trajectory approach, has been to call for two types of apprenticeships: the high-status academic entry kind lasting three years, and the vocational lasting two years and not offering qualified entry.

Germany now shares with Britain the end aim of a flexible, future-oriented and inclusive provision. The starting points and the structural and contextual factors are quite different (Koch and Reuling, 1994). Germany already meets the above criteria for work-based learning, but needs to make its predominant firm-based route to skilled status more flexible, sustaining strong work commitment but able to deal with instabilities in labour markets and the demise of the expectation of stable and continuous upward careers which underlie having a *Beruf*. The options of stratifying the system still further with 'two-tier' apprenticeships feeding into different levels of the labour market is in tune with the trajectory approach but over time may present many of the same drawbacks of the present system.

Moves towards a European model of VET suggest that greater flexibility in ways in which people can draw on combinations of education-based and work-based learning is the direction for both systems. Germany has the advantage of having considerable continuities in VET and the 'anchors' in place enable continuous evolution of the dual system, with mechanisms for a new consensus to emerge. It has much to do, however, in providing social and market support measures for young adults in the new *Länder* which enable and support them to negotiate more flexible structures. These are vulnerable groups with a high risk of social exclusion. Fischer and Zinnecker (1992) suggest that these young people initially embraced Western values and German working values, ethics and identities. Evidence from the current (1998) Anglo-German studies is suggesting that young trainees in the new *Länder* are increasingly confident, but also displaying some resistance to the situation in which they find themselves. The following quote shows how changed behaviour is depicted by one trainer, and his own uncertainty about the relationship involved:

> They have grown much more self-confident in their whole manner and they tackle problems with a carefree attitude – it's just amazing ... Their manners have vastly changed. And the behaviour on the whole, not only their technical behaviour, but ... I also must say that the young people show a strong opposition towards society, which is due to the employment chances after the training. You can talk and talk to motivate them because they have phases, when they say, why am I doing all this, in practice I only lay a cable and when I've finished the training I won't get a job anyway. So I then try to tell them that they are getting a rather broader training and that they should be able to apply that ... Yes, but that occurs more and more often, yes opposition wasn't maybe quite the right word, it's opposition mixed with discouragement, yes a certain attitude of defiance, saying it doesn't make sense anyway.

Young people need coping strategies combined with non-stigmatizing forms of material support to make the full transitions to productive and participative adult roles.

Critical for any country's VET system is a unified qualifications framework through which young people can be guaranteed further progression into higher education or to more specialized vocational study or full adult status in the labour market. For any such system to function, it must be backed by support networks that enable young people to withstand the difficulties of study, that ensure that they are properly supported financially and that they have the right kind of advice when they need it.

In Britain, the potential of a broad-based unified qualifications framework has yet to be realized, with a basis in the needs of *employment* (not just employers) and the longer-term national interests.

Provision should match individual need. Machinery needs putting in place through the formal education system in both countries for developing much greater autonomy in young people in the use of information to make career choices and to enable them to gain the necessary experience inside and outside the educational system to pursue their goals.

The dominant metaphor thus becomes not *trajectory* nor *pathway* but the means for young people to *navigate* their ways towards their life goals with support and without penalties for the changes of direction which are part of the maturational process in extended youth transitions.

Note

1. Comparative studies of employment and life transitions of young people in contrasting labour markets in England and Germany, in Bynner and Roberts (1991); Evans and Heinz (1994), Evans, Behrens and Kaluza (forthcoming, 1998), all supported by the Anglo-German Foundation for the Study of Industrial Society. Also related studies supported by the Leverhulme Trust (Brown, Evans, Blackman and German, 1994) and the Economic and Social Research Council.

References

Ainley, P. and Corney, M. (1990) *Training for the Future: The Rise and Fall of the Manpower Services Commission.* London: Cassell.

Beaumont, G. (1996) *Review of 100 NVQs and SVQs.* Report submitted to the Department of Education and Employment.

Brown, A., Evans, K., Blackman, S. and Germon, S. (1994) *Key Workers: Technical and Training Mastery in the Workplace.* Bournemouth: Hyde.

Bynner, J. and Roberts, K. (1991) *Youth and Work: Transitions to Employment in England and Germany.* London and Bonn: Anglo-German Foundation.

Bynner, J. and Evans, K. (1994) 'Building on cultural traditions: problems and solutions', in K. Evans and W. R. Heinz, *Becoming Adults in England and Germany.* London and Bonn: Anglo-German Foundation,

Dearing, R. (1996) *Review of Qualifications for 16–19-year-olds.* London: School Curriculum and Assessment Authority.

Department of Education and Science (1982) *Experience and Participation* (Thompson Report), Cmnd 8686. London: Her Majesty's Stationery Office.

Evans, K. and Heinz, W. R. (1991) 'Careers and Destinations', in *Youth and Work,* ed. J. Bynner and K. Roberts (1991). London and Bonn: Anglo-German Foundation.

Evans, K. and Heinz, W. R. (1994) *Becoming Adults in England and Germany.* London and Bonn: Anglo-German Foundation.

Evans, K., Hodkinson, P., Keep, E., Maguire, M., Raffe, D., Rainbird, H., Senker, P. and Unwin, L. (1997) *Working to Learn*. London: Institute for Personnel and Development.

Evans, K., Behrens, M. and Kaluza, J. (1998) 'Skill formation, socio-economic attitudes and transition behaviours of young adults in Eastern Germany'. University of Surrey/Zentrum für Arbeits-und Organisationsforschung : Anglo-German Foundation for the Study of Industrial Society (to be published by Macmillan as *Learning and Work in the Risk Society*).

Fischer, A. and Zinnecker, J. (1992) *Jugend '92*. Opladen: Leske & Budrich.

Gillis, J. R. (1975) 'The evaluation of juvenile delinquency in England 1890–1913', *Past and Present*, **67**: 96–126.

Hodkinson, P. and Sparkes, A. C. (1994) 'The myth of the market: the negotiation of training in the youth credits pilot scheme', *British Journal of Education and Work*, **7**(3): 5–19.

Jallade, J. -P. (1989) 'Recent trends in vocational education and training: an overview', *European Journal of Education*, **24**(2): 103–25.

Kerschensteiner, G. (1911) *German Youth and Education for Citizenship*, 5th edn. Erfurt Villaret.

Koch, R. and Reuling, J. (1994) 'The responsiveness and regulation of training capacity and quality', in *OECD Vocational Training in Germany*. Paris: OECD.

National Youth Bureau (1990) *Danger or Opportunity*, Leicester: NYB.

Raffe, D. (1991) 'The "Mixed Mode": social research and the case for reform of 16–18s' education in Britain', in C. Crouch and A. Heath (eds) (1991) *Social Research and Social Reform*. Oxford: Oxford University Press.

Rose, R. (1990) *Prospective Evaluation through Comparative Analysis: Youth Training in a Time–Space Perspective*. Glasgow: Centre for the Study of Public Policy.

Rudd, P. and Evans, K. (1998) 'Structure and agency in youth transitions: students' perspectives on vocational and further education', *Journal of Youth Studies*, **1**(1): 39–69.

Schweitzer, J. (1989) 'Integration of vocational and general education: an educational task and a political challenge for the future', *Vocational Training*, **1**: 35–7. CEDEFOP: Berlin.

Stach, M. (1997) 'The crisis of the dual system'. Paper presented at the international conference sponsored by the *Journal of Vocational Education and Training*, University of Huddersfield, July 1997.

2

Europe's choice: regulation or deregulation of youth labour markets? Old alternatives and new test cases

Ken Roberts and *Klara Foti*

This paper uses the new 'test cases' that have become available as a result of the transformation of former communist states in East-Central Europe to reassess the respective strengths and weaknesses of Germany's regulated, and the UK's unregulated school-to-work regimes. It is argued that the basic characteristics, including the strengths and weaknesses, of each regime remain unchanged, but that their relative weights have shifted as a result of the new global economic conditions, the related economic restructuring, and pan-European changes in young people's transition experiences. Specifically, it is argued that the disadvantages of the German regime are becoming a heavier handicap which can be seen in the difficulties that have been encountered in operating the system in East Germany. Meanwhile, the advantages of the British regime have become more advantageous than formerly, as can be seen in the manner in which the deregulation of their youth labour markets has assisted economic transformation, and enabled many young people to benefit from the opportunities thereby created, in countries such as Poland and Hungary.

Introduction

Youth is an inherently vulnerable life stage. Young people are required to make major status transitions and must deal with these challenges satisfactorily if they are to handle the situations that they will face during the rest of their lives. One of the key status transitions that all young people face is from education into employment, and in every modern country this particular transition has become more complex and risky in recent years. Young people in Western Europe and North America have felt the full effects of technological change and economic restructuring. In the former communist countries the changes have been even more dramatic. Whatever the specific changes, young people have invariably been in the front-line. Hence the widespread interest in which school-to-work transition regimes are best able to protect young people from adversities and enable them to respond positively to the challenges that they face. In addressing these questions Anglo-German comparisons have long been fruitful and this remains the case in the late 1990s.

Anglo-German work on young people's school-to-work transitions has a long history of juxtaposing the well-structured, protective German model with the relatively harsh, weakly regulated UK regime, though, however surprising this now seems, until the Second World War Britain was 'ahead' in regulation in many business sectors (see Clarke, 1993). There have always been domestic critics of Germany's provisions (see Braun, 1977; Heinz, 1985, 1986; Lenhardt, 1977, 1984). As in all other countries, within Germany there has been constant pressure to try even harder and do even better in youth education and training, but until recently external commentary on the German system was repetitively favourable (see Grimond, 1979; Hamilton, 1987; Raggatt, 1988; Rose, 1990). Latterly this has changed as Germany's economy has faltered. Questions have been raised as to whether Germany's youth regime provides the best of all possible preparations for adulthood in post-Fordist economic times (see for example Brown, 1996; Koch and Reuling, 1995; Shackleton, 1997).

The contrasts are as stark as ever. Indeed, during the 1990s some now familiar Anglo-German contrasts have grown even sharper. Germany's tripartite secondary education and apprentice system have survived the post-1970s economic turbulence and the unification of Germany's west and east, while transitions in Britain have become even less regulated. Rather than seeking to import some German practices, the UK has become Europe's self-acclaimed capital of deregulation. Until the 1980s young people in Britain were protected by relatively generous welfare rights (the 'blemish' on the unregulated landscape) but subsequently most of young people's former entitlements have been withdrawn or eroded – student grants, unemployment and housing benefit, for example.

The contrast between these highly and weakly regulated youth regimes makes Anglo-German comparisons interesting for the rest of contemporary Europe; more interesting than ever in the 1990s since they represent the main socio-economic policy alternatives that are being touted for the Union. Should the Union subject its member states' labour markets and employment to common regulations, and bestow similar types and levels of social protection on all workers and citizens, or should it be a minimally regulated single market? And the 1990s have created new test cases. The former German Democratic Republic is undergoing rapid (German-style) Westernization. Meanwhile, other former communist countries have been implementing equally rapid and, in some cases, extreme deregulation. Which transition regime, regulated or unregulated, works best in East-Central Europe will have implications for the entire European Union, given its expected enlargement.

General trends

There have been some common trends since the 1970s in young people's situations in all European countries – north and south, and east and west. First, young people's transitions into their countries' labour markets have been prolonged. Perhaps it is more accurate to say that transitions have become more varied in length but an overall effect has been a net upward movement in the ages at which young people obtain adult employment. One reason has been the higher levels of unemployment than in the 1950s and '60s. Entry jobs have become more difficult to obtain. However, the prolonging of transitions has also owed much to young people's growing appetite for credentials. Even when jobs have been available, many young people have been opting to extend their education in order to become better qualified prior to entering the workforce. It is also relevant that families in most Western countries have become more prosperous and better able to support their children's prolonged transitions. In particular, more married women have been entering and holding onto employment, thus enhancing their households' ability to support young adult members and, simultaneously, making all members aware of the importance of girls' education and longer-term career prospects (see Irwin, 1995).

Second, young people's biographies have been individualized. The sheer variety of the programmes in post-compulsory education, training schemes, part-time and temporary jobs, and periods of unemployment that young people now experience in various sequences is partly responsible. Individualization has also been due to the contraction of the major firms and industries that once dominated many local labour markets, and the weakening of neighbourhood communities as a result of the higher rates of geographical mobility and trends towards home centred lifestyles. A consequence is that young people have become less likely to feel that they share interests and experiences in common with any stable groups, and more likely to feel personally responsible for their current positions and futures (see Roberts, Clark and Wallace, 1994). Another consequence is that it has become difficult to mobilize young people politically in the customary ways – by enlisting them in parties and movements that claim to represent broad classes of people.

A third trend has been towards young people's futures becoming less certain and all the steps that they might take becoming more risky. Uncertain futures are partly a straightforward consequence of individualization. When broad categories of young people travelled towards adulthood together it was relatively easy for them to look ahead, at what had happened to earlier cohorts such as themselves, and thereby glimpse their own most likely futures. Uncertainty is also a product of the large numbers of young people on recently introduced educational programmes and training schemes with no established track records, and equally of the enlarged numbers on well established routes such as higher education. Nowadays there are so many post-compulsory students that it is impossible for them all to have as attractive career prospects as awaited earlier generations of graduates. Perhaps most basically, uncertainty is a product of the sheer pace of economic and occupational change which means that the adult roles that will await many of today's young people are still unknown. An outcome is that all the steps that young people can take have become risky. It may be as vital as ever to complete higher education to maximize one's chances of a high-rising professional or management career, but a university entrant today would be unwise to bank on such a future. Likewise employer-led training may lead into a skilled job, and if so the occupation may last for many years, but there is simply no way today for anyone to be sure. Young people cannot avoid taking risks in which the stakes are their own future lives.

Alongside these trends most countries have experienced a common set of related socio-political developments. The costs of parenting have risen as young people have remained dependent for longer. Young people's family transitions, like their school-to-work transitions, have generally become longer and more complicated than in the past with an intermediate stage between leaving the parental home and marriage.

Most governments have been rethinking young people's welfare rights and attempting to transfer the costs of their support onto young people themselves and their families. Youth cultures have fragmented and have become sites for the creation of proto-communities rather than expressing membership of pre-existent groups. Everywhere there has been concern that young people who fail to survive extended transitions will join excluded groups or underclasses. And all these changes have occurred in a context where governments and businesses have become increasingly concerned about the competitiveness of their own future workforces given the fiercer competition in global economic markets.

East–West contrasts

The above trends in young people's situations have unfolded in Western and post-communist Europe but amid some glaring East–West contrasts. To begin with, there is the sheer pace and degree of change. In the countries that were to become post-communist, change accelerated dramatically after 1989. Until then, despite the unfolding political and economic crises, there was little change in the processes whereby young people moved from education into employment. Subsequently there has been almost total upheaval. This has been due to the massive transfers of economic activity from the public to the private sectors (see Konings, Lehmann and Schaffer, 1995), the loosening of government regulation over the state sectors, steep rises in unemployment or under-employment (people in jobs but without work or wages in some cases), and, in some countries, steep declines in welfare spending, on education among other things. Compared with the East, in the 1980s and '90s the West has been tranquil. The scale and pace of change have been so huge in the former communist countries that it has been impossible for the costs to be passed down to socially disadvantaged groups as has tended to happen in the West. All strata in the Eastern countries have been affected and the costs and benefits of change have been distributed with little regard to former social status. Some, but not all members of the old *nomenclatura* have been able to transform themselves into members of the new business classes (see Ray, 1994). Others have experienced rapid, long range socio-economic demotion. Young people from all types of family and educational backgrounds have been more or less equally at risk of unemployment (see Roberts and Jung, 1995).

A second contrast is that in the East, except in the former German Democratic Republic, overall levels of well-being have declined absolutely. East Germans have not been impoverished, though they have become much more likely to experience job loss, unemployment and downward mobility than Germans in the original Federal Republic (Diewald and Solga, 1996). In Western countries there have been many households whose living standards have fallen, but overall standards have continued to rise, albeit more slowly than in the 1950s and 60s. In contrast, in most former communist societies there have been massive overall declines in economic output and, therefore, in people's standards of living. Precise measurements have been impossible due to the scale of these countries' second economies, but an immediate impact of market reforms was usually to rip around a third from people's living standards. Until communism collapsed, outside wartime no European country had endured such an experience during the twentieth century. In the former communist countries most households have experienced serious reductions in their earned incomes and in their welfare entitlements. Whatever the governments' ideological preferences, they have been unable to afford the former levels of provision. Most households claim to have experienced a decline in their socio-economic levels since the 1980s, prior to when most felt that their positions were improving (Robert, 1996). A symptom of the post-1980s decline in living standards has been the rise in mortality rates (see Kurzynowski, 1993; Makara, 1993). This has been due primarily to the spread of poverty rather than the levels of tobacco and alcohol consumption.

In some countries, including Russia and Ukraine, economic hardship has led to declines in the marriage and birth rates among young adults. Elsewhere young marriage and parenthood have continued without interruption; if they have been unable to build occupational careers and earn economic security young people have been able to create families which, in their countries' experience, provide domestic security. Yet in all the post-communist countries family relationships have come under new strains in the harsher economic conditions. Young people without proper jobs have had no alternative but to remain dependent on, typically living with their parents. Simultaneously their own impoverishment has reduced the older generations' ability to support the young (see Wallace, 1995). Western families for whom the costs of childrearing have risen have not really experienced broadly comparable trends.

A third contrast is that in the East all the countries have either become new sovereign states or are now experiencing considerably greater independence than at any time since 1939–40. Everywhere the collapse of communism was accompanied by an escalation of national consciousness, mass political mobilization, especially among young people, and often by religious revivals. And an older 'nationalities question' was re-opened everywhere. In many places there have been wars between national groups. In the countries that have remained peaceful the political priorities have been to create new, legitimate institutions of government, and to maintain or re-establish law and order across the territories. This has given the 'youth problem' a rather lower political profile than in the West despite the widespread recognition that the experiences and responses of the first post-communist generations are likely to be crucial for the future characters of the countries, and that young people have been exceptionally active in the economies' new market sectors.

A final contrast is that amidst all the economic hardship and, in some places, social and political chaos, there has been an optimism as regards the post-communist countries' futures. Young people in particular have felt that their own adult lives will be better than their parents'. There has been an expectation that the countries will offer their peoples better ways of life in the twenty-first century than would have been possible under the old systems. This is a kind of optimism which, in recent decades, has evaporated from the Western world (see Roberts and Jung, 1995). By the mid-1990s the optimism in much of the East was weakening in the face of persistent impoverishment (see Garami and Toth, 1994) but it was at least still flickering.

Rather than quantifiable comparisons, East–West juxtapositioning produces some glaring contrasts with qualitative differences that are strictly immeasurable. The contrasts are so numerous and stark that it is normally hazardous to assume that youth policies with known effects in the West will have comparable consequences if implemented in the East. Youth unemployment is distributed quite differently, and young people's responses to the predicament in former communist countries have been quite unlike anything encountered in Western social research (see Roberts and Jung, 1995).

Differences among post-communist countries

Needless to say, the former communist countries are not a monolithic group. The former German Democratic Republic has to be treated as a special case. In many respects its institutions remained German under communism just as Poland remained Polish, Hungary remained Hungarian and so on. However, its overriding qualification as a special case is the German Democratic Republic's incorporation into a unified Germany, and thereby into the European Union, in 1991.

It is then possible to identify a group of countries that have experienced rapid Westernization. These include Poland, Slovenia, Hungary and the Czech Republic. By the mid-1990s their private sectors were responsible for most business, and their economies had become primarily market economies and had been growing steadily for several years. Moreover, their political systems had been democratized with governments changing according to how people cast their votes rather than through men with guns occupying parliament buildings, and defeated politicians were entering opposition rather than prison. The progress of these countries towards full membership of the European Union looks assured. In time they may be joined by more former communist countries; the Baltic states, Slovakia, possibly Bulgaria, Romania and Ukraine, and maybe others.

However, by the mid-1990s much of the former Soviet Union was threatened by a new dark age. Some countries' economies had all but collapsed completely. Basic services of electricity, gas and water had become unreliable. In some of these countries the old communist politicians had remained in power having, in many cases, retitled themselves as democrats and nationalists. Some countries had experienced civil wars. One exception on all the national landscapes of political and economic devastation has been that young people remain well educated. The school and higher education systems have been maintained. Maybe the fabric of the buildings has deteriorated along with teachers' salaries. Despite this, there has been no flight from education by young people. In all the former communist countries young people have been staying in education for longer. As in the West, this has been due partly to the absence of jobs, but also to the young people's belief that they need to become as well qualified as possible in order to benefit from what they hope will be their countries' more prosperous futures.

In any East–West comparisons of youth transitions and policies it makes sense to focus on former communist countries that have become fairly close to the West economically, politically and culturally. Any other selection is likely to lead to unmanageable contrasts. The former German Democratic Republic is one obvious choice. Poland and Hungary are others, and these are the new 'test cases' on which the following passages concentrate. The former German Democratic Republic has become a new 'test case' of the regulated dual training system. Simultaneously, Poland and Hungary have become 'test cases' of rapid deregulation. In many respects the latter countries have become examples of extreme deregulation. By the mid-1990s

Poland's professions were less regulated than comparable occupations in any European Union country (see Buchner-Jeziorska and Evetts, 1997). If deregulation can work well anywhere in the post-communist world, Poland and Hungary are arguably such places. By the mid-1990s Hungary had attracted more Western investment than any other ex-communist country, mainly because the government had been willing to privatize businesses to foreigners. The result has been a particularly strong presence of Western (especially German) businesses and business practices in Hungary. Poland is adjacent to Germany and has a significant German population in its western region. Indeed, much of this territory was in Germany until 1945. An even stronger case for considering Poland is that in the first half of the 1990s it recorded the fastest economic growth of all the larger European countries. It has arguably been the former communist world's brightest success story. This success, needless to say, has been strictly relative. In 1995, after several years of economic growth, average living standards in Poland were still 25 per cent down on 1989 levels. Unemployment had been falling for several years but was still above 14 per cent. Likewise inflation was down but was still over 20 per cent (Central Statistical Office of Poland, 1996). In any European Union country such statistics would indicate a crisis.

Differences within the European Union

Maybe the contrasts are not as stark, but there are clear differences in economic and political conditions, and certainly in how youth transitions are organized among the European Union countries. Europe is a Union of countries with distinct languages, cultures and national histories. It is unlikely ever to become the same kind of union as the United States of America. The European Union contains so many countries, all with national peculiarities, that they are impossible to divide into a limited number of groups. For some purposes a north–south contrast proves useful. The main contrasts in levels of economic development follow this axis and likewise in the ages at which couples marry and become parents (generally younger in the south, see Hobcraft and Kiernan, 1995). For other purposes, however, it is the Scandinavian countries that are distinct with their commitment to relatively high levels of social welfare spending. As regards the organization of transitions into employment, a Germanic group of countries can be distinguished where different kinds of secondary schools feed into either higher education or employer-based apprentice training, all routing young people towards specific kinds of employment. The communist countries had a version of this system except that they provided a common schooling up to age 14–16, and in their subsequent dual systems young people were based in education, albeit often in schools which were on the sites of, having been created by, state enterprises. Their similar beginnings have made post-1991 harmonization of education and training in West and East Germany fairly straightforward administratively (Konietzka and Solga, 1995). Within the European Union Britain has been distinctive in recent years by not only practising but espousing deregulation.

In respect of education and training arrangements, there is no obvious pan-European harmonization in process except in so far as the various countries are recognizing equivalents of each other's academic and vocational credentials. In recent years all countries have been adapting their national regimes to the general trends described above – transitions being prolonged, young people's biographies individualized, and their futures becoming less certain. Every country has been developing its national system into an elongated and more flexible version of its former self but without even diminishing let alone obliterating its distinctive characteristics. For example, in (west) Germany all the basic institutions have survived but the links between young people's education and initial training on the one hand, and their first jobs on the other, have become weaker (Konietzka and Solga, 1995). All the systems permit the higher socio-economic strata to transmit advantages to their children whose transitions, therefore, have been shielded from much of the recent turbulence. None of the European Union countries is a clear leader in equal opportunities. Thereafter the differences become overwhelming.

The UK and Germany are not representatives of all other EU countries, or even of groups which in combination account for most members of the Union, but in the 1990s they have come to represent the main socio-economic policy alternatives on the agenda for either an enlarged Union, or one which remains composed of 15 countries. Germany regulates its young people's transitions through a system which has the support of, and is jointly administered by the 'social partners' – government, employers and trade unions. In Germany most education and training programmes lead into specified occupations, and very few occupations can be entered other than through the stipulated education or training. In Germany the links between young people's education and training, and the types of occupations that they enter, have been unusually tight (see Konietzka and Solga, 1995).

The same applies to the links between young Germans' first jobs and their subsequent career development (see Grob, 1997). None of this applies in Britain. The remainder of the Union is not affected directly, yet has good reasons for being interested in the implications of each regime.

German regulation

The German approach to assimilating young people into the workforce has been admired internationally for many years and, despite some internal criticisms, continues to draw support from all sections of the German population. Internal critics invariably want the system to be improved rather than discarded. The basic features of the system have the confidence of all the major political parties, employers' associations and trade unions, plus the overwhelming majority of parents and young people. A common view has been that, 'Germany's relatively strong economic position over the past decades has been due not least to the efficiency of its dual system of training' (Dehnbostel, 1996). This confidence is one reason why the system has worked well in Germany. It is well-established and has developed incrementally throughout the twentieth century. There have been no fresh starts or even pressure for root and branch change (Rose and Page, 1989). The system has so many inter-related parts and socio-economic props that, whatever strains are encountered, it seems certain to adapt rather than collapse (see Brown, 1996).

The main building blocks in the system are tripartite secondary education followed, for most young people, by employer-based apprentice training according to curricula agreed by the social partners. This means that most post-compulsory education and training in Germany is geared to specific occupations or, at least, broad fields of employment. The system aims to give all beginning workers a vocation. This does not mean that young people are forever restricted to the occupations for which they are initially trained, but if they are to switch fields they need formal retraining. The system has in-built flexibility in so far as anyone who has become skilled will be regarded as suitable for conversion training to an cognate field. The links between pre-career education and training, first jobs and subsequent careers are not rigid. Individuals are able to change course according to their aspirations (see Kelle, Witzel and Zinn, 1997), but they must do this in clearly prescribed ways, and within the boundaries set by the highly regulated regime. This regime is enforced not just by culture – the confidence of the population in general – but also by the fact that in Germany it is impossible to practise most occupations (except under supervision) without having achieved the appropriate qualifications through stipulated forms of education or training. In Germany most occupations are formally classified as skilled, albeit at different levels. There are very few officially unskilled jobs. This means that young people are faced by structured routes towards all the more attractive types of employment and they have no option but to enter one of the routes, and complete it successfully, if they are to progress to any decent job (see Roberts, Clark and Wallace, 1994). This regime has ensured that, for several decades, virtually all 16–19-year-olds have worked towards academic or vocational qualifications. A benefit for employers has been that the system produces an abundance of formally skilled labour. German employers are mostly confident that they will be able to keep their workforces abreast of skill demands (see Centre for Exploitation of Science and Technology, 1992). For young people a benefit is that, having completed the prescribed preparation, they will be recognized as skilled workers. In all European countries employer-based training appears to enhance young people's employability (see Sollogoub and Ulrich, 1997; Wolter, Christoffel and Curti, 1997), and a strength of Germany's transition regime has been that most young people have been trained by employers. Moreover, German employers will not normally countenance employing such individuals without offering at least semi-skilled status and pay. At any rate, qualified males of German nationality have been unlikely to be asked to take unskilled jobs.

The dual system has been able to lead to 'good jobs' for virtually all German males who have completed their training partly because of the German economy's strength, but also because since 1945 there have been pools of non-nationals and immigrants who have usually been given less skilled work. After the Second World War many thousands of non-Germans were in the country. Subsequently streams of German adults returned to their homeland, and the country also began to import guest workers, mostly from Mediterranean lands. Since the 1980s, they have been joined by new, legal and illegal migrant workers from Eastern Europe. It is also the case that German females have tended to be tracked into women's occupations with generally lower status and pay than men's jobs. What will happen if and when these sources of compliant non-skilled labour disappear from Germany is unclear.

Many other countries have tried to emulate parts of the German system. The Youth Training Scheme that Britain introduced in 1983 is one example. However, the German system does not travel well, especially when only selected parts are transported, and it is difficult to see how the German training culture could be transplanted instantly (see Deissinger, 1997). One might argue that, if the system can be spread successfully into any new territory, the former German Democratic Republic should be such a case. Since 1991 it has been undergoing wholesale (West) Germanization and it was culturally German to begin with. It is the only example, but arguably the most favourable of all possible test cases for examining whether the German system of regulated youth transitions can work satisfactorily in the new market economies of East-Central Europe.

The reason for suspecting that this attempted transplant may not be entirely successful is that in recent years the entire German system has been encountering new problems, or older problems on a much larger scale. There have always been German and outside critics of the manner in which the country's education and training stratify young people, how some fail repeatedly and face long-term marginalization in the labour market (see Kloas, 1995), and how others become trapped in poor-quality apprenticeships where the training is likely to run into dead-ends (see Evans and Heinz, 1994), but these are not problems specific to Germany; they occur in all countries. Wherever employment is stratified (everywhere in practice) this is reflected in the routes towards different kinds of occupations, and no country's transition regime prevents a 'tail end' of 15 per cent or more failing to reach its basic grade. The proportion of young people who fail to achieve any recognized qualification is in fact much lower in Germany than in most other Western countries (see Oskarsdottir, 1995). However, there are three problems that are more specific to the highly regulated German model.

One is that the regime may be incurably Fordist, geared to preparing workers for crafts. The system may have greater difficulty in producing the kind of flexible workforce, composed of employees who are willing to display initiative and take responsibility for their own careers, rather than just the quality of their work in their vocations, that late-twentieth century work organizations are said to require. A second, related problem is that the German system assumes that the vocations to which young people will devote their futures are known; the regime may be ill-suited to an age in which the future is unpredictable. The third problem is that the German way is expensive, and has grown more expensive over time as more and more young people have striven for the highest qualifications of which they are capable. Nineteen is now the typical age at which apprentices commence training in (west) Germany. Twenty-nine is now the average age of higher education graduates (see Schupp, Buchtemann and Soloff, 1994). The costs of supporting young people through their extended periods of vocational preparation fall mainly on young people themselves and their families. The costs of their education and workplace training are borne mainly by the state and employers. It can be argued that the German system is appropriate only for countries with relatively high living standards and levels of labour productivity. This described (West) Germany from the 1950s to the '70s. Today, however, Germany has higher costs per unit of output than the typical European Union country, not to mention the East European and Asian competitors that have appeared in recent years. Extending the (West) German regime into the former German Democratic Republic could impose intolerable costs on young people and their families. Perhaps equally debilitating, it could raise employers' costs to an extent which blunts their capacity to win markets and attract investment in competition with other post-communist societies.

If the German system is in fact encountering increasingly serious problems the symptoms that one would expect to find are rising numbers of employers and young people seeking ways to avoid all the routes and their costs, and a gradual erosion of confidence in all quarters. One would expect employers to make increasing use of 'non-standard labour' including cheaper (but often well-educated) migrants from the east, possibly alongside rising levels of unemployment among formally skilled Germans. One would also expect increasing numbers of young people to 'vote with their feet' and refuse to enter routes where the outcomes are uncertain or unlikely to be attractive. All these symptoms have in fact become visible in east Germany. Employers have been opting out of regulation; not recognizing trade unions, or not making or, in any event, not observing collective agreements, for example (Hyman, 1996). A shortfall in company-based apprenticeships has led to the opening of numerous training centres. Studies of trainees have not found the training in these centres to be inferior, but the apprenticeships have rapidly been blighted by their unlikelihood of leading to jobs (see Ulrich, 1997). The relatively tight links between initial training, first jobs and subsequent employment that German regulation maintains increase the risks, in tough labour markets, of young people who stumble early-on becoming locked-out for much longer. So in East Germany, since the early 1990s, the pace of dismissals (redundancies) has fallen, but simultaneously the chances of the unemployed obtaining jobs have declined (see Sackmann and Struck-Mobbeck, 1997). This is the context in which young east Germans have been giving the imported dual system the thumbs down. Their main response to the new uncertainties has been to remain in school, continuing their general (academic) education for as long as possible (Grünert and Lutz, 1996).

There have been similar, albeit slower and less dramatic developments in west Germany where the proportion of children entering the *Hauptschule* has declined from around 50 per cent to around 15 per cent over the last 30 years. Young west Germans have been opting for the more academic routes which have always had the highest status, and, in current conditions, could be seen as offering the additional advantage of imparting generic and transferable skills rather than occupation- and industry-specific competencies. As Brown (1996:14) has observed, 'The defining image of the dual system as firm-based training, with part-time vocational education, leading not just to the guarantee of permanent skilled employment, but also carrying the possibility of further firm-based progression to technical or supervisory positions, is increasingly difficult to sustain.' The dual system may have become trapped in an inescapable cycle of degradation. More able young people have been opting for academic routes. Organizational delayering has narrowed the routes upwards from skilled work (Drexel, 1995). Employers prefer to appoint the academically qualified to the middle grade posts that remain. Ex-apprentices find that their skills are under-utilised (Herget, 1987). So young people could become less and less inclined to enter the dual system.

As recognized earlier, adaptation rather than collapse is the most likely outcome of these pressures, in West Germany at any rate. Brown (1996) envisages the status of vocational routes being raised by strengthening their educational content and enlarging the possibilities of switching into higher education. The outcome could be 'a more equal partnership between education and work in the delivery of vocational education and training' (Brown, 1996:15). The dual system is living up to its name, but such developments might simply reinforce the message that it is academic attainment that really counts. If the cycle of decline continues one might expect more young Germans in the eastern and western regions to take non-skilled jobs, possibly 'alternating' while they continue their academic education. Non-skilled employment can offer immediate earnings plus 'experience' which employers may begin to recognize in lieu of formal workplace training. It is in the east of the unified Germany that one would expect to find, and where we do in fact find the earliest and strongest signs of such developments.

British *laisser-faire*

This 'system' was not created by design. It is an outcome of a long-standing preference for voluntarism rather than compulsion, combined with a series of initiatives in education and training, many of which were intended to become the new grand design but which, in total, have created most possible types of provisions, all co-existing alongside straightforward youth employment, from which young people and employers are able to pick and choose.

There are two 'systemic' components which make Britain's transition regime basically unregulated. First, there are few occupations outside the professions for which any specific education or training is absolutely necessary. It is normally up to an employer to decide which types and levels of qualification and experience to require of applicants, and a result is a variety of routes into most kinds of employment. The 'couplings' are much looser than in Germany. Conversely, the young people on most training and educational programmes, even the vocational varieties, subsequently disperse into various fields of employment. Second, there is no requirement on young people to receive any education or training beyond age 16. Correspondingly, there is no requirement or even strong external pressure on employers to train anyone. From time to time governments have introduced various incentives but these have always stopped well short of compulsion. If employers train young people they have enormous discretion as regards who to train and what the training should involve. This has applied even when employers have operated within government programmes such as Youth Training (see Raggatt, 1988). An outcome, needless to say, is that most British employers train for their own specific requirements and rarely deliberately in excess.

In Britain the provision of post-compulsory education and training is left to the market, more so than ever in recent years since the UK government has been trying to introduce market forces into all possible spheres. Employers decide what training to offer, if any. They decide which qualifications and experience to recognize and use in recruitment and promotion. Schools, further education colleges and training 'businesses' decide what to offer, then seek to fill places, the mechanism that triggers state funding. For their part, young people decide which education and training to pursue, if any. The Youth Credits (vouchers which can be used to purchase approved training) that have now been introduced nationwide are intended to encourage young people to 'shop around' and take responsibility for their own career development.

This system offers young people an enormous range of options. They can try to obtain apprenticeships, or less formal training offered by employers, within or outside government programmes, or they might opt for training schemes based in workshops or community projects. Needless to say, regardless of the young people's desires there is no obligation on any employer or trainer to take them on. This applies equally in education where there are scores of academic and vocational courses and qualifications for which young people can enrol in many combinations. Alternatively, at age 16 they may simply seek jobs, and employers are free to employ them with (up to 1998) no legally imposed ceilings or floors on their wages or most other terms and conditions.

There are well-known disadvantages in this British system. These have led to waves of self-criticism usually leading to yet further initiatives which simply add to the options. One problem when all employers try to ensure that they do not train in excess of their own requirements is that the economy as a whole undertrains, and an outcome during every economic upturn is skill shortages. Some argue that this has locked Britain into a low skill, low productivity, low wage niche in international markets (see Brown, 1993; Finegold and Soskice, 1988; Jarvis and Prais, 1988; Prais, 1995; Prais and Wagner, 1985; Soskice, 1995; Steedman, 1988; Steedman and Wagner, 1989). A second problem is that in slack labour markets there are insufficient jobs, with or without training, to absorb all young people, many of whom, therefore, experience unemployment at the very start of their working lives. In Germany this hazard is at least delayed, though not necessarily removed. A third problem is that there is no simple and effective way in which would-be employees can signal their relevant experience and qualifications, or for employers to match jobs with employees' capabilities. Britain's new vocational qualifications, National Vocational Qualifications (NVQs) and General National Vovational Qualifications (GNVQs), may or may not rectify this situation depending on how widely they are taken up and actually used. The prices paid for the defects in the British transition regime are said to be labour market inefficiency, sub-optimal work practices, and a wastage of ability in most work organisations.

To offset these problems British *laisser-faire* can claim three advantages *vis-à-vis* the German model. First, the British way is cheaper, in the short run at any rate. Sixteen-year olds can seek jobs without any investment in their further education or training. Employers whose profit margins are under pressure do not need to train. Second, the system is incredibly flexible. Outcomes are left to the 'hidden hand' of the market and are not imposed administratively. Third, the system requires young people to be resourceful and responsible, and thrusts them into the 'real world' of market forces at a relatively young age, which might be considered the best possible vocational preparation (Bynner and Roberts, 1991).

A normal net result of the pluses and minuses is polarization. The young people in Britain who gain the qualifications that are generally respected by employers, the long-standing academic varieties, are likely to find firms that are willing to employ them and invest in their further training, and nurture them into skilled, core employees who are relatively well-rewarded in pay, fringe benefits and job security. Other young people are liable to find that their training and qualifications are 'not worth the paper'. Their routes into the workforce often prove to be roundabouts which keep them 'in circulation' without lifting them up the labour market. Their exits from education and training are likely to lead only into low skilled, low paid and often insecure employment. However, the weakly regulated British regime enables all young people to benefit from upturns in labour demand, and allows even low skilled, initially temporary jobs to become stepping stones to better things.

The post-communist version

The British approach to vocational preparation has won few international admirers, so its widespread adoption in post-communist countries may appear surprising, especially since the communist education and training systems bore a much closer resemblance to German than British practices. The education and training regimes in East-Central Europe might have evolved smoothly into post-communist versions of the German system. Indeed, the countries may have chosen this path, had they been able. As in Britain itself, the outcomes in most post-communist countries have been unplanned.

Laisser-faire transition systems have developed most rapidly in post-communist countries where market reforms have been introduced most rapidly and extensively, with the exception of the former German Democratic Republic. Becoming more Germanic was never a practical option in most former communist countries on account of the cost, and also because of the free market ideologies amidst which market reforms were set in motion (see Glasman, 1994). Market reforms led to many state enterprises withdrawing support and ceasing recruitment from their linked professional and vocational schools, and an immediate repercussion was a contraction of these educational sectors and an expansion of general (academic) secondary education. Trade unions were disempowered in the course of the reforms. State regulation of the private market sectors, substantial proportions of which remained in the 'second economies', became minimal. Welfare entitlements including unemployment benefits were reduced or withdrawn altogether from some groups which usually included school-leavers. In Hungary school-leavers' unemployment benefits were withdrawn with the intention of recycling the funds to support firms willing to provide apprentice training, but employers have not been required to train young people (see O'Leary, 1995). Employers in Hungary, as elsewhere in East-Central Europe, have become able to hire staff on whatever terms and conditions enable them to attract the required quantity and quality. The fastest growing enterprises, those which have quickly become responsible for high proportions of youth recruitment and employment, have been small locally owned businesses. In most such enterprises formal post-entry training has been minimal. When young people have been sought this has usually been because the employers (with justification) have believed them to be flexible and eager to work (see Roberts and Kurzynowski, 1996). In many parts of the post-communist world self-employment, usually 'trading', has become a common way in which young people earn money. Enterprise skills have been learnt entirely 'on the job' (see Toth, 1995).

If a *laisser-faire* transition regime can work satisfactorily anywhere in the post-communist world one would expect this to be in countries such as Hungary and Poland where economic recovery has been particularly rapid. Within such a context the advantages of a *laisser-faire* system – its low short-term costs to all parties, its flexibility, and the manner in which young people are taught to be resourceful and enterprising – will have played a role in the countries' recovery and may eventually lead to the economies outperforming the unified Germany. This is despite there having been early signs of some characteristically British problems appearing in Poland, Hungary and other post-communist lands where the reforms have taken a similar course as regards the education, training and recruitment of young people into employment. In Poland and Hungary youth unemployment has risen and has stubbornly stuck at roughly double the general level (see Boeri, 1993). In regions where the economies have boomed young people have been fully employed, but in regions with high unemployment the young have suffered disproportionately. Poland has also become aware of the danger of its private enterprises filling a low cost, low wage, low productivity (and low employee commitment) niche in wider markets (see Roberts and Kurzynowski, 1996).

Old issues in changing times

The respective merits of regulated and *laisser-faire* youth transition systems is an old issue that can never be considered closed. The balance of advantages can never be settled for all time because conditions are constantly changing. The current question, 'What are the relative strengths and weaknesses of alternative school-to-work regimes in the new conditions of the 1990s in which transitions have been prolonged, biographies individualized, and individuals' futures have become uncertain?' is best addressed through comparative analysis. And the changing political and economic geography of Europe has created opportunities for exceptionally productive comparative enquiries.

As one would expect, the traditional strengths and weaknesses of the (West) German and British youth transition arrangements remain evident in the 1990s. The issue that needs continuous research is exactly how the balance of advantage is changing in each country, for employers and young people. In both East Germany, Hungary and Poland one would expect the costs and the benefits of their 'reformed' transition systems, and whatever the balance might be, to be more pronounced than in the mature market economies where economic change has been slower and where, in any case, their transition systems have had longer to become embedded and surrounded by coping mechanisms.

There are hazards for the former communist societies in both regulated and *laisser-faire* approaches to young people's transitions. They need to be able to assess the implications of each model within their own specific economic and political circumstances in the 1990s. And the manner in which the former communist societies develop will have implications for the rest of Europe. The course taken in the east will help to determine the kind of wider union that Europe might one day become. Within this context, the issues at stake in debates about regulated and *laisser-faire* youth transition regimes are more important than ever. A wider range of national governments now have stakes in the answers. And the issues have become Euro-politically sensitive since they are now central in debates about the future form of the European Union.

References

Boeri, T. (1993) 'Unemployment in Central and Eastern Europe: transient or persistent?' in S. Ringen and C. Wallace (eds), *Societies in Transition: East-Central Europe Today*. Prague: Central European University.

Braun, F. (1977) 'Youth unemployment in West Germany – the psycho-social aspect', in B. O. Pettman and J. Fyfe (eds), *Youth Unemployment in Britain and the Federal Republic of Germany*. Bradford: MCB Publications.

Brown, A. (1993) 'Employers' approaches to the development of key workers: lessons from Germany, Japan and Holland', paper presented to seminar on Employers' Labour Market Behaviour. Employment Department, London.

Brown, A. (1996) 'Whither the dual system: pressures for change and prospects for the future of vocational education and training in Germany', paper presented to ESRC Symposium on Comparative Skill Formation Processes, Bristol.

Buchner-Jeziorska, A. and Evetts, J. (1997) 'Regulating professionals: the Polish example', *International Sociology*, **12**: 61–72.

Bynner, J. and Roberts, K. (1991) *Youth and Work*. London: Anglo-German Foundation.

Central Statistical Office of Poland (1996) *Social and Economic Situation in Poland in 1995*. Warsaw.

Centre for Exploitation of Science and Technology (1992) *Attitudes to Innovation in Germany and Britain: A Comparison*. London.

Clarke, L. (1993) 'Labour in the construction industry', paper presented to Labour Process Conference, Blackpool.

Dehnbostel, P. (1996) 'Germany: innovative approaches to vocational education and training', paper presented to ESRC Symposium on Comparative Skill Formation Processes, Bristol.

Deissinger, T. (1997) 'The German dual system – a model for Europe?', *Education and Training*, **39**: 297–302.

Diewald, M. and Solga, H. (1996) 'Mobility in East Germany minus mobility in West Germany = transformation?' paper presented to workshop on Transition in Eastern Europe, Berlin.

Drexel, I.(1995) 'The implications of different continuing training systems for corporate work organisation and personnel management policy', in R. Koch and J. Reuling (eds), *The European Dimension in Vocational Training*. Bielefeld: Bertelsmann.

Evans, K. and Heinz, W. R. (eds) (1994) *Becoming Adults in England and Germany*. London: Anglo-German Foundation.

Finegold, D. and Soskice, D. (1988) 'The failure of training in Britain: analysis and prescription', *Oxford Review of Economic Policy*, **4**: 21–53.

Garami, E. and Toth, O. (1994) *Young People's Social and Family Backgrounds and their Political Attitudes in 1993*. Budapest: TARKI.

Glasman, M. (1994) 'The great deformation: Polanyi, Poland and the terrors of planned spontaneity', in C. G. A. Bryant and E. Mokrzycki (eds), *The Great New Transformation*? London: Routledge.

Grimond, J. (1979) *Youth Unemployment and the Bridge from School to Work.* London: Anglo-German Foundation.

Grob, M. (1997) 'Educational systems and occupational attainment', paper presented to International Labour Markets conference on Understanding the School-to-Work Transition, Aberdeen.

Grünert, H. and Lutz, B. (1996) 'A double process of destabilisation in post-socialist societies: the case of Germany', paper presented to workshop of European Science Foundation Network on Transitions in Youth, La Ciotat.

Hamilton, S. F. (1987) 'Apprenticeship as a transition to adulthood in Germany', *American Journal of Education,* **95**: 314–45.

Heinz, W. R. (1985) 'Between school and work: will compensatory training schemes solve the problem of youth unemployment?' in *Thinkers and Makers: Education for Tomorrow's Society.* London: Policy Studies Institute/Anglo-German Foundation.

Heinz, W. R. (1986) 'The transition from school to work: coping with threatening unemployment', paper presented to American Economic Research Association, San Francisco.

Herget, H. (1987) *The Transition of Young People into Employment after Completion of Apprenticeship in the Dual System.* Berlin: CEDEFOP.

Hobcraft, J. and Kiernan, K. (1995) *Becoming a Parent in Europe,* Welfare State Programme 116. London: London School of Economics.

Hyman, R. (1996) 'Institutional transfer: industrial relations in Eastern Germany', *Work, Employment and Society,* **10**: 601–39.

Irwin, S. (1995) *Rights of Passage.* London: UCL Press.

Jarvis, V. and Prais , S. J.(1988) *Two Nations of Shopkeepers: Training for Retailing in France and Britain,* Discussion Paper 140. London: National Institute of Economic and Social Research.

Kelle, U., Witzel, A. and Zinn, J. (1997) 'School-to-work transition and occupational careers – results from a longitudinal study in Germany', paper presented to International Labour Markets conference on Understanding the School-to-Work Transition, Aberdeen.

Kloas, P. W. (1995) 'On the job training: a promising way for young employees to catch up on training qualifications', in R. Koch and J. Reuling (eds), *The European Dimension in Vocational Training.* Bielefeld: Bertelsmann.

Koch, R. and Reuling, J. (eds) (1995) *The European Dimension in Vocational Training.* Bielefeld: Bertelsmann.

Konietzka, D. and Solga, H. (1995) 'Two certified societies? The regulation of entry in the labour market in East and West Germany', paper presented at workshop on Transitions in Youth: Comparisons Over Time and Across Countries. The Netherlands: Oostvoorne.

Konings, J., Lehmann, H. and Schaffer, M. E. (1995) *Employment Growth, Job Creation and Job Destruction in Polish Industry: 1988-91,* Working Paper 38/1995. Leuven Catholic University: Institute for Central and East European Studies.

Kurzynowski, A. (1993) *Main Directions of Systemic Changes and their Effects: Experiences of Poland.* Warsaw: Warsaw School of Economics.

Lenhardt, G. (1977) 'Youth unemployment in West Germany: trends and causes', in B. O. Pettman and J. Fyfe (eds), *Youth Unemployment in Great Britain and the Federal Republic of Germany.* Bradford: MCB Publications.

Lenhardt, G. (1984) 'Between market and welfare state: the social position of young people in the economic crisis', Paper 84/26, *Proceedings of the Standing Conference on the Sociology of Further Education*. Blagdon: Coombe Lodge.

Makara, P. (1993) 'The effect of social changes on the population's way of life and health: a Hungarian case study', paper presented to conference on Social Time – New Problems of Leisure in Contemporary Society, Budapest.

O'Leary, C. (1995) 'Performance indicators: a management tool for active labour programmes in Hungary and Poland', *International Labour Review*, **134**(6).

Oskarsdottir, G. (1995) 'Dropping out in Scandinavia and the USA: a comparative study of dropout patterns', paper presented to workshop on Transitions in Youth: Comparisons Over Time and Across Countries. The Netherlands: Oostvoorne.

Prais, S. J. (1995) *Productivity, Education and Training: An International Perspective*. Cambridge: Cambridge University Press.

Prais, S. J. and Wagner, K. (1985) 'Schooling standards in England and Germany: some summary comparisons bearing on economic performance', *National Institute Economic Review*, **112**: 53–73.

Raggatt, P. (1988) 'Quality control in the dual system of West Germany', *Oxford Review of Education*, **14**: 163–86.

Ray, L. (1994) 'The collapse of Soviet socialism: legitimation, regulation and the state', in P. Brown and R. Crompton (eds), *Economic Restructuring and Social Exclusion*. London: UCL Press.

Robert, P. (1996) 'Perceived mobility in five transition societies', paper presented at workshop on Transition in Eastern Europe, Berlin.

Roberts, K., Clark, S. C. and Wallace, W. (1994) 'Flexibility and individualisation: a comparison of transitions into employment in England and Germany, *Sociology*, **28**: 31–54.

Roberts, K. and Jung, B. (1995) *Poland's First Post-Communist Generation*. Aldershot: Avebury.

Roberts, K. and Kurzynowski, A. (1996) *Young People and their Employers in Present-day Poland*, Occasional Paper 6. Liverpool: University of Liverpool, Department of Sociology, Social Policy and Social Work Studies.

Rose, R. (1990) *Prospective Evaluation through Comparative Analysis*, Studies in Public Policy 182. Strathclyde: University of Strathclyde, Centre for the Study of Public Policy.

Rose, R. and Page, E. C. (1989) *Searching and Acting in Adversity*, Studies in Public Policy 174. Strathclyde: University of Strathclyde, Centre for the Study of Public Policy.

Sackmann, R. and Struck-Mobbeck, O. (1997) 'School to work transitions after the reunification', paper presented to International Labour Markets conference on Understanding the School-to-Work Transition, Aberdeen.

Schupp, J., Buchtemann, C. F. and Soloff, D. (1994) *School to Work Transition Patterns: (West) Germany and the United States*, Working Paper, Network on Transitions in Youth. Strasbourg: European Science Foundation.

Shackleton, J. R. (1997) 'Training in Germany: a view from abroad', *Education and Training*, **8**: 303–8.

Sollogoub, M. and Ulrich, V. (1997) 'The school-to-work transition and the French apprenticeship system', paper presented to International Labour Markets conference on Understanding the School-to-Work Transition, Aberdeen.

Soskice, D. (1995) 'A comparative review: Germany, the UK, the USA and Japan', in R. Koch and J. Reuling (eds), *The European Dimension in Vocational Training*. Bielefeld: Bertelsmann.

Steedman, H. (1988) *Vocational Education and Manufacturing Employment in Western Europe*. London: National Institute of Economic and Social Research.

Steedman, H. and Wagner, K. (1989) 'Productivity, machinery and skills: clothing manufacture in Britain and Germany', *National Institute Economic Review*, **128**: 40–57.

Toth, O. (1995) *Self-employment as a Reality and Perspective in the Careers of Young People*, unpublished typescript, Budapest.

Ulrich, J. G. (1997) 'Non-company based training: the eastern German experience', *Education and Training*, **8**: 309–15.

Wallace, C. (1995) 'Young people and their families in Poland: changing times, changing dependencies', *Journal of European Social Policy*, **5**: 97–109.

Wolter, S. C., Christoffel, J. and Curti, M. (1997) 'Different school systems – different labour market results', paper presented to International Labour Markets conference on Understanding the School-to-Work Transition, Aberdeen.

3

Social structures and individual lives: effects of participation on the institutions of family, education and work

Nicholas Emler

Introduction: social capital and lives in transition

This chapter is concerned with social capital (cf. Coleman, 1988), and specifically with social capital in relation to young people in their late teens, in the transitional phase between childhood and the full rights, responsibilities and opportunities of adulthood. It considers the consequences of access to the major institutional structures which dominate this period of life, those of full-time education and of employment or employment-related training, and compares these with the condition of unemployment. It examines some consequences of being male versus female. Finally, it raises the question as to whether social capital is producer or product of human capital.

The sociologist Louis Wirth (1938) famously observed that social life in the city was 'transitory, segmented, formal, and impersonal'. This was no isolated, whimsical comment. It summed up a consensus among social theorists about the effects upon human relations of the industrial revolution and the mass urbanization it created. The feudal and farming communities familiar to Europeans for centuries as the basis of social life were fast disappearing and for most inhabitants of twentieth century Europe these belonged to the ancestral past. This way of life was no part of the majority's direct experience; it was glimpsed, if at all, in the present only from railway carriage windows. Wirth was simply encapsulating in a conveniently quotable phrase what Wellman (1979) has called the 'community-lost' hypothesis, and others the 'mass society thesis' (Giner, 1976).

The displacement of populations that accompanied the industrial revolution had supposedly broken up the small-scale and largely rural communities of pre-industrial society and progressively replaced them with more anonymous aggregations. Under these new conditions society could no longer be structured around networks of personal ties and relations of personal acquaintance; beyond the increasingly limited confines of families and households, effective social relations could only be based upon formal structures and statuses. Relations between people would be predicated upon the social categories with which they could be identified or the roles and positions they occupied in formalized social institutions and organizations. Relations would not, indeed could not any longer be based upon mutual acquaintance and personal ties. There were after all too many inhabitants of the city; no individual could know personally all those people he or she might encounter on a daily basis. The sheer numbers would rapidly overwhelm each inhabitant's finite 'fund of sociability' (Milgram, 1970). Cognitive economies were required to manage the complexities of modern social life. Social roles and categories provided the basis for those economies.

From the middle of this century, however, the mass society thesis has been in retreat, albeit more rapidly in some of the constituent disciplines of the social sciences than in others. Small scale 'communities'[1] were found to be alive and well even in the hearts of industrial cities (Gans, 1962; Young and Willmott, 1957) and people were found still to be 'dwelling among friends' in urban settings (Fischer, 1981; Mitchell, 1969). This rediscovery of the community and of the ubiquity of personal ties in everyday life also prompted a reassessment of the functions of personal relationships, and a growing recognition that these functions had not been entirely taken over by bureaucratic institutions and formal arrangements. To take some examples, it has become clear that mass media have not entirely replaced personal acquaintances in the exercise of influence (Katz and Lazarsfeld, 1955; Rogers, 1962), that within bureaucratic organizations managers must rely heavily on their personal ties with others and not on their formal authority alone to get their jobs done (Kaplan, 1984), that labour markets continue to depend on personal contacts and recommendations (Granovetter, 1973; Lin, 1982), that alongside money-based, self-contained commercial transactions, there is an extensive economy of informal helpfulness and exchange among kin, friends, and neighbours (Boissevain, 1974), that with respect to social cohesion and social control personal attachments continue to accomplish what neither official agencies of criminal justice nor childhood internalization of behavioural standards can guarantee (Emler and Reicher, 1995; Hirschi, 1969; Sampson and Laub, 1993), that political attitudes and political action are built upon personal ties between actors (Erikson, 1981; Granovetter, 1973; Lalljee and Evans, 1995), and that physical and psychological well-being are a function of the quality of support available through personal relationships and not just degree of access to state- or commercially-proved services (e.g., Brown and Harris, 1978).

The implications of the continuing significance of the community and personal relationships for our understanding of adolescence and youth are extensive. Theorizing about this period of life continues to reflect influences of the mass society thesis. Thus, the transition from child to adult has often been seen as a process of moving out of the informal sphere of the family and into a progressively more formal and impersonal world. Successful management of this transition has been seen to depend on the adequacy of the inner psychological resources built up during the years of childhood. Resources of self-control and intrinsic motivation have been accorded particular importance. Rediscovery of the community shifts the emphasis to the social resources available to adolescents. We might therefore expect that the extent and quality of these resources will be related to successful negotiation of the various tasks of adolescence and youth such as the construction of an adult identity based upon an economic role, formation of a political role and standpoint, and the development of a sexual identity and sexual relationships.

Recently there have been attempts to provide a unifying analysis which can account for the enduring significance of personal relationships in social, political and economic life, and these have further implications for the transition to adulthood. Among these are analyses organized around the concept of 'social capital' (Putnam, 1993; Coleman, 1988; Granovetter, 1985), though many elements of this approach are anticipated in Mitchell's (1969) concept of a personal order, and in Boissevain's (1974) examination of informal networks. Coleman's (1988) own version identifies social capital with a structure of relations between actors that has a degree of closure – some of those to whom any individual actor is linked are also linked to each other. Such structures of relations are claimed to have three important properties: they create trust and they thereby support enduring relations of credit and debt, they allow efficient, low-cost information flow, and they sustain social norms through effective sanctions (Coleman, 1988). Though analytically distinct, these properties are interdependent. Trust is created because sanctions against violations of trust are realistic. The effectiveness of sanctions depends on the ready availability of behavioural information, which ensures that actors are chronically identifiable as the authors of their actions. Trust guarantees confidence in circulated information because sanctions guarantee its reliability. And so on. Additionally, it seems worth recognizing that social capital in Coleman's sense increases the benefit that can be derived from human and material capital. This, in effect, was Boissevain's (1974) point: social capital supports an informal economy in which individuals are able to trade in a range of resources.

Though analytically persuasive, 'social capital' and similar concepts present problems when one tries to translate them into research procedures. The approach taken in this chapter starts from the proposition that the more fundamental consequence of a network of personal ties between actors is information flow and that trust and norm enforcement are more derivative and dependent properties. If one then thinks about how in practice social capital is created by structures of personal relationships, it can be argued that it is created by regular conversational exchanges between people who know one another, but more importantly in which these are exchanges *about* themselves and the people they know in common, about their actions and opinions and relationships (cf. Emler, 1990, 1994). This approach provides a practical starting point for the exploration of research questions, and even helps to identify some of the questions. For example, the more conversations a person has the more information will be available to that person about his or her interpersonal environment. The larger the number of acquaintances with whom these conversations occur the more likely is the structure of relationships as a whole to possess the crucial quality of closure. The closer or more intimate the contacts with others, the more the value of the information exchanged; people disclose more to their close friends (Cozby, 1973) and are more honest with close friends (DePaulo et al., 1997). These variables, frequency of conversational contacts, number of different contacts, and intimacy of contacts, should also have consequences for the position of the individual in the social structure; they should affect the degree to which the individual is a known quantity and thus potentially in a position to benefit from the trust of others.

It should be recognized that the concept of social capital is being interpreted in a particular way here, and that others are possible. For

Coleman (1988) social capital is a property of communities, localities, regions, even nations. At these levels its variability will arise from such factors as patterns and levels of economic activity, the transience or stability of populations, the extent and nature of local resources and amenities to support sociability, the political culture, and even traditions of participation or 'civic engagement' (cf. Putnam, 1993). Thus one might predict – as Coleman does – that young people growing up in a social environment in which social capital is limited will experience less effective informal controls and will in consequence be more likely to drop out of full-time education, will also be more at risk of involvement in criminal activities and/or drug abuse, will have more problems establishing successful personal relationships, and will experience more difficulties gaining access to employment. They will at the same time experience the social environment as a more hazardous and unpredictable place, and we may expect that this experience will reinforce many of the behavioural consequences, as well as reducing feelings of personal efficacy.

In this chapter the individual rather than the collective forms the focus of analysis. In this sense, one could anticipate that individuals will differ in the degree to which they are embedded in or integrated into the *same* collectives, such differences reflecting personal resources of character, temperament, talent and social skill. However, it is likely that personal inclinations and aptitudes will interact with the opportunities available in the social environment in complex ways over the course of adolescence, and an appreciation of the nature of these interactions will require appropriate longitudinal research. But as a first step there is value asking the more modest and manageable questions indicated above, about the frequency, range and intimacy of social contacts. Our own research (e.g. Emler, 1990; Emler and McNamara, 1996) has coupled these basic questions with another: what effects does the status of the young person have upon social contacts? The specific focus of the work to be described here has been upon the different institutional statuses that young people may occupy following the end of compulsory full-time education. In Britain, Germany, and indeed other industrialized countries a range of transitional statuses now intervene between the period taken up by compulsory secondary education and the achievement of full adult status. Although attainment in secondary education powerfully predicts social placement in adulthood, some of the variance in the latter is attributable to these intermediate statuses. But if we accept the import of the foregoing observations about the continuing significance of personal relationships then it is appropriate to ask how the various transitional statuses may shape social contacts and personal relationships.

We know that in Britain after the end of compulsory education the major alternatives are an academic route into higher education, vocation training or further education, some form of work experience possibly involving apprenticeship, and unemployment (cf. Banks et al., 1992). Alongside these transitional statuses into a labour market position, there is also often a transition in domestic arrangements; young people begin living away from the parental home for extended periods, and sooner or later set up more permanent domestic arrangements of their own. In East Germany, reunification has substantially altered the distribution between routes into the labour market, with a fall in the availability of the apprenticeship route and a major increase in youth unemployment. So does access to employment, training or education have effects on the social contact patterns of young people?

Research strategy and methods

Our research on social contacts relies on a methodology that we have evolved over a number of studies. The methodology involves sampling conversational contacts over a week. Among the parameters assessed are the number of conversational encounters over seven days, the range of contacts (how many different people), the nature of the ties between contacts (whether family members, close friends, casual acquaintances, etc.), the stability of ties (how long each contact has been known to the respondent), and the age and sex mix of contacts. A particular focus of our research, however, has been upon the logistics of conversational contacts – how and where do they arise – questions that have been relatively neglected by social scientists after Festinger, Schachter and Back's (1950) pioneering study.

These questions were studied using an event-contingent self-recording (ESR) procedure (see Wheeler and Reis 1991, for a discussion of this approach and its advantages) as a cost-effective means of generating a large and therefore representative sample of social interactions. In this procedure, recording is triggered by a qualifying event. The qualifying event we have used in our research is any conversation in which there is a substantive exchange of information or opinion. Brief service transactions and ritual exchanges of greeting are excluded, as are formal addresses such as lectures in which there is little genuine interaction. Of course, conversation is not the only form of social interaction of any consequence in the lives of young people. A wide range of activities have social and even communicative features as well as being of theoretical interest in their own right (for example, games, sports, hobbies, dancing, hiking and other joint leisure activities, and working with or alongside others). Moreover, other ESR methods, notably the widely used RIR (Rochester Interaction Record; Wheeler and Reis, 1991) define qualifying events in other ways.[2] Nonetheless, as already indicated, there are reasons for regarding conversational exchanges as having special significance in social life, and our method does sample such exchanges.

In this chapter I want to describe the social contact patterns in five distinct groups of young people, all resident in the east of Scotland at the time they were studied, and representing four key transitional statuses. The first was a group of 50 18- to 19-year-old males and females in full-time education, attending a university in the region and living away from their family home. The second was a group of 28 attending the same university, but living at home with their parents. The third were a group of 20, with the same age range, living in parental homes, and attending local colleges of further education; such colleges tend to offer vocational rather than academic training. Students at these colleges do not on average have academic records as strong as those at university and do not come from such advantaged backgrounds. Inclusion of these three groups gave some opportunity to distinguish the effects associated with level of post-compulsory education from those associated with living away from the parental home. The fourth group of 47 were again in the same age range, living in the same area of Scotland in the parental home, but in full-time employment. Their jobs reflected their limited academic and vocational qualifications; these were unskilled, low pay jobs. The fifth group of 36 were resident in the same area but distinguished in terms of employment status; they were unemployed, though a few had occasional part-time work. However, they also tended to have the poorest educational qualifications.

The ESR procedure involves recording conversational contacts in a small, diary-like booklet, using simple letter codes for much of the information. The recording procedure is introduced at an initial meeting with participants in which detailed written instructions are provided and discussed and potential recording problems considered. The diary itself includes an *aide-memoire* to the recording procedure. The seven day sample of conversations provided by our ESR procedure is a short enough interval for the motivation and commitment of participants to be sustained (see Stone, Kessler and Haythornthwaite, 1991), but it is also an appropriate sampling interval given the weekly cycle of much routine activity.

Patterns of conversational contact

Consider first the simplest descriptive statistic derived from the research, namely the average numbers of conversational encounters in each of the five groups (Table 3.1).

What is immediately apparent from this table is the massive advantage of those in full-time education as compared to the unemployed. Moreover, the values for the college group are comparable to those of the university groups, which suggests that it is something about the social environment created by full-time education and not purely the ability or social background of those involved in it, or even the fact of living away from home, which generates more extensive social contact. Turning to the employed group, employment does generate more social contact than unemployment, or to put it another way the enforced leisure time of the unemployed is not used for increased social contact. Table 3.1 also shows, however, that full-time education is associated with more opportunities than full-time employment (the difference is statistically significant).

Consider next the kinds of relationships these young people have with their social contacts. Table 3.2 breaks down contacts into six principle categories[3] of relationship. I would draw attention to two features of the overall pattern. The first is that social life for all these groups seems to occur very largely within a known social world of family, friends and acquaintances. Of the different people encountered over the seven days, strangers form a very small proportion for all but those at university. In other research we have been able to establish that at most one third of this category of strangers will lie entirely outside the

Table 3.1 Total number of conversational encounters over seven days as a function of status

	Females	Males
University Away from home	206.5	182.5
University Living at home	181.4	165.1
College Living at home	179.1	154.8
Employed Living at home	125.1	126.2
Unemployed Living at home	75.6	78.5

Table 3.2 Numbers of different people encountered in each relationship category

Relation to self		UA	UH	COLL	EMP	UNEM
Close friend	M	6.9	6.0	8.7	7.9	4.3
	F	6.4	5.9	8.5	4.2	4.1
Other friends	M	17.3	16.4	18.9	15.9	12.2
	F	18.4	13.2	16.5	12.3	10.6
Casual acqs	M	17.1	17.7	12.9	7.2	4.2
	F	17.6	17.7	14.8	10.1	5.9
Family	M	2.5	3.5	2.9	2.9	2.7
	F	2.8	5.6	4.2	3.4	3.8
Formal	M	5.8	3.7	7.6	6.4	1.0
	F	3.8	4.5	7.1	10.0	1.3
Stranger	M	8.2	3.8	0.6	1.4	1.1
	F	8.6	7.3	2.4	3.3	1.7
Total no. of people	M	54.6	52.7	56.2	44.2	28.0
	F	66.3	52.5	59.7	46.5	30.6

UA: University, living away from home; UH: university, living at home; COLL: college, living at home; EMP: in full-time employment, living at home; UNEM: unemployed, living at home.

known social worlds of the respondents. Many of the 'strangers' are people they already knew about before the encounter occurred or were known to a mutual friend who made the introduction. Contacts that are purely formal – people encountered in business and service transactions and based only on organizational roles – also form a small proportion of the total. In other words, most encounters were not the impersonal, role- or status-based contacts anticipated in Wirth's (1938) vision of city life. It remains possible of course that Wirth was correct about much larger cities than those our respondents lived in, but I would argue this is now a hypothesis that needs to be tested empirically rather than a fact to be assumed *a priori*.

The second feature relates to effects of status on the distribution of contacts across different kinds of relationship. Marked differences between males and females are largely absent. But, compared to this biologically-based status, institutional status has a substantial impact on social life. Again the college group are very similar to the university group in most respects whereas both are strikingly different from the unemployed group. In no individual category of relationship does the average number of different contacts of the college group differ substantially from the corresponding average of the university group, except for contacts with strangers. One might expect, however, that the college group will have fewer of the 'weak ties' identified as economically and politically significant by Granovetter (1973); this seems likely given that the university group living away from home have at least two distinct sets of contacts, only one of which is represented fully in the recorded sample of their conversations. The other set would predominate during the university vacations when they are back at the family home.

The unemployed group do not differ dramatically from the employed group with respect to any individual category of relationship. The most marked differences are with respect to the formal and stranger categories, although the unemployed males also had contacts within a smaller circle of friends (X = 16.5) than their employed counterparts (X = 23.8). The small differences in most categories are nonetheless, with one exception, in the same direction and accumulate to substantial and statistically significant overall differences between these two categories. Overall, the university groups in full-time education have a range of social contacts about twice the average for the unemployed group.

The evidence presented up to this point indicates that official status within the principle institutions of society – as student in an educational establishment, as employee in an organization, as a member of a family household – have a major impact upon the 'unofficial' lives of young people, upon their contacts with people regarded as friends and acquaintances. Moreover, such official statuses have a much greater impact than biological status as male or female, a fact which perhaps points to the important role access to education and to employment have had in the emancipation of women over this century. I would further argue that social background and educational ability have effects on the range and intensity of young people's social relationships which are mediated by the social structures to which these personal and social attributes give or deny access, and I will return to this point towards the end of the chapter. For the moment it indicates that one important question must concern the determinants of, for example, voluntary participation in full-time further and higher education by young people.

The next obvious question is why these formal institutions have these effects on informal lives. Information provided by the contact records offers two kinds of clue. The first of these comes from evidence about where contacts take place. Table 3.3 gives the mean numbers of

Table 3.3 Frequency of conversational encounters as a function of setting

Setting		UA	UH	COLL	EMP	UNEM
Own home/residence	M	60.3	49.7	38.1	30.3	31.3
	F	95.9	43.9	44.2	32.6	26.3
Others' homes/res.	M	26.0	36.7	7.4	12.0	13.9
	F	24.5	24.3	17.3	11.9	19.9
University/college	M	34.7	24.6	71.1	1.0	0.0
	F	31.2	31.7	82.2	1.6	0.2
Workplace	M	4.2	0.0	10.9	39.3	0.9
	F	2.9	0.2	5.2	42.3	2.0
Street	M	9.3	7.0	5.6	7.4	5.7
	F	9.6	7.3	6.6	5.2	4.0
Club	M	4.4	2.4.	1.2	4.7	1.7
	F	4.3	3.2	2.3	3.8	2.0
Bar/pub	M	25.2	18.3	6.7	8.6	5.8
	F	23.8	5.6	3.3	11.8	4.1
Travelling	M	4.7	11.6	10.1	5.4	1.9
	F	2.9	6.6	5.9	5.4	1.9
Telephone	M	4.1	4.9	3.1	4.2	4.2
	F	5.1	16.7	4.5	6.7	5.2
Shopping	M	2.0	4.2	3.1	3.2	2.6
	F	2.6	4.5	5.2	4.3	2.6
Party	M	2.1	2.6	0.0	0.9	2.7
	F	3.2	5.1	1.1	1.5	0.9

contacts of the different groups across eleven different settings.[4] Various features are worth noting here. First, several kinds of settings are relatively unimportant, at least in terms of sheer numbers of contacts. Thus, none of the groups depended for social life primarily upon meetings or contacts at parties or clubs, or over the telephone. Neither were the public settings of the street, travelling, or shopping important. Bars and pubs, represented in beer commercials as the heart of social life in Britain, were only of much significance for the university group. Second, and in sharp contrast, homes or places of residence were very important, both others' homes/residences and particularly own home/residence. Third, the physical premises of the institution itself, whether university, college, or place of work, was of great significance for those with an official status in that institution. This is one feature which dramatically sets the unemployed group apart from all the others. Fourth, however, it is clearly not all that sets them apart. The effects of institutional status spill over into many of the other settings for social interaction. Across the various non-work settings of clubs, travel, street, bar and shopping, for example, the employed females recorded 30.5 contacts as against 14.6 for the unemployed females. This suggests that young people's official roles in education and employment allow them to generate and sustain social relationships which then spread into other spheres of their lives. The greater generative power of education as compared to employment is more apparent in its impact on the number of contacts which occur within a domestic or residential setting.

The second clue to the impact of institutions is provided by evidence about the circumstances under which encounters arose. The records kept of conversational encounters included information about how each such encounter arose. Encounters were recorded as either *appointed* (arranged in advance), *intended* (in so far as one or other of the participants had intentionally sought out the other), *chance* (encounters perceived as unforeseen or fortuitous), or *predictable* (encounters which were not deliberately sought out but which were perceived as foreseeable; in effect, these are encounters which arise because individuals have habits and routines which intersect at various times and locations with those of others and these points of intersection become predictable).

I would draw attention to five features of the pattern in Table 3.4. The first is the prevalence of predictable encounters. For all groups this

Table 3.4 Frequency (*and percentage*) conversational encounters as a function of circumstances

	Chance	Arranged	Intended	Predictable
University	58.6	18.7	40.5	81.4
Away from home	*(29.4)*	*(9.4)*	*(20.3)*	*(40.9)*
University	33.0	19.8	31.2	91.2
Living at home	*(18.8)*	*(11.3)*	*(17.8)*	*(52.0)*
College	29.2	15.4	11.6	109.4
Living at home	*(17.6)*	*(9.3)*	*(7.0)*	*(66.1)*
Employed	27.5	17.3	13.4	66.9
Living at home	*(22.0)*	*(13.8)*	*(10.7)*	*(53.5)*
Unemployed	16.7	15.3	13.3	31.5
Living at home	*(21.7)*	*(19.9)*	*(17.3)*	*(41.0)*

is the most commonly recorded circumstance under which encounters arise and for one group, those at college, it accounts for fully two thirds of all their encounters. The second is that making arrangements in advance has only minor importance in social life as a whole (though the qualification must be added that these data show only raw numbers of encounters, not their individual psychological or social importance; it is just possible that the small numbers of arranged encounters include all those which have the greatest importance for the individuals involved). A third noteworthy feature is the relatively high frequency of chance encounters among the group attending university away from home. I would suggest that this reflects the quite densely populated and, for this group, relatively new social environment (most had been at the university for about four months at the time of the study). Fourth, the university group has, compared to the others, relatively high numbers of intended encounters. There is a striking parallel here with managerial staff who, we have found, have more encounters in this category than in any other (Emler, 1996). Is it possible that the university group is somehow anticipating or rehearsing a task-oriented social strategy which will equip them for future managerial level work? Alternatively this strategy may reflect a form of cultural capital, derived from family background.

The fifth and final feature, perhaps the most significant, is reflected in the small absolute numbers of both chance and especially predictable encounters among the unemployed group. This supports the conclusion that unemployed youth have limited social contacts because they lack both routines outside the home such as are provided by education and work, and the chance opportunities which arise simply through regular presence in workplace and educational settings.

Such settings appear to be dense in legitimate interaction opportunities.

Sources of variance in contact patterns: caveats and possibilities

At this point something must be said about the validity of the evidence. As with the other methods available to the social researcher who wishes to study social contact patterns – self-reports in surveys or interviews, direct observation – this too is liable to error. Two kinds of error are likely in particular. One is under-recording; it is rather more likely that some interactions which actually occurred will not have been recorded than that interactions will be recorded which did not take place. It is impossible to be precise about the degree of under-recording but we are reasonably confident that it is less than that which is typical with other event self-recording methods. Wheeler and Nezlek's (1977) RIR produces much smaller mean numbers of both people and contacts for similar populations, which in part reflects the requirement of their method that only interactions of ten minutes or more should be recorded. Signal-contingent recording (e.g., using bleepers) has the advantage of allowing direct quantification of under-recording; it has been shown that this can run as high as twenty percent (Raffaelli and Duckett, 1989). Reasons for under-recording with this method include forgetting to carry the bleeper or the record forms. Our strategy for reducing under-recording has been to simplify the recording process as much as possible and to make the diary exceptionally compact and therefore portable. In its current form it is similar in size to a pocket diary, 15 cm × 10 cm.

Second there may be errors of categorization. Factual details can be wrong, such as a person's age which may often be guessed at by the recorder, how long the recorder has known a particular person, or where or when a contact occurred. Potentially more problematic, however, are the categorizations of relationships and encounter circumstances. These require interpretation by the recorder; there are no factually correct responses so in each case it is a matter of the recorder's judgement. We can hope that different recorders interpret such categories as 'close friend' or 'predictable encounter' or even what counts as a qualifying encounter (itself a potential source of either under- *or* over-recording) in the same way, but we cannot be certain that this will invariably happen. Some ambiguity is inevitable as well as some inter-individual variation in the interpretation of categories; for example, it is possible to imagine at one extreme a person who perceives almost every acquaintance to be a close friend and at the other an individual who regards no one as a friend. Nonetheless, some confidence that these sources of error are not so great as to render the data worthless is provided by the infrequency of reported difficulties in using the categories, by a consistent tendency for different relationship categories to be associated with different periods of acquaintance, and by direct inspection of the individual diaries which revealed that mean values were not merely based on extreme patterns.

There were, however, high variances *within* groups for many of the indices derived from the diaries and the question must be raised as to how much of the inter-individual variation is true variation and how much is error. There are four possible sources of the total variation, three of which reflect true variance. Variation across individuals in recording practices would constitute error; one individual may, for example, record more interactions than another because he or she is more conscientious or has a lower threshold for recognizing the occurrence of qualifying interactions. A source of true variance is temporary change in circumstances. Several respondents reported that the recorded week had been atypical, for example because they were sick and in bed for a part of it, because they were travelling away from home or because they had attended some major social gathering. There may be no such thing as a typical week, but some determination of this could be provided by comparing records collected by the same sample from two sufficiently separated weeks. Third, variation will arise from more stable characteristics of individuals themselves, including aspects of their personalities. We would expect on the basis of other research that, for example, extraverts and those who are more socially skilled would be more likely to convert potential opportunities into actual interactions. And we have indeed found in our own work that extraversion is correlated with number of encounters recorded (e.g., Emler, 1984). We also found that extraverts both interact more often with the people they know and interact with more people. We anticipate that further analysis of these data will provide additional clues as to how extraverts generate more social interaction, for instance whether they convert more of their chance meetings into conversational encounters, whether sheer interaction rate increases the predictability of the social environment, or whether they make greater use of particular settings.

Whatever the case, variance due to personality would nevertheless be true variance, unless personality is also correlated with recording errors. Perhaps the most significant threat to the external validity of our results, however, is that recording error is correlated with status. Is it possible that the very much lower totals recorded by the unemployed group as compared to all other groups reflects an exaggerated tendency to under-record produced by the condition of being unemployed? If this were so then a consistent depression of all values would be expected. This is not what we find; the differentials between this and other groups vary across categories in a coherent way.

Finally, variations may reflect more enduring differences in individual circumstances – in effect, a third source of true variance and the kind of effect to which our own data point with respect to institutional status. But the issue here is variance within these statuses. Thus, for example, not all jobs are the same. Mars (1981) has distinguished an occupational type he calls the 'donkey' job; it isolates the employee from regular social contact. Other jobs, identified by Mars as 'wolf-pack' jobs, ensure frequent interaction but with the same small group of individuals who form one's work team. So, the crude distinctions of status – in full-time education, in employment, unemployed – capture some of this circumstance-related variation, but not all. Additionally, if personality theorists are right that individuals select themselves into settings that are congenial to their temperaments then individual circumstances are likely to be correlated with personality.

For the present I would argue that although this method of studying social interaction will, in common with any method, involve a degree of error and although more research is needed to evaluate reliability and validity, our procedure does provide evidence about characteristics of social interaction that would be difficult to obtain in any other way. And it is already providing new and useful information about patterns of social life. For example, so far as I am aware this is the first research to quantify the circumstances of encounters, to show in detail how social life is being generated, for any human population. The method also is relatively straightforward to use and can generate a large amount of data from samples of a reasonable size for a modest cost.

The impact of status on social contacts: implications and directions for future research

The data I have described offers essentially descriptive statistics on various features of young people's social contact patterns. It relates these to the statuses of the young people and shows that status does produce some variation in rates of contact. But it does not relate rates or other features of contacts to significant psychological or social outcomes, such as identify formation, psychological health, political participation, behavioural habits or adult labour market position. Finally, therefore, I would like to return to some of the implications of, and as yet unanswered questions raised by, the kind of findings described in this chapter, and to relate these to the broader themes of this book. This concluding section is organized under four headings, concerning respectively the household, relationship quality, class divisions, and the link between human and social capital.

The enduring importance of the household

We now know that reports of the terminal decline of the family were premature. What the present results show is the enduring importance of the physical settings associated with families, namely households. In every group we studied a place of residence was one of the most frequent settings for routine social contacts. One implication is that a close link should be expected between housing policies affecting young people and their capacity to sustain social relationships. That domestic settings emerge in this work as so important may reflect the progressive privatization of social life that some observers of contemporary society have claimed to identify. Thus it may indeed be true that public life, relationships conducted in streets, markets, and cafés, and with these the arts of conversation, have been withering away in western society for the last century, as people have more and more retreated indoors to their television sets and other privately consumed entertainments. It is certainly true that public settings provided relatively infrequent venues for social contacts. But it also has to be said that the privatization of social life is at best a hypothesis and one difficult to test without comparable historical data on contact settings. What I think should be of more immediate interest and concern is the impact of poor housing, of overcrowded, temporary or inconveniently located accommodation, and especially of homelessness on the social isolation of young people (see also Coles, this volume).

Quantity and quality

The data presented relate primarily to the quantitative aspects of social contacts and therefore tell us nothing directly about the quality of the relationships young people have with those to whom they talk in the course of a week, nor about the social value or psychological significance of particular encounters. One might suppose that many of the crucial psychological functions of personal ties – their capacity to sustain personal integration, to shape beliefs and life choices, to buffer against stresses, to assist in coping with emotional crises and negotiation of life transitions – will depend on the quality of the relationship. Indeed, this is what other research leads us to expect: relationships which are more enduring, intimate and harmonious will deliver more benefits. But it does not follow that the quantity of interaction is without psychological or social significance. Thus, for example, we have been able to establish in other research that young people who interact more frequently with acquaintances are more accurately appraised by them (Tarry, Soat and Emler, 1998). And as I argued earlier, being a known quantity is a foundation for trust in social relations. As regards young people's range of contacts – the number of different people involved – there are potential implications for both deviance and social attitudes. We have found that young people more heavily involved in delinquency have a more restricted range of social contacts (Emler and Reicher, 1995). With respect to attitudes towards ethnic minorities, Altemeyer (1996) talks of right-wing authoritarians as moving in tight circles of acquaintances, while Pettigrew et al. (1998) report that racism is associated with lack of diversity in friendships. If the economic transition in East Germany pushes more young people into unemployment and so a more restricted range of social contacts, a rise in support for racist positions might not be entirely unexpected.

What can be said about the quality of encounters on the basis of the evidence presented in this chapter is necessarily more speculative, but not entirely so. Participants did, in effect, provide some evidence on their perceptions of the quality of their relationships; they had to judge whether contacts who were not family members, strangers or purely formal contacts were friends or only acquaintances and, if friends, whether they were particularly close friends. The unemployed group stand out as distinctive in the smaller number of close friends with whom they have contact, though the employed females are similar in this respect. It seems likely that if young people have contacts with fewer close friends they will enjoy less social support and will in consequence be more at risk of depression and the damaging effects of stress. In this context we might also recall the emphasis in Hirschi's (1969) control theory of delinquency, the importance of strong attachments to others (cf. also Sampson and Laub, 1993).

Class divisions

If the data presented in this chapter demonstrate the impact of formal institutions on personal lives, they also indicate how these institutions reproduce class divisions. It has long been established that friendships and partnerships are overwhelmingly homogamous; personal ties are most likely to be found between people with similar social backgrounds (Hollingshead, 1949; Kahl and Davis, 1955; Kerchoff, 1974). Many social scientists have argued that these class-based patterns of affiliation reflect preference for social similarity and a range of hypotheses have been offered about the formation and operation of such preferences. But this argument assumes people choose friends and potential marriage partners from the population on the basis of match with relevant social qualifications. Our data suggest opportunity plays as large a part as does deliberate choice; young people form relationships – whether of friendship or other kinds – with the other people they encounter in the institutional settings to which they share regular access and in which they have legitimate opportunities for informal interaction. The formal, institutionally-based statuses of young people, whether as students, trainees or employees, do give them access to a range of other people. The point, of course, is that this range is systematically restricted. A university student will regularly interact with other people who are largely the same age, from very similar social backgrounds, and of course possess very similar levels of education. The social mix of contacts available to the college group will be very different and much more local in origin. It will be different in other ways from that available to the employed group. The only clear signs of deliberate choice operating are with respect to gender; males are more likely to interact with other males and females with other females, but even some of this variation may reflect the gender composition of different degree courses, vocational training courses and employment sectors.

If there is class-based segregation of personal lives mediated by social institutions this is likely to have a range of significant consequences. For example, the various manifestations of political engagement – interest in politics, attentiveness to information about politics, political knowledge, coherence of political opinions, participation in politics – are strongly associated with education (e.g., Nie et al., 1996). It seems likely that at least part of this effect is mediated by the access that participation in full-time education, and particularly further and higher education, provides to a social milieu in which politics is regularly discussed and political identities are salient (Frazer and Emler, 1997). This segregation of personal lives will also produce differential access to human and material capital. The informal economy, in other words, will show the same kind of stratification as the labour market.

The relation between human capital and social capital

The title of Coleman's (1988) influential paper on social capital is explicit about its role in the creation of human capital. In the paper he develops the argument that social capital enhances young people's prospects of developing their talents (human capital) through education and then profiting from these through employment. If Coleman is correct in this then it also needs to be recognized that the relations between social and human capital may also be recursive and so involve vicious and virtuous cycles. So far as the social capital of young people is concerned it would appear that this is likely to be a *consequence* of their educational attainment and labour market participation as much as it is a cause. Thus, for example the child poverty described by Nauck (this volume) will be accompanied by limited social capital among the single mothers bringing these children up, and they in their turn risk poorer educational qualifications, more restricted opportunities for employment (cf. Diewald, this volume), and consequently more limited social capital of their own. In general, to the extent that social exclusion, the theme of Part 3 of this volume, is exclusion from the institutions of education, training, employment and, in the extreme, the family and its household, then the effects of social exclusion must be counted in terms of unrealized social capital. Ultimately, social exclusion is exclusion from all the material, social and psychological resources that support any reasonable quality of life.

At this point I wish to return briefly to the dramatically disadvantaged position of the unemployed group, compared to all others. It has been claimed that adults experiencing unemployment do not suffer the same degree of social isolation. Though this has yet to be confirmed using comparable methods to assess social contacts, it raises the possibility that young people who move directly from education to unemployment may experience a particular disadvantage if this transition denies them the opportunity to develop social capital that is not reliant on school-based contacts. In other words, this transitional phase of life is perhaps crucial in the opportunities it provides, or lacks, to form relationships that will carry over into adult life.

The social isolation of the unemployed also points to the profound repercussions of labour market conditions for young people. But this brings us to the credibility of the crucial counterfactual in this analysis. I have implied that if this unemployed group were instead in employment or some form of training then their contact patterns would largely resemble those of the groups of young people in our sample who did occupy such statuses. I do believe this is a reasonable claim. However, those young people with the lowest levels of educational attainment and the most limited cognitive skills will be heavily represented in the unemployed category. Without further appropriate research we do not yet know what role the same cognitive skills that underlie educational attainment also allow individuals to generate social contacts. Some of the variance in contact patterns may arise from personal qualities – social and intellectual skills – that are correlated with institutional status.

Notes

1. Note, however, that 'community' itself has become a contested concept (e.g. Stacey, 1969).

2. For the RIR a qualifying event is any face-to-face interaction between two or more people lasting ten or more minutes. We took the view that such a qualification leaves out too much of importance and burdens the recorder with an additional, distracting task, namely monitoring the length of any interaction.
3. In the records, boy- and girl-friends were distinguished from other kinds of friend, and relatives such as aunts, uncles and grandparents were distinguished from immediate family members (mothers, fathers, brothers, sisters).
4. One other setting, church, was recorded but the frequencies were exceptionally low across all groups.

References

Altemeyer, B. (1996) *The Authoritarian Specter.* Cambridge, MA: Harvard University Press.

Banks, M., Bates, I., Breakwell, G., Bynner, J., Emler, N., Jamieson, L. and Roberts, K. (1992) *Careers and Identities.* Milton Keynes: Open University Press.

Boissevain, J. (1974) *Friends of Friends: Networks, Manipulators and Coalitions.* Oxford: Blackwell.

Brown, G. W. and Harris, T. (1978) *Social Origins of Depression: A Study of Psychiatric Disorder in Women.* New York: Free Press.

Coleman, J.S. (1988) 'Social capital in the creation of human capital', *American Journal of Sociology,* **94** (supplement): S95–S120.

Cozby, P. C. (1973) 'Self-disclosure: A literature review', *Psychological Bulletin,* **79**: 73–91.

DePaulo, B., Kashy, D, Kirtendol, S. E., Wyer, M. et al. (1996) 'Lying in everyday life', *Journal of Personality and Social Psychology,* **70**: 979–95.

Emler, N. (1984) 'Personality and social participation', paper presented at EAESP General Meeting, Tilburg.

Emler, N. (1990) 'A social psychology of reputation', in W. Stroebe and M. Hewstone (eds), *European Review of Social Psychology,* vol. 1. Chichester: Wiley.

Emler, N. (1994) 'Gossip, reputation and social adaptation', in R. F. Goodman and A. Ben-Ze'ev (eds), *Good Gossip.* Kansas: University of Kansas Press.

Emler, N. (1996) *Social Contact Patterns among a Group of Managers.* Unpublished manuscript, Oxford University.

Emler, N. and McNamara, S. (1996) 'The social contact patterns of young people', in H. Helve and J. Bynner, (eds), *Youth and Life Management.* Helsinki: Yliopistopaino.

Emler, N. and Reicher, S. (1995) *Adolescence and Delinquency: The Collective Management of Reputation.* Oxford: Blackwell.

Erikson, B. H. (1981) 'Networks, ideologies and belief systems', in P. V. Marsden and N. Lin (eds), *Social Structure and Network Analysis.* Beverley Hills: Sage.

Festinger, L. Schachter, S. and Back, C. (1950) *Social Pressures in Informal Groups: A Study of Human Factors in Housing.* New York: Harper.

Fischer, C. (1981) *To Dwell among Friends: Personal Networks in Town and City.* Chicago: University of Chicago Press.

Frazer, L. and Emler, N. (1997) 'Participation and citizenship: A new agenda for youth politics research?' In J. Bynner, L. Chisholm and A. Furlong (eds), *Youth, Citizenship and Social Change in a European Context.* Aldershot: Ashgate.

Gans, H. J. (1962) *The Urban Village*. New York: Free Press.
Giner, S. (1976) *Mass Society*. London: Martin Robertson.
Granovetter, M. (1973) 'The strength of weak ties', *American Journal of Sociology*, **78**: 1360–80.
Granovetter, M. (1985) 'Economic action and social structure: The problem of embeddedness', *American Journal of Sociology*, **91**: 485–510.
Hirschi, T. (1969) *Causes of Delinquency*. Berkely, CA: University of California Press.
Hollingshead, A. B. (1949) *Elmtown's Youth*. New York: Wiley.
Kahl, J. A. and Davis, J. A. (1955) 'A comparison of indexes of socio-economic status', *American Sociological Review*, **20**: 317–25.
Kaplan, R.E. (1984) 'Trade routes: the manager's network of relationships', *Organizational Dynamics*, **12**: 37–52.
Katz, E. and Lazarsfeld, P.F.(1955) *Personal Influence: The Part Played by People in the Flow of Mass Communications*. Glencoe, IL: Free Press
Katz, D. and Kahn, R. L. (1978) *The Social Psychology of Organization*. New York: Wiley.
Kerchoff, A. (1974) 'Patterns of homogamy and the field of eligibles', *Social Forces*, **42**: 289–97.
Lalljee, M. and Evans, G. (1995) 'Talk and attitude stability in the political arena', paper presented at EAESP workshop on political participation, Milan, September.
Lin, N. (1982) 'Social resources and instrumental action', in P. V. Marsden and N. Lin (eds), *Social Structure and Network Analysis*. Beverley Hills, CA: Sage.
Litwak, E. and Szelenyi, I. (1969) 'Primary group structures and their functions', *American Sociological Review*, **35**: 465–81.
Mars, G. (1981) *Cheats at Work: An Anthropology of Work-place Crime*. London: Unwin.
Milgram, S. (1970) 'The experience of living in cities', *Science*, **167**: 1461–8.
Mitchell, J. C. (1969) *Social Networks in Urban Situations*. Manchester: Manchester University Press.
Nie, N., Junn, J. and Stehlik-Barry, K. (1996) *Education and Democratic Citizenship in America*. Chicago: University of Chicago Press.
Pettigrew, T. F., Jackson, J., Ben Brika, J., Lemaine, G., Meertens, R. W., Wagner, U., and Zick, A. (1998) 'Outgroup prejudice in Western Europe', in W. Stroebe and M. Hewstone (eds), *European Review of Social Psychology*, Vol. 8, Chichester: Wiley.
Putnam, R. D. (1993) *Making Democracy Work: Civic Traditions in Modern Italy*. Princeton University Press: Princeton.
Raffaelli, M. and Duckett, E. (1989) '"We were just talking": Conversations in early adolescence', *Journal of Youth and Adolescence*, **18**: 567–82.
Reis, H. T. and Wheeler, L. (1991) 'Studying social interaction with the Rochester Interaction Record', in M. Zanna (ed.), *Advances in Experimental Social Psychology*, Vol. 24. New York: Academic Press.
Rogers, E. M. (1962) *Diffusion of Innovations*. New York: Free Press.
Sampson, R. J. and Laub, J. H. (1993). *Crime in the Making: Pathways and Turning Points through Life*. Cambridge, MA: Harvard University Press.
Stacey, M. (1969) 'The myth of community studies', *British Journal of Sociology*, **20**: 134–47.

Stone, A. A., Kessler, R. C. and Haythornthwaite, J. A. (1991) 'Measuring daily events and experiences: decisions for the researcher', *Journal of Personality*, **59**: 574–607.

Tarry, H., Soat, C. and Emler, N. (1998) 'Evaluation of leadership potential: A social relations analysis', paper presented at British Psychological Society, Social Psychology Section annual conference, Kent, September 1998.

Tonnies, F. (1957) *Community and Society*. New York: Harper. (First German edition, 1887).

Weber, M. (1947) *The Theory of Social and Economic Organization*. New York: Free Press.

Wellman, B. (1979) 'The community question: The intimate networks of East Yorkers', *American Journal of Sociology*, **84**: 1201–31.

Wheeler, L. and Nezlek, J. (1977) 'Sex differences in social participation', *Journal of Personality and Social Psychology*, **35**: 742–54.

Wheeler, L. and Reis, H. T. (1991) 'Self-recording of everyday life events', *Journal of Personality*, **59**: 339–54.

Whyte, W. F. (1943) *Street Corner Society*, 2nd edn. Chicago: University of Chicago Press.

Wirth, L. (1938) 'Urbanism as a way of life', *American Journal of Sociology*, **44**: 3–24.

Young, M. and Willmott, P. (1957) *Family and Kinship in East London*. Harmondsworth: Penguin.

Part 2

Social change and individual development

4
Subjective experience of social change in individual development[1]

Gisela Trommsdorff

Until recently social change processes were usually studied at a macro level, focusing on social, political and economic phenomena such as changes in social institutions, political power, or economic disparities. However, such changes are not independent of individual behaviour (or vice versa). Therefore, the interrelations between social change and individual action need to be studied in more detail. Macro level changes cannot be explained by psychological theorizing, and individual behaviour cannot be explained by sociological theorizing; however, both perspectives can be fruitfully connected in order to understand possible interrelations between social change and individual behaviour. Here, such conceptual bridging will be explored by focusing on individual development in particular contexts.

Only in recent years have the effects of social change on individual development been discussed, relating, on the one hand, social (and historical) phenomena occurring on different levels, in different areas, with varying intensity and speed, and, on the other hand, individual developmental processes of persons of different cohorts and sex. Elder's (1974) famous study, *Children of the Great Depression*, has contributed impressively to the difficult question of connecting social and psychological theorizing. This study showed that social categories like cohort, sex and social status have to be transformed into psychological variables to enable us to understand the differential effects of social change on individual development. Furthermore, clarification is needed of the processes which transform social change into subjectively meaningful events (or sequences of events) which activate a person's behaviour.

This is related to a basic question for psychologists: whether and in which way objective life circumstances (economic status, level of education, material well-being and so on) and the changes in one's immediate life conditions (such as financial and social support) affect a person's behaviour and course of development. At least for a basic variable reflecting psychological health – psychological well-being – empirical research indicates that the effects of socio-demographic variables are small; most people in all groups feel quite happy. (For a summary, see Suh, Diener and Fujita, 1996). Does this also apply to the experience of social change? Previous research on stress, coping, and well-being has shown that individuals exhibit very different cognitive and emotional reactions to seemingly similar events (cf. Folkman and Lazarus, 1991). If this also applies to the experience of social change, how can such differences be explained? What are the psychological processes whereby persons negotiate social change?

There are several problems to be dealt with when the effects of social change on individual lives are studied. First, the concepts, social change and individual development, and their relationship are discussed in the introductory section. In the second and third sections, we shall deal with theoretically relevant factors which may filter the effects of social change on the subjective experience of change and on the individual negotiation of change. In the fourth section, some studies on psychological aspects of social change in East Germany are discussed.

Social change and individual development

Social change usually consists of a multitude of interrelated events which occur at different points of time, with different speed, strength and effects in different levels of a society. Usually there is no single event which can be regarded as a sufficient indicator of a change; certain events (such as changes in a society's constitution) are usually connected to other changes which either support or hinder the effectiveness and speed of any repercussions; for example, other changes in women's rights may be, but not necessarily, related to the legal status of abortion.

Also, the onset of social change does not necessarily affect people directly. All changes have latent and manifest consequences, and their effects on individuals can be rather indirect. They can be moderated and mediated by institutions and contexts, for example, the political system; changes affecting immediate contexts, which are more directly related to the person's everyday life, can be increased or buffered by 'proximal' contexts of workplace or family. Furthermore, the effects of social change are dynamic and interrelated over time; certain effects may increase, or decrease, or compensate for each other, or have a joint accumulative effect on a person's distant or immediate context. Accordingly, the effects of a social change may differ in their impact on people's beliefs and behaviour.

Why do certain social changes affect people differently? Are certain people more affected by changes on the macro level because they are more sensitive to social change? Changes at the level of market systems have multiple implications for activating, frustrating, and satisfying individual needs. Changes in individual behaviour can be induced, for example, by the internationalization of consumer behaviour (travelling, fashions, leisure etc.). However, a person need not be aware of such new behavioural options deriving from global changes. The implications of changes at the level of international economic relations can be merely perceived as theoretical scenarios, which may or may not affect meanings and induce action. Therefore, not all members of a population will experience the effects of a social change at the same time, to the same degree, with respect to the same aspects, or in the same way. Even in times of fundamental socio-economic change (e.g., changes in the world economy, and internationalization of the market system during globalization), only certain people will actually experience such macro level changes as events which affect their individual lives. Even when people are objectively affected by certain changes, they need not necessarily be aware of the changes, or of any changes in their own beliefs and behaviour.

Individual development is understood here as a life-long process which is actively negotiated in changing environments (Lerner, 1986). Starting from a contextual approach to individual development (cf. Bronfenbrenner, 1979; Silbereisen, Eyfert and Rudinger, 1986), certain interrelations between individual behaviour and characteristics of the context are assumed. Development is based on changes and stabilities; thus, individuals may expect more or less predictable ways of interaction with their environments. Individual development implies that the person acts in changing ecological contexts in ways which are related to changing developmental demands and outcomes. Therefore, the experience of change is one aspect of a person's life-long experience.

While people experience contextual changes throughout their lives, these changes need not be related to social change. Thus, people may experience contextual changes as 'normal' events during life-long development. It therefore seems useful to differentiate between life events in developmental transitions (e.g., entering school or work), and certain life events which occur as consequences of social change and which constitute non-normative events ('exogenous shocks') disrupting the person's established way of thinking and behaviour. Though both normative and non-normative events constitute objective changes, it is questionable whether they also induce a *subjective experience* of change. The quality of such experience, and people's ways of *negotiating* such changes are likely to differ.

Obviously, certain changes in a person's social, economic and political environment may cause significant changes in an individual's behaviour and their evaluation of the self in relation to the environment, including their life goals, future outlook, and control orientation. Therefore new interaction processes between a person and his/her environment may occur while he/she acts on and is affected by social change.

In times of social change certain unpredictable contextual changes in the proximal environment may occur, and induce problems that can be solved only by changing previously established behaviour patterns. This may be the case when a person undergoes normal transitions in his/her biography (e.g. having children), and at the same time experiences drastic changes in his/her proximal environment on account of social change (e.g., economic hardship, changes in the demands of the labour market, increased unemployment). The accumulation of contextual changes may induce uncertainty due to lack of experience of how to cope with such changes.

It therefore seems necessary, first of all, to study the conditions which affect the *perception* and *subjective experience of change*. An awareness of change could be induced, for example, by the disruption of well-established person-environment relations such as an increased or reduced socio-emotional and physical availability of attachment figures. Social systems on the micro level, the family for instance, can mediate the meaning and effects of socio-economic changes. Attachment figures may transmit a certain meaning of ongoing changes in such a way that the control beliefs of children are reduced or stabilized. How the changes in a person's context are perceived and evaluated by relevant others may affect the way the person experiences the social changes (see Figure 4.1).

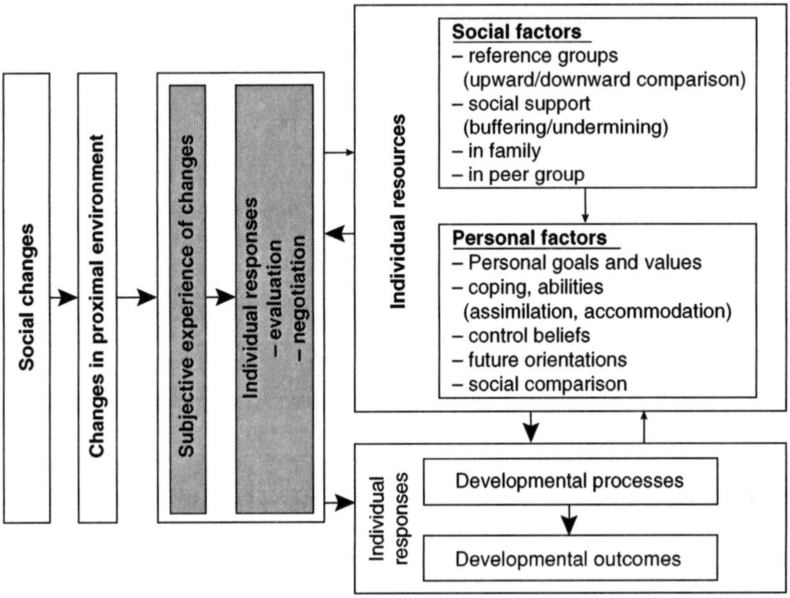

Figure 4.1 Subjective experience of social change and individual development

Individual differences in the subjective experience of social change: socio-psychological factors influencing the subjective meaning of social change

When dealing with the subjective meaning of social change and socio-psychological processes which affect these meanings, data on the aggregate level can only provide general information and assist in formulating hypotheses about individual processes. In the following, we will discuss some theoretical aspects of how social change is experienced and handled by the individual, thus turning from studies on the broad effects of social change to studies of *intervening psychological processes* which may account for inter-individual differences in the experience of change.

Individual differences in the experience of change

Social change can affect different persons in different ways. For instance, late adolescence is a critical time for forming one's identity and for commitment to values and ideologies. Therefore, historically significant changes experienced during this period should affect the identity of adolescents from the same cohort in a similar way. According to Mannheim (1928/1952), the combined effects of the circumstances of the historical moment in which a cohort enters adolescence, the shared socialization and the specific demographic characteristics of the cohort, build up a potential for dealing with social change. However, this does not preclude individual differences. Certain subgroups of a particular cohort may deal with life events in different ways depending, for example, on their specific socialization experiences and related social and personal resources. The impact of social change on people at different stages in the life course is likely to be related to the kind, the strength, and also the sequential processes of such social changes. For example, during times of economic recession, unskilled workers may be the first to be affected, followed by female workers, adolescents, then highly skilled personnel. For other kinds of social change such sequential processes of impact may follow different routes. For example, in the transformation of East Germany, and even more so, in Eastern Europe, the political elite was hit first; however, this group then had a good chance to recover first from the upheaval by using experience and well-established networks for effective coping strategies.

An important variable is the period of change, and how in their individual and family lives, people experience particular effects (Trommsdorff, 1994b; 1998a). How these events are dealt with will presumably have consequences for subsequent development. The following differentiations are therefore necessary:

(a) *different people* (e.g., different cohorts; people from different educational backgrounds) will experience social change in different ways, depending on their past and present experiences and their related resources;

(b) at *different stages of individual development* in the life course, any changes will be experienced differently, depending on the particular stage of life a person has reached (developmental age), and on their life history up to that date, including the development of their roles, statuses and resources;

(c) at *different points in a process of social change*, different social groups and individuals can be affected differently (period effects). All these factors will contribute to differential subjective experiences of social change. Therefore, combined cross-sectional and sequential studies of individual development in relation to the experience of a given change are necessary.

Future research thus needs to study subjective experience of social change as part of the specific developmental process, based on interactions between the social context and intra-individual factors. This may permit predictions of whether, and how far, social change imparts risks or challenges, and what the developmental outcomes (including coping) are like.

Social influences on individual differences

It is assumed here that individual differences in the experience of social change depend on the person's goals and belief systems and on the reference group he/she adheres to. Individual goals and values, and the relevance of a certain reference person or group, are not independent of each other (as in model learning). A reference person or group fulfills several functions in a person's development (for example, identity formation) and for their everyday activities (orientation; evaluation). Here, processes of comparison play an important role. Especially in situations of increased imbalance between past and present experiences, reference groups gain more importance. This should especially be the case in times of social change (see Figure 4.1).

Social comparison and reference groups

Depending on their subjective evaluations of different aspects of life quality, people will experience different levels of overall satisfaction. Public opinion polls demonstrate a decrease in satisfaction among East Germans during the years since reunification. Subjective well-being and satisfaction were much higher immediately after the collapse of the former GDR than currently. Even though the objective situation with respect to democracy, freedom and mobility has dramatically improved, other aspects of life quality have deteriorated. These include general job security and women's chances in the job market. May such changes in life satisfaction depend on changes in the environment and on the indicators selected for comparison?

Subjective evaluations of the effects of social changes depend on the goal structures (and value systems) of individuals; these affect the relevance to the person of any aspects of social change and also the person's baselines for comparison. There are two bases for anchoring comparisons: intrapersonal and interpersonal experiences in the past, and expectations for the future (and their interrelations). The interpersonal level embraces the individual's own position and the position of their reference group with respect to a given social context. The intrapersonal level includes evaluations of past, present and future experiences. The subjective meaning of social change, with respect to goal attainment and related subjective well-being, for example, comprises multiple components and criteria for evaluation that depend on processes of comparison.

The effects of social change become psychologically relevant only when the environment acquires a new subjective meaning. This meaning may be modified and mediated by relevant others – the family, friends or other reference groups (political party) – and used for comparisons (see Figure 4.1). One aspect of the subjective meaning of social change is the person's satisfaction with respect to goal attainment and need fulfillment; this may affect the person's subjective well-being. The reference group gives a certain meaning to social change providing an anchor for evaluating present conditions with respect to personal goal attainment.

When most of a population is affected by change, the individual can more easily compare his/her situation with that of other group members. In the case of negative changes, as in times of economic depression, when other people also suffer from economic decline, the individual does not feel alone. This helps people to feel not responsible for the economic hardship of their families; attributions of its causes to other factors serve to preserve self-esteem which is an important factor in coping. Thus besides providing criteria for the evaluation of social change, the reference group has additional functions. The reference group can provide socio-emotional support and self-concept enhancing effects.

However, a reference group does not necessarily provide resources for coping. Coping is more difficult when the comparison results in perceiving oneself as a loser while neighbours and friends are perceived as winners. Also, the reference group may affect attribution processes and related control beliefs in a negative way, as when the belief is supported that nobody acting alone or with others can control the present economic situation. In this case, relinquished control and anomie exemplify the derogating effects of reference groups. When the entire reference group loses out from social change, identification with this group can hurt self-esteem. Identification with a highly devalued reference group may increase stress, while identification with a highly valued reference group may serve as buffering factor when coping with social change.

Social support

As we have seen, reference groups mediate the effects on the subjective experience of social change, thus contributing to individual differences in response to it. In this section the focus is on social support and its psychological effects on the experience of change. Individual differences are explained here by the availability and psychological function of social support.

In times of social change, particularly when critical life events accumulate, perceived and/or experienced social support become all the more relevant. The protective effects of social support among adults can be demonstrated with variables such as the size of social networks. The psychological function of social support is related to emotional, instrumental and affirmative support (Wills, Mariani and Filer, 1996). For example, emotional support enhances a person's well-being and coping ability in stressful situations. Awareness of being part of a social group and being cared for by members of this group has considerable importance for people undergoing stressful events. Instrumental and affirmative support – perceived help for dealing with problems – is especially relevant for persons who lack the personal experience and knowledge to deal with stressful events.

Social support and social undermining. A significant mediating factor predicting whether a person will cope with social change and related critical life events is the quality of social interactions. Certain social interactions can provide emotional, instrumental and self-support, whereas others can be detrimental and have adverse effects. While social support serves as a buffering factor in coping with critical life events, social undermining is a risk factor which can build up stress and frustration (see Figure 4.1). The positive psychological functions of social support do not, however, depend on the size of social networks or the existence of (multiple) interpersonal relations alone; the types of peers and the quality of interactions are also crucial. It should be noted that taking into account only 'objective' social resources and disregarding 'subjectively' perceived support can lead to false conclusions.

Social support in the family. For example, it is necessary to take into account whether males and females differ in the quality of support perceived from their marital partners (Brunstein, Dangelmayer and Schultheiss, 1996). Whether a critical life event such as economic hardship really affects a person negatively, can depend on the quality of their intimate social relations. These, in turn, can be affected by economic hardship through mediating chains of events such as the subjective experience of financial strain and related increase of hostile family interaction (Conger et al., 1990). Early research on the 'great depression' showed that one person's unemployment can affect the entire family (Jahoda, Lazarsfeld and Zeisel, 1972).

Stressful life events, such as unemployment, can affect the mental health of the person negatively and may extend beyond the unemployed person, driving other critical life events. Growing frustration among the unemployed may give rise to destructive interaction patterns, increased marital dissatisfaction and conflict among family members. The effects of the associated financial strain can generate a spiralling negative interaction process and dysfunctional exchanges (social undermining) between partners (or family members) which increase symptoms of depression and may lead to further conflict and eventual separation. In contrast, the emotional and instrumental quality of experienced social support contributes to coping with stress.

Following this line of reasoning, the perceived withdrawal of supportive behaviour can be a further (independent) contributor to the stress caused by economic hardship and socio-economic change. Conger et al. (1990) have tested these hypotheses in a cross-sectional study of samples in rural communities, where males were usually the employed breadwinners. Vinokur, Price and Caplan (1996) extended the generality of the process model using longitudinal data on urban samples with recently unemployed wives and husbands. These authors demonstrate that people experiencing recent unemployment also tend to experience increased depression and decreased relationship satisfaction as a function of financial strain; the same persons also experience less social support and more social undermining (as assessed by both partners).

Using the same line of reasoning for children and adolescents, the family and peer group may both be a source of further stress or a social resource which can be utilized to deal with stress. Especially in a situation where the whole family experiences critical life events such as experiencing economic hardship, emotional support from other family members may contribute to the improvement of social and personal resources.

The positive function of supportive parents has been shown for adolescents at risk (Wills, 1991). For example, affiliation with peers who reject mainstream values turns out to be a risk factor for adolescents (Jessor and Jessor, 1977). However, parental support can protect adolescents from affiliation with deviant peers. Stress-buffering effects of emotional support from parents reduce the often demonstrated relationship between negative life events and adverse effects for adolescents. Moreover, Wills and Cleary (1996) have demonstrated in a large and representative sample of adolescents (from early to middle adolescence) that substance use was inversely related to parental support. High support increased the impact of protective factors like behavioural coping; it also reduced the impact of negative events, and moderated the effects of risk factors.

Parental support as a protector will be based on the particular parent–child relationship which operates as a mediating factor. The psychological processes involved in parent–child relations allow for a better understanding of the resilience of certain children, and how the buffering effects against problem behaviour operate. Parent–child relationships cover multiple types of support, the monitoring of a child's behaviour, companionship with the child, providing warmth and emotional support. These help strengthen secure attachment relations between parent and child. Furthermore, parents can demonstrate effective task-oriented problem-solving and serve as models for effective coping.

Empirical evidence shows that a close and supportive parent–child relationship strengthens a positive self-concept by providing secure attachment, including a certain 'inner working model' comprising a positive view of oneself and one's relation to the wider social world (Bowlby, 1969; Ainsworth et al., 1978). Persons who conceive others as friendly are less likely to attribute hostile intentions and react aggressively (Kornadt, 1982). A positive and trusting 'inner working model' should prevent an adolescent engaging in conflicting interactions. Rather it predisposes him or her to establish rewarding intimate relations which provide further protective social support. Close parent–child relationships increase the effectiveness of socialization through the child's acceptance and internalization of the parents' values. These help prevent the child affiliating with deviant groups. Furthermore, a close parent–child relationship encourages the development of better skills for self-regulation and emotional control in stressful situations (Friedlmeier and Trommsdorff, 1997). A close parent–child relationship promotes abilities for coping with stressful events, and for developing resistance to problem behaviour.

In cases of social change inducing stressful life events for family members (eg unemployment), parents' effective coping can be achieved while supportive communication among family members is maintained. This gives a child the chance to observe empathy, co-operation, and problem-solving behaviour in the family in this critical period. Parental warmth and problem-solving presumably serve as a model for the child's effective coping with negative life events, and contribute to the transmission of protective factors for children in times of social change.

Personal factors in experiencing change and coping with stress: personal goals, future orientation and control beliefs in times of social change

So far we have discussed how social factors mediate and moderate the effects of social change. In the following, we will deal with the way the individual experiences and acts upon the effects of social change. This will lead us to ask which personal factors are most relevant and how they function in the process of experiencing change.

From a motivation theory point of view, people's actions are structured around their dominant goals which make up the core of their identities. Such goals ('current concerns', 'personal projects') represent what people want to achieve or wish to become. In periods of social change, such goals, and also ways of achieving these goals, may be affected. This will affect the way social change is experienced psychologically. From a motivation theory point of view, one can assume that experience of frustration in achieving important goals will induce negative emotions and activate psychological processes. These impel individuals to find ways of overcoming such imbalances in person–environment relations. They engage in problem-solving and coping behaviour in order to achieve the goals or to search for new goals. In the case of subjectively experienced changes as barriers to goal achievement, evaluations of alternative goals and ways of achieving them can be expected. This may encourage active pursuit of these new goals or ruminations about lost opportunities. Depending on the experience of the effects of social change and on the available social and personal resources for coping (for example, family support, attribution of causes of events, control beliefs, self-esteem) individual responses to change will differ (see Figure 4.1).

Therefore, it has to be clarified whether a social change is perceived by the individual as an event affecting his or her goals and ways of achieving them. This motivation theory approach differentiates between the negative and positive experience of social change. Social change can be subjectively experienced as improvement or as a threat to achieving personal goals. Accordingly, social changes (or changes in the economic system) will have different effects on individual behaviour.

Control beliefs and coping. When social change affects the pursuit and realization of personal goals, a belief in self-efficacy to regulate any discrepancy between personal goals and the given situation may be activated. When the goal-directed behaviour arising from previous plans is affected by social change, goals, plans, and parts of the goal-directed behaviour are likely to be reorganized in certain ways (see Figure 4.1). Carver and Scheier (1990) assume that goal disruptions induce a state of self-focused attention in which the person compares their present state with their personal goals. When these do not fit, they engage in one of two different forms of coping: one of these is to try again to achieve the goals (assimilative control), the other is to change the importance of the goal or to redirect the focus of attention (accommodative control).

Several theoretical approaches including theories of cognitive dissonance (Festinger, 1968), and theories of habituation (Suh, Diener and Fujita, 1996) provide hypotheses to explain accommodation. For example, from studies of habituation we know that the psychological effects of negative (and also positive) life events may eventually wear off. From longitudinal studies Suh, Diener and Fujita (1996) demonstrate that the psychological effects of life events on subjective well-being diminish once adaptation takes place. Another interesting finding from this study is that good and bad events tend to occur together rather than apart within an individual lifecourse. Also, theories of self-enhancement provide examples of how accommodation processes are activated. A cognitive interpretation of the self and the environment in a self-supportive way improves adaptation to, and coping with, objectively negative life circumstances.

Processes of accommodation and assimilation reduce the negative feelings arising from goal disruption; if such processes are not successfully activated, self-focused attention and negative affect may increase or reduce the individual's positive self-concept. The question remains as to whether assimilative or accommodative control is more successful for coping. For a long time, primary (assimilative) control (changing one's environment according to one's own goals) was seen as being more useful than secondary (accommodative) control, (changing one's goals according to expectations of the environment) (cf. states of coping: Flammer, 1990). However, recent cross-cultural studies have demonstrated that no single model of coping can be applied in cultures where different values for primary or secondary control exist (Weisz, Rothbaum and Blackburn, 1984; Essau and Trommsdorff, 1996; Trommsdorff and Essau, 1998).

Furthermore, recent studies of control orientation demonstrate that successful coping depends on a certain balance between primary and secondary control orientation which again is affected by the cultural context and related values. In a culture where secondary control (changing one's own goals according to expectations of the context) is dominant, this strategy will be more useful than primary control (changing one's context according to one's goals), and vice versa (Seginer, Trommsdorff and Essau, 1993).

In addition, studies of control orientation over the life-span indicate that, depending on the stage reached, primary or secondary control strategies change in their functional effectiveness for coping. Although at a younger age primary control may be more adequate, at an older age, the functional value of secondary control may increase (Heckhausen and Schulz, 1995). The self-regulatory function of psychological control is used by children in ways different from those adopted by adults when confronted by stressful events. Lopez and Little (1996) reported more personal and control expectancy beliefs, more activation of various coping strategies, and more primary control among younger children (about age 8) compared with older children (about 11 years). These results are in line with the findings of Band and Weisz (1988) who found that younger children prefer primary control coping strategies more than older children do. Secondary control strategies increase during middle childhood. These results are consistent with the results from our own studies of self-regulation, control beliefs and the future orientations of children in middle and late childhood (Trommsdorff et al., 1978). In these studies it was shown that young children's unrealistic internal attribution of control is reduced when approaching adolescence; this is when self-regulating behaviour increases.

Future orientation and coping. Social change may bring about changes in concrete 'current concerns' arising from changes in perceived opportunities and social expectations. Such changes can eventually affect the direction and content of more general personal goals, projects and life tasks. In cases where such goals have become part of the person's future orientation (Nuttin, 1984; Trommsdorff, 1984; 1994c) and their self-identity changes, a new developmental task has to be achieved (see Figure 4.1).

From a motivation theory perspective, personal goals and related control beliefs, and future orientations, predict people's behaviour (Heckhausen and Schulz, 1995; Trommsdorff, 1986; 1994a; 1994c). Conceiving a person's future orientation as including a structured system of personal goals, which individuals hope to achieve in the near or distant future (Trommsdorff, 1986; 1994c), the study of future orientation in times of social change can give insights into the impact of such changes on individual development. An optimistic future orientation, strong goal-commitment and favourable situational conditions for attaining personal goals allow for successful goal achievement, personal satisfaction and well-being. Brunstein (1993) was able to demonstrate that optimistic expectations of goal attainability, belief in outcome control, and the experience of social support increased the likelihood of goal attainment and personal satisfaction. According to Scheier and Carver (1992), pessimistic persons have more difficulties in coping with problems because of their lower expectations of future success, while persons with optimistic attitudes and a belief in control are better able to cope with stressful life events. Bandura's (1994) studies of self-efficacy and the related belief in control are in line with this thesis. Strong belief in self-efficacy is conceived of as a functional precondition for successful adaptation to changes in the personal environment.

However, recent studies point out that simple relations between optimism and coping do not hold. First, we should differentiate between strategies for coping. So far, the coping literature has identified two groups of strategies: activities aiming at self-improvement or preparation for certain events, and activities aimed at the regulation of emotions (Folkman and Lazarus, 1991). Effective coping is reduced by insufficient regulation of negative effects, and is enhanced by problem-solving. Coping activities which aim at self-improvement make use of mental simulations such as downward social comparisons or defensive pessimism. Downward social comparison can function as a self-enhancing strategy because we compare ourselves to others who are worse off. Coping with negative life events can be successful in the case of a downward focus ('others suffer more than I do') (Wills, 1981). In contrast, upward comparisons may induce dissatisfaction and feelings of deprivation, especially when people perceive their failure and misfortune as unjustified and difficult to change. On the other hand, upward social comparisons (comparisons with others who are better off) can provide the best information for self-betterment (Taylor and Lobel, 1989). Thus, the same behaviour can have two different functions.

Second, we need to differentiate between the various functional aspects of pessimism and optimism. Functions similar to those for coping strategies can be observed in the mental simulation of future events. Such anticipations can be based on optimistic or pessimistic attitudes. However, both optimistic and pessimistic expectations may have a self-serving function: defensive pessimists would prefer a negative view of the future while optimists would prefer positive expectations. For both the defensive pessimist and the optimist, the underlying strategy is highly functional for problem-solving. Defensive pessimists and optimists display different but potentially equal functional responses, in attempting to cope with negative life events (Cantor and Norem, 1989). One of the major ways in which both may vary is in their use of anticipatory vs. retrospective coping strategies in order to protect self-esteem. Defensive pessimists may use anticipatory thinking-through strategies and set low expectations before action; optimists may use retrospective strategies and restructure their performances (Seginer, 1997). Mental simulations such as social comparison, and anticipatory vs. retrospective evaluation of performance, allow for self-improvement and affect regulation – two important activities in coping. Thus a singular view of the relations between an optimistic versus pessimistic future orientation and coping can lead only to inconsistent results. It is necessary to distinguish 'true' pessimists from 'defensive' pessimists and from optimists. Defensive pessimists may be more ready than optimists to delay gratification by experiencing a short-term negative effect in order to solve an upcoming problem more efficiently. It may be useful to study not only the direction (and context) but also the timing of people's mental simulations. Especially in times of social change, a complex dynamic sequence of changing events over a long period of time is to be expected. In this case, starting one's mental simulation too early (before the stressful events really become manifest) may render coping procedures less effective.

To summarize, personal goals and values, and mental simulations (with respect to social comparisons, evaluating the past and future and personal control) can serve as important personal resources for coping with stressful life events in times of social change (cf. Figure 4.1). Upward and downward social comparisons, optimistic and pessimistic individual expectations, and primary and secondary control beliefs can be combined to optimize coping. Since ability and preference for the direction and timing of such mental simulation differ between people, individual differences with respect to responses to social change can be expected.

Psychological aspects of social change in East Germany

In this section, empirical studies on the subjective experience of social change in East Germany and some implications for individual development are discussed in relation to the theoretical frame of reference just outlined. The methodological shortcomings of the empirical data do not yet allow a systematic testing of the theoretical propositions. However, empirical studies of the processes of transformation in East Germany can help in the formulation of some hypotheses about the effects of social change on individual behaviour and development.

The transformation has been seen as a challenge for some people and as a risk for others; accordingly, changes after it may have produced losers and winners. It is assumed here that whether, and in which way, social change influences individual lives depends, on the one hand, on the way the person experiences certain aspects of the change, and, on the other hand, how the person negotiates and deals with changing contexts. How can the subjective experience and psychological effects of social change on individual development be studied? First, some methodological problems have to be taken into account (cf. Trommsdorff, in press-b).

Methodological issues

In order to measure the effects of specific social changes, 'natural experiments' are useful. They avoid some problems of the confounding effects of ongoing contextual processes. The transformation of the former German Democratic Republic (GDR) has sometimes been regarded as a 'natural experiment', because a complete restructuring of all social, political and economic institutions took place after the former GDR broke down and they were taken over by the West German system. Therefore, comparative studies on East German people before and after the unification should be valuable in measuring the effects of social change. Can the East German transformation really serve as a quasi natural experiment to measure the effects of social change on individual development?

The methodological requirements are not really fulfilled. The first constraint is the incomplete data set on individual beliefs and behaviour before unification. In order to measure its effects, it would be necessary to have data on hand from the time of the old GDR, and to follow up the same people over time, during the process of transformation, and during their development.

Such studies, however, are rare. First, few data exist from the time of the former GDR that can be used as baseline for comparison. This is due to restrictions on polling for political reasons in the former GDR. Furthermore, it is difficult to identify samples for which repeated measures (on the same persons) have been carried out. Some of the longitudinal studies which have been started only after unification may fulfil the conditions of an 'after-only' design, but they cannot give information on the really striking effects because of the lack of an adequate control group. One could argue that West Germans provide an adequate control group: both East and West Germany shared the same cultural and historical background until the end of the Second World War. Then the governments in East and West Germany went in antagonistic directions and their populations were socialized in very different contexts. Therefore, the effects of these different socialization experiences have to be taken into account when using West Germans as a control group.

In order to measure the subjective effects of social change, public opinion polls are often used. It is usually difficult to decide whether such information on attitudes can be interpreted as the effects of social change or as depending on other factors, education or media, for example. Also, it is unclear whether public opinion polls taken at different points of time can measure the stability or change in individual attitudes. Only repeated measures of the same people over a period of time are useful for this purpose (panel). However, panel studies produce only data on the aggregate level. Their designs are not necessarily appropriate to measure the effects of social changes on individual beliefs. Consequently, they usually do not tell us which aspects of a social change were influential, and under what conditions in the individual life course these influences occurred. Also, most of the panel studies since unification yield little data on psychological variables regarding individual development. Only some of them give information on stabilities and changes in the attitudes in East and West Germany which are needed to derive hypotheses on the possible effects of socio-political change on psychological variables.

East Germans' perception and evaluation of change after the unification

Let us first turn to the question whether social change as such has been acknowledged by East German people, and how such changes were evaluated and experienced.

Studies by Zapf and Habich (1995) demonstrate that during the first years after reunification East Germans perceived their situation as having improved significantly, while the majority of West Germans perceived their situation as unchanged. Also, West Germans reported significantly less change compared with East Germans as measured by the number of life events which were mentioned as having occurred in recent years. These changes were usually evaluated by East and West Germans as positive rather than negative. East Germans reported more positive and also more negative events. Later on, however, it seems that East Germans evaluated their situation differently. A generalized experience of dissatisfaction and reduced sense of control can be observed after a short period of happiness. Opinion polls show that responsibility was attributed by East Germans to external powers (such as the state or government) to a significantly higher degree than by West Germans (61 vs. 32 per cent). The individual person was seen as less responsible (39 vs. 68 per cent) (Zapf and Habich, 1995). Moreover, trust in (present) public institutions was significantly lower in East Germany compared with West Germany (Gensicke, 1996). In line with these data, political participation (for example, political involvement and political influence) was less highly valued by East Germans compared with West Germans.

Ongoing social changes may have affected people's anchors for social comparisons. Changes in the anchor may induce changes in the experience of social change. The loss of one's reference group may accentuate the negative effects of social change. In East Germany active work groups (brigades) and other social organizations (*Junge Pioniere*, for example), which served as reference groups and social resources in the former GDR, disappeared after reunification. Several studies point to the negative effects of losing these social resources (e.g. Zinnecker and Silbereisen, 1996; Trommsdorff and Chakkarath, 1996; Trommsdorff, in press-a). Therefore, a need to find substitutes for such reference groups, in order to gain cognitive and emotional support, should have developed. However, the West German system so far has not yet become a system with which large numbers of East Germans can identify. This may be another reason for individuals to search for familiar groups for identification. For example, the former socialist party which has transformed itself into the so-called PDS (Partei des Demokratischen Sozialismus – Party of Democratic Socialists) has gained increasing acceptance (cf. Trommsdorff, 1994b).

Depending on the evaluations, and the related comparison processes, which different people carry out in different ways (comparisons of present with past situation; comparisons between present situation and expected future situation; comparison between East and West Germans), the outcomes should be different. The results should differ between people from different age groups, gender, and educational status. In other words, individual differences in evaluations of social change must be taken into account.

The subjective experience of social change is affected by cohort, age and gender. A striking example of these effects is the results of the study by Roether and Kunze (1995) on male and female older people in East and West Germany (mean age: 77 years). This study demonstrated not only that certain older people in East Germany were better off than their same-aged peers in West Germany but also that they were more likely to experience their age positively and as less of a burden. The experience of old age was more positive for old women from East as compared to West Germany. This also held for the experience of past events; while East and West German women did not differ with respect to reporting past negative events, East German older women remembered more positive events than West German women. Also, East German women reported more consistency between their expectations and life experiences with respect to work and family. The East German women were less depressed than the West German women and they seemed better equipped to deal with old age. Ongoing social changes did not affect East German older women negatively. On the contrary, as compared with West German women, East German older women seem to have profited from the changes after reunification, and also from their past experience, when they had to deal with ongoing changes in the former GDR.

The subjective experience of objective changes may induce an accentuation of previously held values. One of the most dramatic aspects of objective socio-economic change in East Germany included economic unification and the breakdown of state-supported job security and the state-regulated labour market. Therefore, growing unemployment should have affected the well-being, and work-related goals and values of East Germans. Several opinion polls have shown that East and West Germans differ in work-related value orientations. For example, East Germans held the more achievement-oriented childrearing goals and showed a higher preference for family and work values (cf. Gensicke, 1996; Meulemann, 1996). These differences in value orientations seem to be related to socialization conditions before unification; they have not changed since it took place. Past socialization and present insecurity in the labour market may both have reinforced or stabilized the importance of work values in East Germany. The experience of change in the labour market presumably has reinforced work values. As a matter of fact, while the overall subjective well-being declined for East Germans, the subjectively perceived importance of work for subjective well-being remained quite stable and was higher than for West Germans after unification (SOEP, 1995).

Further reanalyses of data from the German Socio-Economic Panel show that the relevance of family, work and leisure for overall satisfaction differed significantly between East and West Germans, and also between males and females and between different cohorts. East German females (in all age groups) had a stronger work orientation than West German females. Their life satisfaction was to a stronger degree affected by work rather than by leisure and informal social relations. In contrast, for West German males and females, work, as compared to leisure, was less important than for East German males and females, especially for people between 30 and 60 years old. We shall have to study over a longer period whether, and in which way, inconsistencies between high work values on the one hand, and low job opportunities in the labour market on the other hand, will eventually affect the value orientations and behaviour of East Germans.

The subjective experience of social change is mediated by the family. The family as a private niche which provides security was an important social resource in a socio-political context of restricted individual freedom in the former GDR. Possibly, basic functions of the family (such as providing emotional support) have gained even more importance in times of radical socio-economic change (Trommsdorff and Chakkarath, 1996). For East German people, the positive effect of perceived socio-emotional support has been shown in the 'Rostock study'. East Germans experienced socio-emotional support during the former GDR from their families and work groups. However, after reunification both microsystems lost some of their functional quality. The work teams were disrupted by the restricted job market; and many families suffered through economic insecurity. Data from the longitudinal study of adolescents and young adults in Rostock (Reis, 1993) demonstrated that the need for emotional support gained in importance after reunification while its quality decreased.

Future research will have to show whether families in East Germany will provide social support in cases of a conflict of values between the younger and older generation. For the younger East German generation, a shift towards 'postmodern' (individualistic and hedonistic) value orientations can be observed (Gensicke, 1996; Schnabel, Baumert and Roeder, 1994). These 'postmodern' value orientations have been visible among East German adolescents since the 1980s when significant value changes occurred in the former GDR (Friedrich and Griese, 1991). Therefore, it may not be surprising that East German adolescents were more susceptible than their parents to the 'postmodern', hedonistic values promoted since reunification. Whether, and how far, such different goals and values may induce a generation conflict in East Germany and reduce the quality of social support from the family is an important topic for future study.

Individual differences in subjective experience of social change: comparisons between East and West Germans – cohort and gender effects

We now turn to parts of our own longitudinal studies on the subjective experience of social change. The focus is on individual differences in social and personal factors as part of individual resources. These resources are related to assumed differences in socialization with respect to growing up in East or West Germany, as female or male, as a member of a certain cohort, and as a child, an adolescent, or adult.

One study is based on data from the representative German socio-economic panel study (SOEP) which was originally designed to study changes of social and economic conditions of the West German population.[2] Since unification, data collection has been extended to representative samples from East Germany. Also, recently, psychological indicators for well-being have been included, which partly allow us to measure the subjective experience of socio-economic and political conditions and their changes. In the following, we focus on the study carried out in 1995, six years after unification, which included some psychological indicators of interest.[3]

Adjustment to social change and subjective wellbeing: Recent empirical studies

East and West Germans obviously differed when being asked how they had adjusted to the experience of social change. East Germans as compared to West Germans reported more difficulties in adjusting to changing contexts. East German women born between 1930 and 1950 reported the highest incidence of difficulties in adjustment (see Figure 4.2).

These results demonstrate that the objectively more dramatic social changes in East Germany affected subjective experience. Further data demonstrate that the life satisfaction of East Germans, as compared to West Germans – again of females born around 1940 – was lower (see Figure 4.3).

These results underline the differential effects of social change among people differing in *gender* and *age*: working women have been the most negatively affected by the changing work situation. East

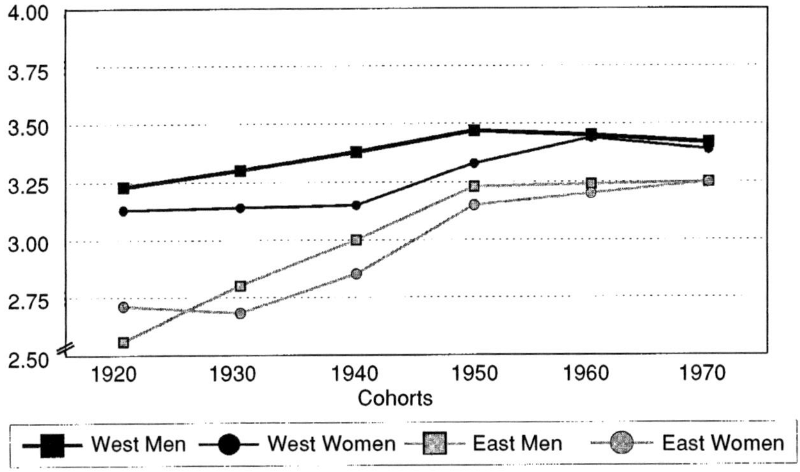

Scale: 1 = agree to 4 = disagree
Source: SOEP, 1995

Figure 4.2 Difficulty in adjusting to changing contexts: a comparison of East and West German cohorts

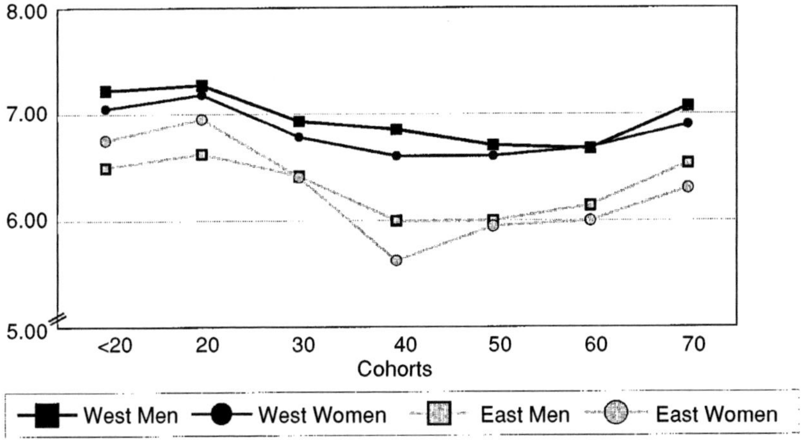

Satisfaction related to various domains of life
Scale: 0 = dissatisfied to 10 = satisfied
Source: SOEP, 1995

Figure 4.3 Life satisfaction of East and West German cohorts

German women were guaranteed life-long employment under the former GDR system; after re-unification they lost their economic security, and they also lost the advantages of being embedded in informal social networks at the workplace. In general, East German women, especially the 1940 cohort, seem to be the main losers. On the other hand, East German women above the age of 60 report significantly higher satisfaction. Retired people have often been considered 'winners'.

The data from the SOEP (1995) on gender differences with respect to personal resources indicate that East German females were experiencing more difficulties in response to the social change. This is further supported by data on control beliefs. East German females were more fatalistic than any other group (see Figure 4.4).

Furthermore, the East German females' future orientation was more pessimistic as compared to the other groups (see Figure 4.5).

The results from this analysis reveal that East Germans, as compared to West Germans in general, were less optimistic. The most striking differences occurred for the young adults (1970 cohort): East German females were significantly more pessimistic than West German females or males from either East or West Germany.

These results are in line with those from another recent longitudinal study. We compared the future orientation (optimism/pessimism) of

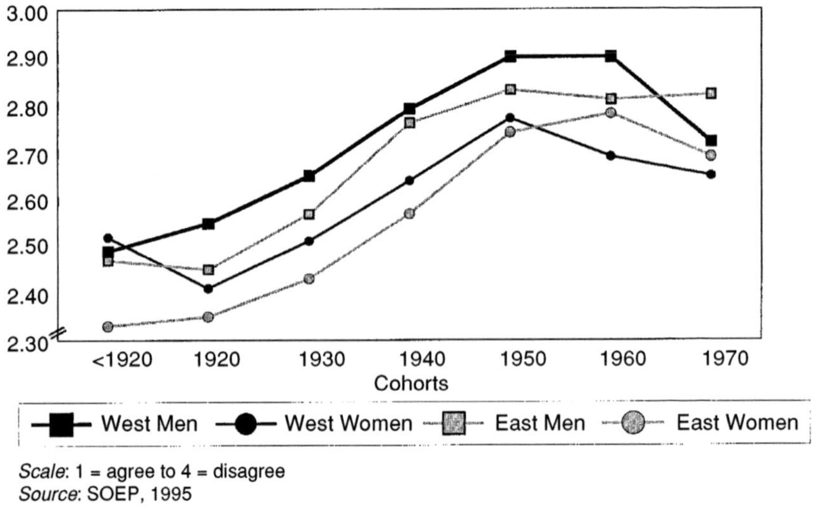

Figure 4.4 Belief in external control of East and West German cohorts

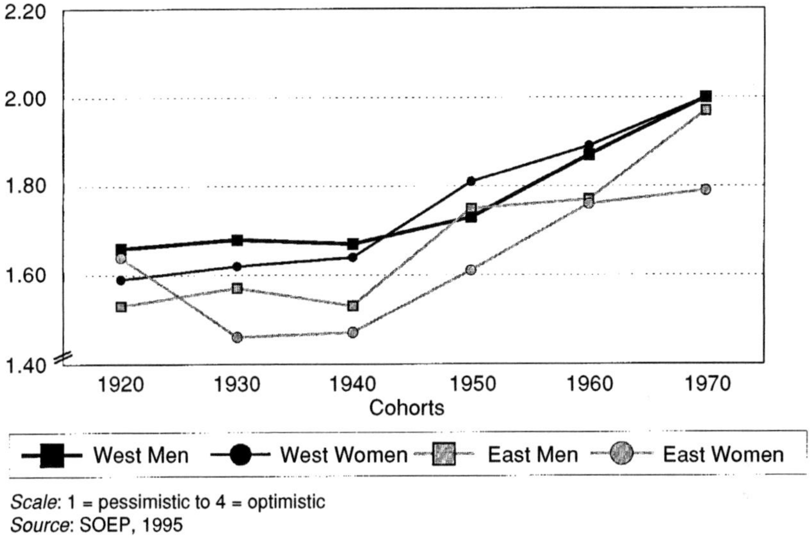

Figure 4.5 Optimism of East and West German cohorts

East and West German adolescents. (N = 80 West German (Saarbrücken, Konstanz) and N = 60 East German (Brandenburg) adolescents (16-years-old) participated in this study.) The instrument used was the Life Orientation Test (LOT) by Scheier and Carver (1985). The results revealed significantly higher pessimism among East as compared to West German adolescents with respect to achieving their life goals. This difference was due to higher pessimism among East German females (Trommsdorff and Kornadt, 1995). Three years later, we used the same instrument a) with the students from the first study and b) for a control group of 16 year old students (N = 54 students from East Germany, N = 73 students from West Germany). The younger cohort from this second study revealed no significant difference between East German as compared to West German adolescents, while the older cohort from East Germany was still more pessimistic compared to the same cohort from West Germany (Trommsdorff and Kornadt, 1998) (see Figure 4.6).

It is unclear whether the East German older cohort of adolescents in our study had been affected more negatively by the ongoing social changes, or whether they had held more pessimistic attitudes before unification, or whether such pessimism was related to their specific developmental tasks. Another follow-up of these groups of adolescents

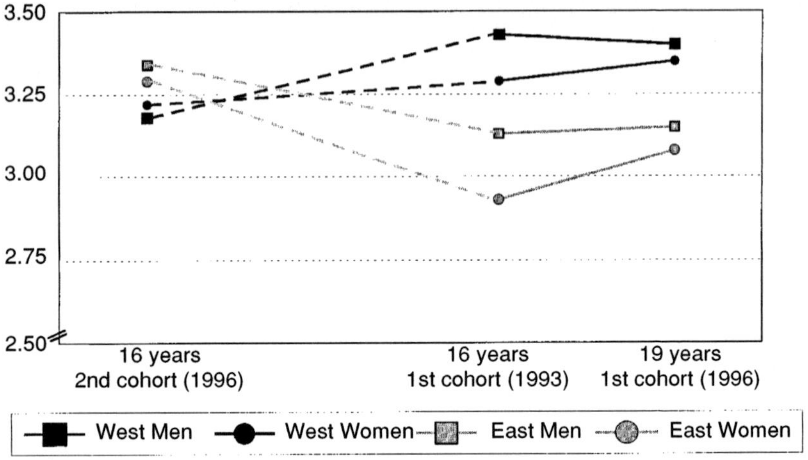

Scale: 0 = no optimism to 4 = high optimism

Figure 4.6 Optimism of two cohorts of East and West German adolescents

is underway in order to test the stability of future orientation and its function in the process of adapting to ongoing social changes.

Summary: effects of cohort, age, and gender: winners and losers of social change

The subjective experience of social change depends on gender, age, and cohort; it is mediated by, and it affects, personal factors. However, the directions of the effect are difficult to interpret: differences in personal factors between East and West Germans may indicate effects of social change and/or previously established resources for coping. Even when studies on control and future orientation are based on longitudinal designs, information on attitudes *before* unification are not at hand. Also, no differentiation between the various functions of control and future orientation, including mental simulation for coping, is usually available. So far, little information about the experience of social change and individual differences is available.

The results from the SOEP indicate only that East Germans, as compared to West Germans, have difficulties in adjusting to ongoing changes; they also experience less satisfaction and more pessimism. However, East German women reveal relatively high life satisfaction during retirement and very low life satisfaction at the age of about 50 when options in the labour market are reduced. Retired people (including women) above the age of 60 can be considered winners: they receive a stable pension which is much higher than under the former GDR system. It often occurs that East German grandparents' monthly incomes are higher than the incomes of their working adult children and grandchildren. However, this way of defining winners and losers according to income and employment is too simplistic and only partly accounts for the *subjective* experiences of social change after the collapse of the former GDR.

Here the question arises as to whether older East Germans are profiting more from their past experience in the former GDR, which provided numerous challenges for problem-solving (cf. Holahan and Moos, 1985, for a 'personal growth model'), or whether they are profiting mainly from the objective increase in material well-being after unification. To summarize, the timing of transition in East Germany is positive for the older age group while it is obviously more problematic for their children who are about 50 years of age, and for the young generation of adolescents. Longitudinal studies of these cohorts may clarify particularly the role of social and individual factors in contributing to individual resources when negotiating social change.

Effects of developmental age and timing of social change on social behaviour

From a developmental point of view, the effects of social change on social behaviour are of special interest. In our longitudinal research[4] we studied the development of pro-social and anti-social motivation in children and adolescents (Trommsdorff and Kornadt, 1995; 1998; Trommsdorff, Kornadt and Hessel-Scherf, 1998).

(a) As we have seen from the panel studies, persons of *different developmental ages* can be affected differently by various features of social change. The impact of social change depends on the time of its occurrence in individual development. In our longitudinal research we studied 5- and 8-year-old children and their mothers, and 16- and 19-year-old adolescents from East and West Germany with respect to pro-social and anti-social motivation in interaction with peers (main study: first measurement, 1992; second measurement, 1995; third measurement, 1998). In the following account, the focus is only on children. The subjects included N = 40 5-year-old and 29 8-year-old boys and girls from Brandenburg and N = 54 5-year-old and 34 8-year-old boys and girls from Konstanz and Saarbrücken. As instruments, scenario techniques to measure pro-social behaviour (APS) and aggression (AS) were used (picture stories of different interaction situations between two children). The answers of the children were coded into the following categories: pro-social behaviour (APS); (verbal and behavioural) aggression, neutral behaviour (verbal and behavioural), pro-social behaviour (AS). The results demonstrated that the 5- and 8-year-old children from the two regions did not differ with respect to aggression but East German, as compared to West German, children showed significantly less pro-social behavior at the age of 5 years while these differences had disappeared by the age of 8 (see Figures 4.7a, 4.7b). Furthermore, the internal structure of the aggression motive was similar for East and West German children: e.g., negative evaluations of the aggressor and the attribution of negative intentions correlated with aggressive tendencies. Also, mothers' socialization behaviour was related in the same way to children's proneness to aggression; these specific aggression-related socialization conditions did not differ between the East and West German samples. It seems that East and West German children at the age of 5 years had experienced similar mother–child interactions. Whether socialization conditions changed later on is presently being investigated in our study.

(b) People encountered the effects of social changes at *different stages*. Three years after the first measurement, we studied a comparable sample of 5-year-olds in order to control for possible period effects. We used the same instruments in order to ascertain comparability between the age groups. (N = 21 East German children and N = 44 West German children participated in this second study.) Socio-demographic data were similar to those of the 5-year-olds studied three years before. The East German 5-year-old control group showed more pro-social behaviour compared with the same-aged East German children studied three years previously. On the other hand, the same control group of 5-year-old children who were tested in 1995 showed significant differences with respect to aggression: East German children preferred aggressive behaviour more frequently than West German children (see Figures 4.7a, 4.7b). These results show that in the course of individual development the ongoing social changes were producing both negative and positive effects for the social behaviour of East German children.

East German preschool children who encountered the effects of the social changes at an earlier stage in the transformation preferred less pro-social action and more aggression compared with a control group of children who experienced the effects of social change at a later

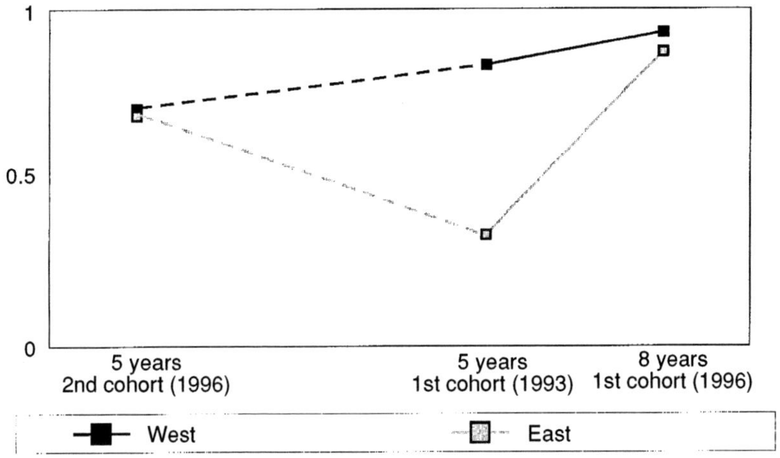

Scale: 0 = no pro-social behaviour to 1 = pro-social behaviour in all situations

Figure 4.7a Pro-social behaviour of two cohorts of East and West German children

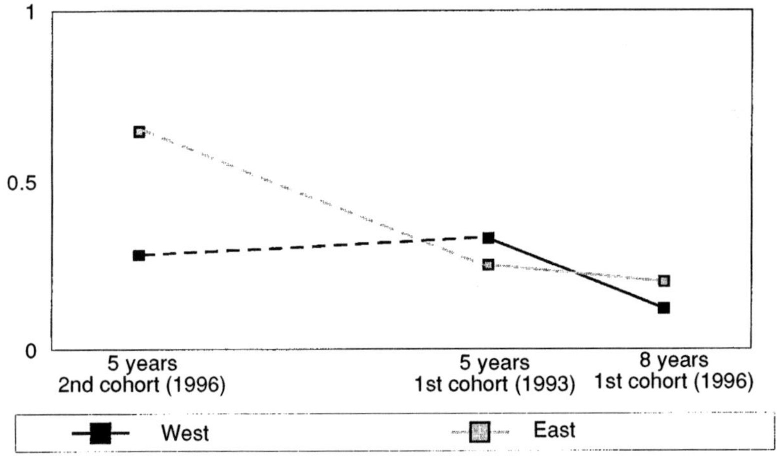

Scale: 0 = non-aggressive behaviour to 1 = aggressive behaviour in all situations

Figure 4.7b Aggressive behaviour of two cohorts of East and West German children

stage. Obviously, the children had experienced different challenges at different stages of ongoing changes which affected their social behaviour and development differently.

The quality of socialization of both cohorts of children in East Germany was different: the older cohort experienced early childhood in the relatively stable environment of the former GDR (including day care), and had experienced the effects of the transformation only after the second year of life or even later. The younger cohort had, from the beginning, grown up in an environment which had undergone continuous socio-economic change. These children had presumably experienced more changes in their immediate environment in the family and in their peer group in the course of their early development compared with the older cohort, and compared with the West German children. Possibly, such changes may have been connected with higher rates of social support, and hostility, and thus may have contributed to their experience of both types of social behaviour – pro-social and aggressive.

Future research is needed to show whether the preference for both pro-social and aggressive behaviour remains stable for this cohort of East German children. For East German adolescents, comparable results are reported by Sturzbecher (1997). Currently, more anti-social behaviour and, at the same time, more incidents of pro-social behavior, such as solidarity, can be observed than several years earlier. Do the experience of social change, related stress, and the need for coping, increase both pro-social and anti-social motivation: the need for solidarity and social support on the one hand, and the need to harm others on the other? Also, we may ask whether these two systems of motives represent specific resources for coping which are of differential functional value at different times of development (cf. Zahn-Waxler, Cummings and Iannotti, 1986).

When social change has induced significant changes in children's proximal social environments, in and outside the family, both challenges and risks for children's emotional and social development can arise. These contribute to the higher preference for pro-social and also for aggressive action. However, it still has to be seen how stable such effects are, and whether ongoing social change on the one hand, and changes in children's proximal environments arising from transitions (entering school and experiencing other socialization effects outside the family) on the other, may increase or compensate for developmental risks. The third measurement of our main sample and the second measurement of our control group (when these children will also be

8 years old) are in process and will contribute to the testing of the effects of developmental age, cohort, and period of social change.

Conclusion and outlook

Social change affects people at different developmental ages and from different cohorts at different periods during the course of the change in different ways. It is assumed that this results from different experiences of the social change and the different uses made of coping strategies. The subjective dimensions of social change alert us to the fact that people may experience and evaluate changes in their proximal environments as threatening and stressful life events or as promising challenges. Both the experience and the way of negotiating social change will be related to the way the person makes use of his or her individual resources. These include goals, competence, beliefs and perceived social resources. Studies of the effects of social change should focus more on the internal processes of experiencing and negotiating the change and how these are mediated and modified by social conditions and personal factors.

Studies of social change in East Germany rarely deal with questions concerning the psychological experience of changes in the period of transition. These include what kind of changes are experienced in which way, whether persons experience more negative or more positive changes, and whether the experience of change changes its meaning in the context of other experiences. Social change events will be interpreted not only once, at the time of their first appearance, but, when the person is aware of such changes, on successive occasions in the process of change, and while other events are happening. Social change events which may have been experienced originally as negative may, in the light of later experiences, lose their negative meanings, or the other way round. Also, ongoing social changes, including objective changes in a person's proximal environment, may lose their character of novelty, and may thereby change their subjective meaning.

People can adjust to social changes and increase their individual resources by activating, for example, social support and/or by intra-individual processes of habituation, mental simulation and so on. People can accommodate and habituate to all kinds of changes in their environments on the basis of multiple processes of balancing inconsistencies by changing their goals, control beliefs, or behaviour. When experiencing events which block goal attainment, people may re-arrange their goal structures and disengage from unattainable goals (secondary control), or they may actively change their situations in search of supportive or new positive events (primary control). Obviously, individual differences in negotiating social change have to be taken into account. Therefore, beside a stress-buffering model of coping with negative events (through perceived social support, for example), a personal growth model may be applicable when studying the subjective aspects of social change. From a developmental point of view, the experience of social change (and related positive and negative events) may create opportunities for psychological growth. Thus, human plasticity may enable individuals to negotiate the effects of social changes in ways that allow for successful coping and the ultimate improvement of their social and personal resources.

Notes

1. Parts of this study were supported by the Deutsche Forschungsgemeinschaft (DFG).
2. The SOEP is a project at the Deutsches Institut für Wirtschaftsforschung (DIW), Berlin. The SOEP is partly supported by the Deutsche Forschungsgemeinschaft, the Federal State of Berlin, and the German Government (Ministry of Technology, Research and Education, BMBF).
3. I am indebted to Friedhelm Löffelhardt who carried out the difficult task of secondary analyses of the data from the SOEP.
4. The longitudinal study reported here refers to our project 'Pro- and antisocial motivation of children and adolescents in the old and new German federal states' and was supported by the Deutsche Forschungsmeinschaft (DFG).

References

Ainsworth, J., Blehar, M., Waters, E. and Wall, S. (1978) *Patterns of Attachment: A Psychological Study of the Strange Situation.* Hillsdale, NJ: Lawrence Erlbaum.

Band, E. B. and Weisz, J. R. (1988) 'How to feel better when it feels bad: Children's perspectives on coping with everyday stress', *Developmental Psychology*, **24**: 247–53.

Bandura, A. (1994) *Self-efficacy: The Exercise of Control.* New York: Freeman.

Bowlby, J. (1969) *Attachment and Loss:* Vol. 1: *Attachment.* New York: Basic Books.

Bronfenbrenner, U. (1979) *The Ecology of Human Development: Experiment by Nature and Design.* London: Harvard University Press.

Brunstein, J. C. (1993) 'Personal goals and subjective well-being: a longitudinal study', *Journal of Personality and Social Psychology*, **65**: 1061–70.

Brunstein, J. C., Dangelmayer, G. and Schultheiss, O. C. (1996) 'Personal goals and social support in close relationships: effects on relationship mood and marital satisfaction', *Journal of Personality and Social Psychology*, **71**: 1006–19.

Cantor, N. and Norem, J. K. (1989) 'Defensive pessimism and stress and coping', *Social Cognition*, **7**: 92–112.

Carver, C. S. and Scheier, M. F. (1990) 'Origins and functions of positive and negative affect: A control-process view', *Psychological Review*, **97**: 19–35.

Conger, R. D., Elder, G. H., Lorenz, F. O., Conger, K. J., Simons, R. L., Whitbeck, L. B., Huck, S. and Melby, J. N. (1990) 'Linking economic hardship to marital quality and instability', *Journal of Marriage and the Family*, **52**: 643–56.

Conger, R. D., Ge, X., Elder, G. H., Lorenz, F. O. and Simons, R. L. (1994) 'Economic stress, coercive family process, and developmental problems of adolescents', *Child Development*, **65**: 541–61.

Elder, G. H. (1974). *The Children of the Great Depression: Social Change and Life Experience.* Chicago: University of Chicago Press.

Essau, C. and Trommsdorff, G. (1996) 'Coping with university-related problems: a cross-cultural comparison', *Journal of Cross-Cultural Psychology*, **27**: 315–28.

Festinger, L. (1968) *A Theory of Cognitive Dissonance.* Stanford, CA: Stanford University Press.

Flammer, A. (1990) *Erfahrung der eigenen Wirksamkeit: Einführung in die Psychologie der Kontrollmeinung* [Experience of own efficacy: introduction to the psychology of control beliefs]. Bern: Huber.

Folkman, S. and Lazarus, R. S. (1991) 'Coping and emotion', in A. Monat and R. S. Lazarus (eds), *Stress and Coping: An Anthology* (3rd edn: 207–27). New York: Guilford Press.

Friedlmeier, W. and Trommsdorff, G. (1997) Preferences of individual control strategies in a cultural perspective. Paper presented at the 8th European Conference on Developmental Psychology, Rennes, France, 3–7 September.

Friedrich, W. and Griese, H. (Hrsg.) (1991) *Jugend und Jugendforschung in der DDR. Gesellschaftspolitische Situationen, Sozialisation und Mentalitätsentwicklung in den achtziger Jahren* [Youth and youth research in the German Democratic Republic. Adolescents' social situation, socialization, and mentality in the 1980s]. Opladen: Leske & Budrich.

Gensicke, T. (1996) *Von der Transformation zur Integration. Die Ostdeutschen an der Schnittstelle zwischen individueller Anpassung und Vergesellschaftung im neuen Deutschland* [From transformation to integration]. Unpublished doctoral dissertation, Hochschule für Verwaltungswissenschaften Speyer.

Heckhausen, J. and Schulz, R. (1995) 'A lifespan theory of control', *Psychological Review*, **102**: 284–304.

Holahan, C. J. and Moos, R. H. (1985) 'Life stress and health: personality, coping, and family support in stress resistance', *Journal of Personality and Social Psychology*, **49**: 739–47.

Jahoda, M., Lazarsfeld, P. F. and Zeisel, H. (1972) *Marienthal: The Sociology of an Unemployed Community*. New York: Aldine–Atherton.

Jessor, R. and Jessor, S. L. (1977) *Problem Behavior and Psychological Behavior: A Longitudinal Study of Youth.* New York: Academic Press.

Kornadt, H.-J. (1982) *Aggressionsmotiv und Aggressionshemmung* [Aggression motive and aggression inhibition]. Bern: Huber.

Lerner, R. M. (1986) *Concepts and Theories of Human Development* (2nd edn). New York: Random House.

Lopez, D. F. and Little, T. D. (1996) 'Children's action-control beliefs and emotional regulation in the social domain', *Developmental Psychology*, **32**: 299–312.

Mannheim, K. (1952) 'The problem of generations', in K. Mannheim, *Essays on the Sociology of Knowledge* (pp. 276–322). London: Routledge & Kegan Paul. (Original work published 1928)
Meulemann, H. (1996) *Werte und Wertewandel: Zur Identität einer geteilten und wieder vereinten Nation* [Values and value change: identity of a divided and reunited nation]. Weinheim: Juventa.
Nuttin, J. (1984) *Motivation, action, and planning: a relational theory of behaviour dynamics*. Leuven, Belgium: Leuven University Press.
Reis, O. (1993) *Risiken und Ressourcen für die Persönlichkeitsentwicklung im Übergang zum Erwachsenenalter: Die Rostocker Längsschnittstudie nach 20 Jahren* [Risks and resources of the development of personality in transition to adulthood]. Unpublished doctoral dissertation, Universität Rostock.
Roether, D. and Kunze, H. (1995) 'Lebenssituation alter Menschen: Ein Ost–West-Vergeich' [The life situation of the elderly: A comparison between East and West Germany], *Zeitschrift für Gerontopsychologie und -psychiatrie*, **8**: 263–72.
Scheier, M. F. and Carver, C. S. (1985) 'Optimism, coping, and health: assessment and implications of generalized outcome expectancies', *Health Psychology*, **4**: 219–47.
Scheier, M. F. and Carver, C. S. (1992) 'Effects of optimism on psychological and physical well-being: theoretical overview and empirical update', *Cognitive Therapy and Research*, **16**, 201–28.
Schnabel, K., Baumert, J. and Roeder, P. (1994) 'Wertewandel in Ost und West: Ein Vergleich von Jugendlichen und Erwachsenen in den neuen und alten Bundesländern' [Value change in East and West: a comparison of adolescents and adults in the Western And Eastern German states], in G. Trommsdorff (ed.), *Psychologische Aspekte des sozio-politischen Wandels in Ostdeutschland* (pp. 77–93). Berlin: DeGruyter.
Seginer, R. (1997) *Defensive Pessimism and Optimism Correlates of Adolescent Future Orientation: A Domain-specific Analysis.* Manuscript submitted for publication, Haifa University.
Seginer, R., Trommsdorff, G. and Essau, C. A. (1993) 'Adolescent control beliefs: cross-cultural variations of primary and secondary orientations', *International Journal of Behavioral Development*, **16**: 242–60.
Silbereisen, R. K., Eyfert, K. and Rudinger, G. (eds). (1986) *Development as Action in Context: Problem Behavior and Normal Youth Development.* New York: Springer.
SOEP: Sozio-ökonomisches Panel [Socio-economic panel] (1995) Berlin: Deutsches Institut für Wirtschaftsforschung.
Sturzbecher, D. (ed.) (1997) *Jugend und Gewalt in Ostdeutschland: Lebenserfahrungen in Schule, Freizeit und Familie* [Youth and violence in East Germany: life experiences in school, leisure time and family]. Göttingen: Hogrefe.
Suh, E., Diener, E. and Fujita, F. (1996) 'Events and subjective well-being: only recent events matter', *Journal of Personality and Social Psychology*, **70**: 1091–102.
Taylor, S. E. and Lobel, M. (1989) 'Social comparison activity under threat: downward evaluation and upward contacts', *Psychological Bulletin*, **96**: 569–75.
Trommsdorff, G. (1984) 'Familiale Sozialisation im Kulturvergleich: Japan und Deutschland' [Cross-cultural comparison of socialization in the family: Japan and Germany]. *Zeitschrift für Sozialisationsforschung und Erziehungssoziologie*, **4**: 79–97.

Trommsdorff, G. (1986) 'Future time orientation and its relevance for development as action', in R. K. Silbereisen, K. Eyferth and G. Rudinger (eds.), *Development as Action in Context* (pp. 121–36). Berlin: Springer.

Trommsdorff, G. (1994a) 'Future time perspective and control orientation: social conditions and consequences', in Z. Zaleski (ed.), *Psychology of Future Orientation* (pp. 39–62). Lublin, Poland: TN Kul.

Trommsdorff, G. (1994b) 'Psychologische Probleme bei den Transformationsprozessen in Ostdeutschland' [Psychological aspects of sociopolitical change in Eastern Germany], in G. Trommsdorff (ed.), *Psychologische Aspekte des soziopolitischen Wandels in Ostdeutschland* (pp. 19–42). Berlin: DeGruyter.

Trommsdorff, G. (1994c) 'Zukunft als Teil individueller Handlungsorientierungen' [The future as part of individual action orientations], in E. Holst, J. P. Rinderspacher and J. Schupp (eds), *Erwartungen an die Zukunft* (pp. 45–76). Frankfurt: Campus.

Trommsdorff, G. (in press-a). 'Effects of social change and individual development: the role of social and personal factors, and the timing of events', in L. Crocket and R. K. Silbereisen (eds), *Negotiating Adolescence in Times of Social Change*. Cambridge: Cambridge University Press.

Trommsdorff, G. (in press-b) 'Social change and individual development in East Germany: a methodological critique', in R. K. Silbereisen and A. von Eye (eds), *Growing Up in Times of Social Change*. Berlin: de Gruyter.

Trommsdorff, G., Burger, C., Füchsle, T. and Lamm, H. (1978) *Erziehung für die Zukunft* [Socialization for the future]. Düsseldorf: Schwann.

Trommsdorff, G. and Chakkarath, P. (with the collaboration of P. Heller) (1996) 'Kindheit im Transformationsprozess' [Childhood in the process of transformation], in S. Hormuth, W. R. Heinz, H.-J. Kornadt, H. Sydow and G. Trommsdorff (eds), *Individuelle Entwicklung, Bildung und Berufsverläufe*, Vol. 4, pp. 11–77. Opladen: Leske & Budrich.

Trommsdorff, G. and Essau, C. A. (1998) Adolescents' control orientation: a cross-cultural study. In G. Trommsdorff, W. Friedlmeier, and H.-J. Kornadt (eds), *Japan in Transition – Psychological and Sociological Aspects*. Lengerich: Pabst Science Publishers.

Trommsdorff, G. and Kornadt, H.-J. (1995) 'Prosocial and antisocial motivation of adolescents in East and West Germany', in J. Youniss (ed.), *After the Wall: Family Adaptations in East and West Germany. New Directions for Child Development*, No. 70, pp. 39–56. San Francisco, CA: Jossey-Bass.

Trommsdorff, G. and Kornadt, H.-J. (1998) *Pro-social and Anti-social Motivation of East and West German Children and Adolescents*. Manuscript in preparation.

Trommsdorff, G., Kornadt, H.-J. and Hessel-Scherf, M. (1998) 'Soziale Motivation ost- und westdeutscher Kinder' [Social motivation of East and West German children], *Zeitschrift für Sozialisationsforschung und Erziehungssoziologie*, 18, pp. 121–36.

Vinokur, A. D., Price, R. H. and Caplan, R. D. (1996) 'Hard times and hurtful partners: how financial strain affects depression and relationship satisfaction of unemployed persons and their spouses', *Journal of Personality and Social Psychology*, **71**: 166–79.

Weisz, J. R., Rothbaum, F. M. and Blackburn, T. C. (1984) 'Standing out and standing in: the psychology of control in America and Japan', *American Psychologist*, **39**: 955–69.

Wills, T. A. (1981) 'Downward comparison principles in social psychology', *Psychological Bulletin*, **90**: 245–71.
Wills, T. A. (1991) 'Social support and interpersonal relationships', in M. S. Clark (ed.), *Review of Personality and Social Psychology: Vol. 12: Prosocial Behavior* (pp. 265–89). Newbury Park, CA: Sage.
Wills, T. A. and Cleary, S. D. (1996) 'How are social support effects mediated? A test with parental support and adolescent substance use', *Journal of Personality and Social Psychology*, **71**: 937–52.
Wills, T. A., Mariani, J. and Filer, M. (1996) 'The role of family and peer relationships in adolescent substance use', in G. R. Pierce, B. R. Sarason and I. G. Sarason (eds), *Handbook of Social Support and the Family* (pp. 521–49). New York: Plenum.
Zahn-Waxler, C., Cummings, E. M. and Iannotti, R. J. (1986) *Altruism and Aggression: Biological and Social Origins*. Cambridge: Cambridge University Press.
Zapf, W. and Habich, R. (1995) 'Die sich stabilisierende Transformation – ein deutscher Sonderweg?' [Stabilizing transformation – A specific German way?], in H. Rudolph (ed.), *Geplanter Wandel, ungeplante Wirkungen. Handlungslogiken und -ressourcen im Prozess der Transformation* (pp. 137–59). Berlin: Edition Sigma.
Zinnecker, J. and Silbereisen, R. K. (1996) *Kindheit in Deutschland: Aktueller Survey über Kinder und ihre Eltern* [Childhood in Germany: a current survey of children and their parents]. Weinheim: Juventa.

5

Adapting to social change: Adolescent values in Eastern and Western Germany[1]

Matthias Reitzle and *Rainer K. Silbereisen*

Values can be regarded as a key concept in understanding the interplay between social change and individual development. For example, the steadily growing economic affluence and improvement of the educational systems in postwar Western industrialized countries were held responsible for individuals' increasing endorsement of postmaterialistic value orientations (Inglehart, 1977, 1990). Value orientations supposedly have implications in a large variety of behavioral settings such as family, social relationships and work (Fijnman, Willemsen and Poortinga, 1996). This does not mean that every facet of an individual's behaviour can be predicted directly from values. The value system characteristic of each society, however, provides a climate for individual behaviour and development. Competitive behaviours, for example, should be more salient in a society endorsing individual achievements than in a society of ideologically mandated status equality.

Research on the impact of social change on individual development, such as Elder's landmark studies of the Great Depression (1974, 1979), demonstrated that cohorts can differ in the ease of adaptation to macrolevel change (Elder and Caspi, 1992). According to the 'life stage principle', individuals' positions in the life cycle in terms of age-graded roles, tasks and experiences largely determine the nature and size of effects that social change has on their development across the life-span.

German unification represents a unique situation for the study of the interplay between social and individual change. The fall of the Berlin instantaneously changed the economic and societal context for

Easterners, entailing effects on careers, education and social relationships. As holds true for the Great Depression, unification is one of the rare instances of sufficiently discrete macrolevel change (Schulenberg, O'Malley, Bachman and Johnston, in press; Shanahan and Elder, 1997) that allows for clear demarcations of cohorts who experienced change at different stages in the life-cycle.

After the breakdown of the socialist system, comparisons between Western and former Eastern Block countries based on survey data became possible. In a recent cross-cultural study on work-related values, Smith, Dugan and Trompenaars (1996) found that adult employees from former Eastern block countries ranked higher on a dimension of conservatism versus egalitarian commitment than did their Western counterparts. Conservatism implied status ascription, particularism (i.e., granting close friends privileges even under violation of common rules), the unquestioning acceptance of authority, and the expectation that companies are in charge of the social security and well-being of their employees. Within the former Eastern block, East Germany ranked higher on conservatism than Hungary, the former Czechoslovakia and Poland, thereby revealing an even larger difference from Western Germany. The fact that common history and language did not provide for a greater similarity underscores the impact of the different political and societal macrocontexts characteristic of the two parts of Germany.

Smaller, or even no value differences were found among adolescents. For instance, in a study of materialistic and postmaterialistic orientations, Schnabel, Baumert and Roeder (1994) reported no value differences between Eastern and Western samples of 10th-graders. The authors compared their findings for adolescents to data from a representative survey of German adults aged 18 to 79 years. In contrast to adolescents, a higher percentage of adults from former East Germany as compared to Westerners were categorized as materialistic, thereby emphasizing the importance of social order and economic stability. Interestingly, the East–West differences in the percentage of materialists increased almost linearly with the age of the respondents. The general picture of age-graded value differences supports the view that particularly Eastern teenagers had increasingly turned to Western-like values and lifestyle before unification (Friedrich and Foerster, 1994, 1997). Although Eastern adolescents may have felt attracted to the Western media and pop culture, the completely different living contexts should have preserved some value differences between Eastern and Western young people in other value domains.

The present study is concerned with value differences between adolescents and young adults from the Eastern and Western parts of Germany shortly after unification, and, even more interesting from a developmental perspective, with changes of value orientations across different cohorts. More precisely, we assumed that social change would affect young peoples' lives and value systems differently depending on their particular developmental stages. We compared Eastern and Western young peoples' values in terms of individualism and collectivism (Schwartz and Bilsky, 1987; Schwartz, 1990) using data collected in 1991, but additionally analysed another cross-sectional set of value data gathered in 1996. In combining these two cross-sectional studies, we tested two hypotheses, the first concerned with value differences between the political regions, and the second focused on changes in values across time. Primarily, we expected that adolescents and young adults from the Eastern and Western parts of Germany could clearly be distinguished by their value orientations shortly after unification in 1991.

Hypothesis 1

According to the theoretical framework of Schwartz and colleagues (Schwartz, 1990; Schwartz and Bilsky, 1987), individualism and collectivism represent broader domains into which the ten universal types of values identified by Schwartz can be categorized according to whose interests these value types primarily serve. Values relating to hedonism, stimulation, achievement, self-direction, and social power are deemed to primarily serve personal goals and hence are subsumed under individualistic value types. Prosocial values, values aiming at restrictive conformity and security, and values indicating high regard for tradition predominantly aim at the welfare of others, whether it be one's own family or society as a whole. Therefore, values of these four types are collectivist in their orientation. Values relating to maturity, such as broadmindedness, wisdom, and aesthetic values, are deemed to contribute equally to individual and to collective goals.

Although individual and collective interests are not necessarily in conflict, societies can be described in terms of the degree of their members' preferences for collectivist as compared to individualistic values. So-called collectivist societies, better termed 'communal societies', can be characterized by people's commitment to extended primary groups such as kinship, neighbourhoods, or work groups, based on ascribed statuses (Schwartz, 1990:152). In individualist societies, roles, statuses, and related commitments beyond the scope of the nuclear family are matters of negotiation and undergo frequent change.

Fitting into the picture of communal societies, the former East Germany provided many supervised opportunities for adolescents and young adults to adopt preformed roles and functions in school, in one of the numerous party-related organizations, or at the workplace for which there were no equivalents in Western Germany. Employed work itself was regarded as a societal duty above and beyond being a means of improving one's individual standard of living (Resetka, 1997). Hence, it was quite common and ideologically desirable for Eastern youngsters to take over collective responsibilities at a rather early age. In addition, Eastern young adults also made earlier commitments in the realms of marriage and parenthood, and thus acquired family roles and responsibilities earlier than their Western peers (Strohmeier and Schulze, 1995). Given this higher degree of organized public life and the earlier commitment to adult roles in one's own family, according to Hypothesis 1 we expected Eastern young people *to endorse values from the collectivist domain to a greater degree than their Western counterparts in 1991.*

Hypothesis 2

The fundamental change from a socialist system to a competitive market economy in former East Germany, beginning in 1989, should be reflected in changes of value orientations, thereby rendering the values of Easterners and Westerners more similar. Large-scale social changes, such as those experienced by the entire population of former East Germany, represent situations of uncertainty and potential loss of control (Elder and Caspi, 1992). In the case of unification, Easterners faced completely new requirements concerning their job qualifications (Sackmann and Wingens, 1996), such as a greater demand for individual decisions and competition in the labor market than they were accustomed to. They were confronted with the economic concomitants of a Western value system widely identified with individualism, self-direction and competition without having had the previous experience of applying these values in their everyday lives.

In a situation marked by a mismatch between competencies and emerging demands, value changes may represent an attempt to regain control (Elder and Caspi, 1992), if the new value orientations appear adaptive to the new conditions and promise gratification and success. Note that in the case of unification, this means a gradual shift towards more individualism rather than a complete reversal of values young people were used to. Depending on their particular stage in the life-cycle, however, individuals change more or less easily because the susceptibility to macrolevel changes largely depends on opportunities for change which are not equally distributed across different developmental stages (Elder, 1979).

Developmentalists have suggested several models for individual change versus stability at different periods of the life-span (for a detailed discussion see Alwin, 1994). According to the 'impressionable years' model, changes in personality including value systems and political orientations are most likely to occur during adolescence and young adulthood. What makes adolescents and young adults so impressionable or flexible, may be their freedom to experiment in various fields including values, worldviews, and politics before they become constrained by the demands of work and obligations towards spouse and children (Van Snippenburg and Hendriks Vettehen, 1992). These authors showed that during a transitional phase into adulthood, reminiscent of the moratorium stage of identity development (Marcia, 1980), young people were more inclined to adhere to new worldviews and ideas than older cohorts or those among their peers who were already committed to work and family responsibilities. In essence, early adulthood can be seen as a 'watershed' experience, in political socialization (McAdam, 1989).

The impressionable years model suggests that value changes are most likely to occur among those Eastern youth who were still in the phase of identity formation at the time of unification. For instance, Eastern adolescents who had not yet completed their education or training, had the opportunity to revise initial career plans, could profit from new training programs, or even had the chance to choose career tracks which were previously inaccessible. Briefly, they could integrate the demands of social change without calling their prior lives into question. In contrast, young adults who were already committed to an occupation, had started their own family, and had achieved an acknowledged status in the socialist society before unification, were less able to adapt to macrolevel changes (Hormuth and Heller, 1996; Trommsdorff, 1994).

In more precise terms, according to Hypothesis 2 we expected that by 1996 *the values of those Easterners who had not yet completed their entire transition into adulthood before unification would converge substantially with those of their Western peers*. In contrast, relatively little value convergence was expected among Eastern young adults who had experienced the crucial part of their transition into adulthood (including vocational training or college studies, achieving the majority age of 18, and, for males, completing the obligatory military service) under socialist conditions.

Both hypotheses will be tested with cross-sectional data on value preferences, gathered in 1991 and 1996. As is well known, such information represents the joint outcome of trends due to age, cohort and period of measurement (Schaie, 1965; Glenn, 1974, 1980). In order to analyse cohort-specific changes in East–West value differences, we had to assume that at least one of the potential effects is irrelevant in size relative to the effects of interest. Concerning age, this seems indeed to be the case according to previous research. Glenn (1980) reported that most studies on value change had not found maturational effects. The increasing endorsement of social order among older people, for instance, is mainly due to the fact that they did not tune in to the societal trend of increasing liberalism to the same extent as younger people. Thus, older people's values appear to have become more conservative with age. Seen against this backdrop, the expected smaller value convergence between 1991 and 1996 among older as compared to younger cohorts was conceived as indicating the impact of social change (predominantly affecting young Easterners' values) rather than differential maturation.

Method

Sample

In 1991, a study of adolescents and young adults was conducted in the newly unified Germany (Jugendwerk der Deutschen Shell, 1992). Data were collected from a large sample which was stratified by community size, age, educational level, and gender in order to represent the composition of the German population of the age range from 13 to 29 years. Participants from the East were oversampled because using the actual proportion of Eastern Germans (22 per cent) would have provided an insufficient sample size for subgroup comparisons within the Eastern sample. Only German nationals were used in the study. Adolescents residing in institutions were not selected.

The study comprised 1,656 adolescents, ranging from 13 to 19 years of age (1,074 from the West: mean age 16.5 years, standard deviation (SD) 2.1 years; 582 from the East: mean age 16.4 years, SD 2.2 years) and 2,174 young adults aged 20 to 29 years (1,471 from the West: mean age 24.4 years, SD 2.7 years; 703 from the East: 24.1 years, SD 2.7

years). Among the Western adolescents, 41 per cent attended or had completed academic school tracks as compared to 38 per cent in the East. The remaining adolescents were from vocationally oriented schools. In the young adult samples, 35 per cent of the Westerners had completed academic tracks, with the corresponding figure in the East being 30 per cent.

Participants were interviewed by trained interviewers who were employed by a reputable commercial survey research company. This company was hired to carry out the field work under the direction of a consortium of three German universities. The interviewers were asked to identify four to eight individuals who were suitable for inclusion in the study. According to a predefined profile, they were given instructions regarding how many males and females from which age stratum and educational level they should interview. As is common in quota-based survey studies, interviewers continued their work until they obtained the requested number of interviews. All participants were interviewed in their homes.

In 1996, an equivalent cross-sectional survey was conducted, aiming at the same age groups as in 1991, utilizing the same procedures as described above. The 1996 survey, however, was aimed at Eastern and Western subsamples of equal size. The resulting sample included 1,424 adolescents (694 from the West: mean age 16.5 years, standard deviation (SD) 1.9 years; 730 from the East: mean age 16.6 years, SD 2.0 years) and 1,809 young adults (959 from the West: mean age 24.6 years, SD 2.8 years; 850 from the East: mean age 24.8 years, SD 2.9 years). In the adolescent samples, 37 per cent of the Westerners and 33 per cent of the Easterners were from academically oriented schools, whereas the corresponding rates among young adults were 40 per cent in the West and 23 per cent in the East.

For the purpose of the present study, it was crucial to exclude cases who were identified as having migrated from the Western to the Eastern states of Germany, and vice versa. In 1991, this applied to only 9 out of the 2,174 young adults; 8 Easterners had moved to the West, but only one Westerner had moved to the East at the time of the study. By 1996, however, mobility between the two parts of Germany had increased: 34 adolescents and 113 young adults were identified as migrants, almost half of them (71) being Easterners recruited for participation in the study in one of the Western states.

As these migrants and participants below age 15 were excluded from the study for design reasons (see below), the actual sample sizes, gender distributions, and mean ages that are summarized in Table 5.1 differ

Table 5.1 Sample sizes, gender distributions, mean ages, and percentage of completed transitions into adulthood by survey and region

	Males		Females		Age		Transitions into adulthood				
	N	%	N	%	Mean	SD	Left home %	Qualified %	Self-supporting %	Cohabit./married %	Own children %
1991											
West											
Age 15 to 19	367	49.3	378	50.7	17.6	1.5	10.2	9.3	12.9	4.0	0.8
Age 20 to 24	451	50.1	449	49.9	22.6	1.5	54.2	65.8	63.4	24.3	6.3
Age 25 to 29	286	50.8	277	49.2	27.3	1.5	81.5	87.2	87.9	54.7	27.9
East											
Age 15 to 19	189	48.3	202	51.7	17.7	1.5	14.1	26.3	22.0	7.9	1.8
Age 20 to 24	242	52.3	221	47.7	22.4	1.4	53.8	82.1	74.7	36.9	19.4
Age 25 to 29	121	50.6	118	49.4	27.2	1.5	82.4	92.5	92.1	70.7	56.9
1996											
West											
Age 15 to 19	249	50.5	244	49.5	17.4	1.5	6.9	7.3	11.4	4.5	0.4
Age 20 to 24	245	47.0	276	53.0	22.5	1.4	56.2	53.4	57.0	23.6	8.4
Age 25 to 29	187	48.2	201	51.8	27.5	1.4	85.3	79.9	82.2	51.3	24.5
East											
Age 15 to 19	268	49.6	272	50.4	17.4	1.5	11.9	9.3	13.5	6.9	1.1
Age 20 to 24	215	49.4	220	50.6	22.5	1.5	62.8	70.6	70.1	35.4	14.5
Age 25 to 29	163	46.3	189	53.7	27.6	1.4	87.2	92.9	93.2	64.2	47.4

from the size of the overall samples surveyed. To allow for a comparison of life stages represented in different cohorts, Table 5.1 also reports the percentage of young people who had completed vocational training (i.e. were 'qualified'), were financially self-supporting, were cohabiting or married, or had children, separately by survey year, region and cohort. Cohort differences regarding these transitions are described in greater detail in the following section.

Study design

In order to address our expectations concerning cohort-specific decreases in value differences between East and West from 1991 to 1996, the repeated cross-sectional studies were arranged in a so-called standard cohort table, commonly used for the study of age, cohort and period effects in sociological research (for a detailed description see Glenn, 1974, 1980). Although such cohort trend studies do not follow the same individuals through time, they are also 'longitudinal' by virtue of ascertaining average or typical change within identical birth cohorts (Jackson and Antonucci, 1994). In a standard cohort table, the time intervals used to delineate the age groups (and cohorts, respectively) are chosen so that they correspond to the time interval between the measures, in our case five years (15–19 years, 20–24 years, and 25–29 years). These age groups represent the different life stages at the time of unification, referred to in Hypothesis 2. Following the rationale of a standard cohort table, our design allows for tracing intracohort trends because 15–19-year-olds in 1991 and 20–24-year-olds in 1996 represent the same birth cohorts of 1972–76. Similarly, 20–24-year-olds in 1991 and 25–29-year-olds in 1996 represent the birth cohorts of 1967–71. Additionally, this setup allows for the analysis of cross-sectional age trends (15–19-year-olds, 20–24-year-olds, 25–29-year-olds in 1991 and 1996, respectively), and for tracing trends at each age level, as one cohort replaces another (e.g., 15–19-year-olds in 1991 as compared to 1996).

As shown in Table 5.1, among Easterners only 14 per cent of the youngest group had left home, about a quarter had completed vocational training, less than a quarter were financially self-supporting, only 8 per cent lived with a partner or were married, and less than 2 per cent had a child by 1991, i.e., one year after unification. In contrast, the vast majority of 20- to 24-year-old Easterners had completed vocational training and had already achieved financial self-support before 1991. More than a third of them were living with a married or unmarried partner, and about 20 per cent already had children. In sum, most members of these birth cohorts had taken major steps into adulthood before unification. In the West, the differences in transition rates between 15- to 19-year-old adolescents and the 20- to 24-year-olds were similar. The absolute percentages of completed transitions, however, were lower in the West across all ages, indicating that the pace of development into adulthood was generally slower in the West as compared to the East (Silbereisen, Schwarz and Rinker, 1996).

Measures

Values were assessed using 18 statements of terminal values derived from the research of Schwartz and Bilsky (1990), most of them dating back to Rokeach's (1973) work. Respondents in the 1991 and the 1996 surveys were asked: 'In the following list, there are some issues which may have importance for your life, things you are striving for or guidelines for your life. Please tell me how important the issue referred to is in your life.' Participants rated the items on a 7-point rating scale (1 = 'not important at all' to 7 = 'extremely important'). The wording of the items and their categorization into individualistic and collectivist value types are reported in the Appendix. Individualism and collectivism represent constructs at a very high level of abstraction which do not easily translate into measures (Fijnman, Willemsen and Poortinga, 1996). Because different individuals may express their individualism or collectivism through the endorsement of quite different subsets of individualistic or collectivist values, the respective value items are not so highly correlated as to form homogeneous individualism or collectivism scales. Even attempts to fit these value data to four more fine-grained subtypes of individualism and collectivism suggested by Schwartz (1990) remained unsatisfactory (Krebs, 1992). Hence, we did not form value scales but used the whole set of single items to determine value differences between East and West. The broad motivational categories 'individualism' and 'collectivism', however, remained in use as an organizing principle for the classification and interpretation of our findings.

Preliminary analyses revealed that Easterners, on average, tended to agree to all value statements more than did Westerners (1991: $p < .001$; 1996: $p < .01$), thus indicating a context-typical response set. As we could also not rule out that age-specific tendencies in responding would be confounded with actual age-related trends in value preferences, a within-subject standardization across the 18 items was performed. Such a procedure is highly recommended in cross-cultural research if there are culture-specific response sets (Leung and Bond,

1989; Hofstede, 1980). Hence, for each value item a new scale was formed by subtracting the within-subject mean from the raw score, and dividing the result by the respective standard deviation across the 18 answers. Only respondents with complete data for the value items (98.3 per cent of the sample described in Table 5.1) were included in the analyses.

As a consequence of within-subject standardization, each of a respondent's new value scores is linearly dependent on the remaining 17 scores, i.e., knowing 17 scores of a respondent renders the 18th score redundant. Thus, in order to avoid linear dependency among the value scores in the following analyses, one of the values had to be excluded. Preliminary analyses revealed that by omitting the item 'A world of beauty (beauty of nature and arts)' we would not lose any information on value differences between East and West (this item proved unrelated to the region).

Results

Using the SPSS statistical package (SPSS Inc., 1994), logistic regression models were estimated that predicted respondents' being either Easterners or Westerners based on their value orientations. By using items instead of scales as predictors for the region of origin, we allowed for the possibility that one or only few single values optimally distinguish between East and West. Although such issues are usually addressed via discriminant analysis, logistic regression was preferred as a more robust tool requiring neither a multivariate normal distribution nor equal covariance matrices in the groups under study (for a detailed discussion see Hosmer and Lemeshow, 1989).

Hypothesis 1: initial value differences 1991

The results of the logistic regressions for the three different age groups (in 1991) are given in Table 5.2. The coefficients Exp(B) represent factors by which the odds ratio of the probability of being an Easterner divided by the probability of being a Westerner is increased (coefficients > 1) or decreased (coefficients < 1) as a result of a one-unit change in the predictor. For example, the coefficient of 1.54 for Authority (in the age group 15 to 19 years) indicates that high scores on Authority were associated with a greater likelihood of being an Easterner, whereas the coefficient of .75 related to Inner Harmony corresponds to a smaller likelihood of being an Easterner, or a greater likelihood of being a Westerner, respectively. In short, coefficients greater

Table 5.2 Values predicting region (West = 0; East = 1): logistic regression models in different age groups in 1991

	Age 15 to 19 (born 1972–76)	Age 20 to 24 (born 1967–71)	Age 25 to 29
Predictors	*Exp(B) p*	*Exp(B) p*	*Exp(B) p*
Individualistic values			
Freedom (to do and think as one pleases)	.78†	.77†	.52§
Creativity (originality, imagination)	.87	.86	.78
Social power (control or dominance over others)	.81†	.69‡	.68*
Authority (the right to lead and to decide)	1.54§	1.28*	1.06
Wealth (material property, money)	.91	.91	.83
Stimulating life (stimulating experiences)	1.07	1.19	.90
Variety in life (filled with challenges, novelty and change)	1.42*	1.53‡	1.43†
Collectivist values			
World at peace (void of war and conflict)	.80	1.19	.83
True friendship (close, supportive friends)	.85†	.75†	1.26
Politeness (good manners)	1.53‡	1.45‡	1.32
Family safety (security for loved ones)	1.54‡	2.14§	1.75‡
National security (protection of one's nation against enemies)	1.08	.80†	.71*
Social order (stability of the society)	1.40*	1.19	1.28
Respect for tradition (conservation of venerable customs)	1.38‡	1.34†	1.18

Table 5.2 Continued

	Age 15 to 19 (born 1972–76)	Age 20 to 24 (born 1967–71)	Age 25 to 29
Predictors	*Exp(B) p*	*Exp(B) p*	*Exp(B) p*
Mixed-type maturity values			
Inner harmony (a balanced personality)	$.75^{*}$	$.57^{§}$	$.64^{*}$
Being one with nature (blending into nature)	1.14	.88	.83
Not categorized			
Detachment (from worldly wants)	.88	$.74^{‡}$	$.72^{*}$
N	1123	1357	799
–2LL	1447.81	1739.27	974.97
Model improvement (Chi^2/17 df)	$174.79^{§}$	$228.32^{§}$	$115.04^{§}$

Note: 'A world of beauty (beauty of nature and arts)' was removed from analyses to avoid linear dependency among predictors.
$^{†}p < .10$ $^{*}p < .05$ $^{‡}p < .01$ $^{§}p < .001$

than one indicate Easterners' higher endorsement of a particular value, whereas coefficients smaller than one reflect Easterners' lower endorsement as compared to Westerners.

Supporting our first hypothesis, the significant chi-squares for model improvement (compared to a model including only the constant) indicated that, in 1991, respondents' region of origin could be predicted by their values. Acknowledging that some differences in the significance levels of predictors across age groups may be partly due to different sample sizes, a rather coherent pattern emerged. As was expected, Eastern adolescents and young adults endorsed to a higher degree collectivist values such as Politeness and Family Safety. In the two younger groups, Respect for Tradition also proved more salient for Easterners. It was only the Eastern adolescents aged 15 to 19 years, however, who put more emphasis on Social Order.

At the same time, Eastern adolescents as well as young adults were less likely than their Western counterparts to subscribe to individualistic values such as Social Power and Freedom. Finally, Inner Harmony, representing a mixed-type maturity value, was also consistently less appreciated in the East. Surprisingly, Variety in Life, another individualistic value, gained more regard from Easterners across all age groups. Additionally, in the two younger groups the same held true for Authority, i.e., 'the right to lead and to decide'.

In order to test whether the entire predictive pattern applied equally to all age groups, the following strategy was pursued. For each pair of age groups, the model was first estimated in a single run, but with separate coefficients for each group (S-Plus for Windows, Module GLM; Mathsoft Inc., 1995). In a second step, equality constraints were imposed on all regression coefficients. If the equality constraints result in a significant worsening of the model chi-squares, the assumption of equal predictive patterns must be rejected. Results of all tests following this rationale are reported in Table 5.3. None of the pairwise comparisons reached the 5 per cent level of significance (see Table 5.3, upper left quadrant) indicating that the general picture of Easterners' higher endorsement of some collectivist values and lower appreciation of individualism applied across all ages in the 1991 data.

Hypothesis 2: changes in value differences 1996[1]

The logistic regression analyses were repeated with the 1996 data. Again, significant chi-squares for model improvement in all age groups revealed that value orientations still helped to identify participants' region of origin (Table 5.4). However, it was no longer the greater

Table 5.3 Pairwise tests of equality of predictive patterns: chi-square change after imposing equality constraints between groups (P-values in parentheses)

		1991			1996		
		Age 15 to 19	Age 20–24	Age 25–29	Age 15 to 19	Age 20–24	Age 25–29
	Age 15 to 19	–	–	–	30.86 (.0208)	–	–
1991	Age 20 to 24	26.07 (.0732)	–	–	–	52.18 (.0000)	–
	Age 25 to 29	21.84 (.1911)	16.23 (.5080)	–	–	– (.0197)	32.08
	Age 15 to 19	–	–	–	–	–	–
1996	Age 20 to 24	37.12 (.0032)	–	–	17.24 (.4380)	–	–
	Age 25 to 29	–	46.45 (.0001)	–	16.46 (.4913)	23.58 (.1314)	–

Table 5.4 Values predicting region (West = 0; East = 1): logistic regression models in different age groups in 1996

	Age 15 to 19	Age 20 to 24 (born 1972–76)	Age 25 to 29 (born 1967–71)
Predictors	*Exp(B)* *p*	*Exp(B)* *p*	*Exp(B)* *p*
Individualistic values			
Freedom (to do and think as one pleases)	.72*	.71*	.48§
Creativity (originality, imagination)	1.05	1.00	.63‡
Social power (control or dominance over others)	.78*	.81†	.59§
Authority (the right to lead and to decide)	1.27*	1.31*	.93
Wealth (material property, money)	1.08	1.10	.77†
Stimulating life (stimulating experiences)	1.07	.90	.77
Variety in life (filled with challenges, novelty and change)	1.29†	1.05	.96
Collectivist values			
World at peace (void of war and conflict)	1.24	1.08	1.00
True friendship (close, supportive friends)	1.13	.92	.64*
Politeness (good manners)	1.22	.98	.99
Family safety (security for loved ones)	1.16	1.12	.85
National security (protection of one's nation against enemies)	1.00	.97	.89
Social order (stability of the society)	1.48‡	1.05	1.36†
Respect for tradition (conservation of venerable customs)	1.19	1.05	.79†

Table 5.4 Continued

Predictors	Age 15 to 19 Exp(B) p	Age 20 to 24 (born 1972–76) Exp(B) p	Age 25 to 29 (born 1967–71) Exp(B) p
Mixed-type maturity values			
Inner harmony (a balanced personality)	$.79^{\dagger}$	$.77^{\dagger}$	$.61^{\ddagger}$
Being one with nature (blending into nature)	.97	1.05	$.65^{*}$
Not categorized			
Detachment (from worldly wants)	1.00	$.75^{*}$	$.63^{\ddagger}$
N	992	934	722
– 2LL	1372.68	1288.93	999.11
Model improvement (Chi^2/17 df)	$76.31^{\S}$	$60.01^{\S}$	$89.97^{\S}$

Note: 'A world of beauty (beauty of nature and arts)' was removed from analyses to avoid linear dependency among predictors.
$^{\dagger}p < .10$ $^{*}p < .05$ $^{\ddagger}p < .01$ $^{\S}p < .001$

emphasis on collectivist values that distinguished Eastern adolescents and young adults from their Western counterparts. All formerly significant coefficients from the collectivist value domain referring to Politeness, Family Safety, and Respect for Tradition were markedly attenuated. Instead, the cross-sectional picture in 1996 was one of Easterners' endorsing individualistic values such as Freedom and Social Power to a lesser degree than did Westerners. In this regard, findings resembled those found in the 1991 samples. As in 1991, there were no indications that the overall predictive pattern substantially differed between age groups. None of the corresponding pairwise tests proved significant (Table 5.3, lower right quadrant). Note, however, that these tests have less power as compared to those of the 1991 samples due to smaller sample sizes and a greater number of insignificant coefficients.

Referring to the second hypothesis, the major focus is on differential change between the 1972–76 and the 1967–71 birth cohorts. Among the former, aged 15 to 19 in 1991 and 20 to 24 in 1996, all the previously significant coefficients pertaining to collectivist values such as Politeness, Family Safety, Social Order and Respect for Tradition completely vanished in 1996, indicating that, regarding collectivism, the Eastern and Western members of these younger cohorts had become more similar. Moreover, Easterners' former greater regard for Variety and Authority was also gone (from 1.42 to 1.05), or at least attenuated (from 1.54 to 1.31). However, the initially lower endorsement of individualistic and maturity values such as Freedom and Social Power and Inner Harmony among the Eastern young persisted.

In the older birth cohorts of 1967–71, aged 20 to 24 years in 1991 and 25 to 29 in 1996, Easterners' previously greater emphasis on collectivist values had also disappeared by 1996. Their initially lower commitment to individualistic and maturity values, however, not only persisted, but even seemed accentuated. Particularly the coefficients for Freedom, Creativity and Social Power reached higher significance levels (lower probability values) despite the markedly smaller sample size (722 in 1996 versus 1357 in 1991) indicating that these individualistic values were better predictors discerning Easterners from Westerners in 1996 as compared to 1991.

The general impression of changes in the predictive patterns from 1991 to 1996 was corroborated by pairwise testing across measurement occasions, both for the same birth cohorts (Table 5.3, lower left quadrant), and for the same age groups (Table 5.3, upper right quadrant). Each of these five tests was significant at the 5 per cent level or less. Thus far, it could be concluded that in 1996 there were still value differences between East and West, but not the same as those identified in 1991.

Whether these findings actually implied a decrease in East–West value differences from 1991 to 1996 exclusively among younger cohorts and a persistence of differences among the older ones, as predicted by Hypothesis 2, could not be directly inferred from comparisons of predictive patterns. In order to test our second hypothesis properly, it had to be shown that values predicted the region of origin with significantly lower accuracy in 1996 when compared to 1991, but only in the younger cohorts.

A simple approach to assessing differences in predictive accuracy between the 1991 and 1996 models is provided by the use of predicted probabilities of being an Easterner, derived from each of the six logistic regressions. The East–West mean difference in these probabilities can be used as an indicator of the predictive accuracy of a particular model, or put differently, the difference can be used as a comprehensive measure of the overall East–West value difference in this model. This is based on the following considerations. In a perfect model that optimally discriminates between East and the West, all Easterners would yield predicted probabilities close to one, whereas all Westerners would have predicted probabilities close to zero. As a result, the difference between the average Eastern and Western probabilities would approximate 1. In a completely failing model with no predictive information gained by values, all predicted probabilities would have the same value (the observed probability of Easterners) with the difference between the average Eastern and Western probabilities being zero, of course. The actual East–West mean differences in predicted probabilities from the six logistic regressions are depicted in Figure 5.1.

These mean differences representing overall value differences can be used to test Hypothesis 2. Tests were performed with a set of Analyses of Variance (ANOVAs) including the factors Region, Period, Cohort, and Age Group. However, the predicted probabilities of being an Easterner only technically served as the dependent variable. The measures of interest, though, were not Easterners' and Westerners' absolute levels, but the East–West mean differences in these probabilities (graphically speaking, the value gap). These differences are represented by the Region effect. The crucial question was how the Region effect would *interact* with the factors Period, Cohort, and Age Group.

The first expected data pattern was one of a differential intracohort trend, that is, a decreasing value gap among younger cohorts and persistence of value differences among older cohorts at the same time. An

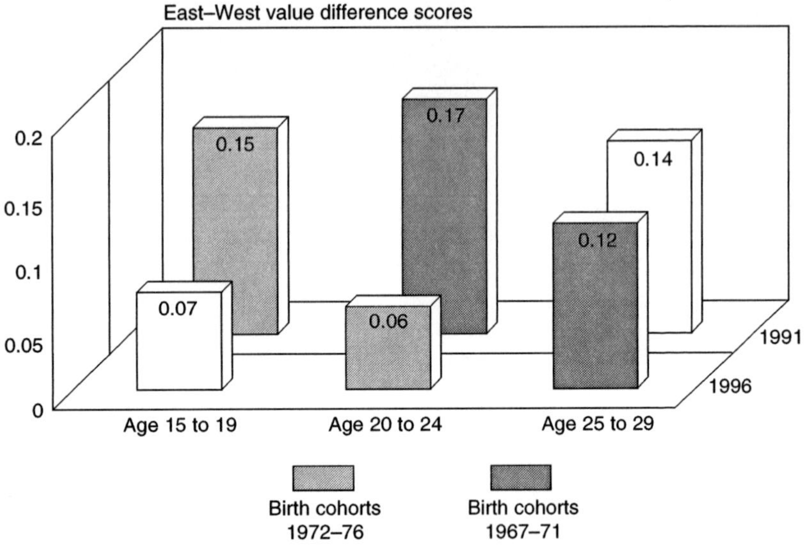

Figure 5.1 East–West mean differences in value orientations

ANOVA with the factors Region, Period, and Cohort (1967–71, 1972–76) was run. A significant triple interaction of the Region effect (value gap) with Period and Cohort ($p < .05$) reflected the fact that differences in value orientations had decreased particularly among the younger cohorts aged 15 to 19 in 1991, and 20 to 24 in 1996, respectively.

Additionally, in order to render maturation effects unlikely, it was expected that initially (1991) there could be no cross-sectional age effects, thus supporting the view that the different societal contexts operated similarly across all ages studied. In the second ANOVA on the 1991 data with the factors Region, and Age Group (15–19, 20–24, 25–29), there was no cross-sectional age trend supporting a maturation effect. As expected, the Region by Age group interaction was not significant ($p > .40$), indicating that the initial value gap between East and West was of a uniform size across all age groups studied.

Finally, the basic idea of cohort-specific changes in East–West value differences also translates into cohort replacement trends. More specifically, it was expected that the two younger age groups (15–19 and 20–24 years) in 1996 should exhibit smaller East–West value differences than their 1991 predecessors. Persistence of value differences was expected for the oldest age group (25–29 years) replacing their 1991 predecessors. In an ANOVA with the factors Region, Period, and Age Group, these differential cohort replacement trends were most comprehensively reflected in a significant triple interaction of Region (value gap), Period, and Age Group ($p < .01$).

Discussion

Differences in value orientations between adolescents and young adults from East and West Germany were tested. Using data from two representative samples with more than 6,900 respondents assessed in 1991 and 1996, we found empirical support for our hypotheses. First, values significantly distinguished between Easterners and Westerners in 1991, irrespective of the age group under study. Eastern adolescents and young adults put a greater emphasis on collectivist values such as Family Safety, Politeness, and Respect for Tradition than their Western peers, while assigning less importance to individualist and maturity values such as Freedom, Social Power, and Inner Harmony. Second, in line with the impressionable years model of individual change, value differences between East and West were attenuated in 1996 particularly among younger birth cohorts who had not yet completed their transitions into adulthood by the time of unification. More specifically, the younger cohorts born between 1972 and 1976 had become more similar to their Western peers in the domain of collectivist values. Although this also proved true for the older cohorts born between 1969 and 1971, their overall East–West value difference decreased only modestly. That no greater similarity was achieved among the older cohorts was due to an even accentuated dissimilarity between Easterners and Westerners in the individualism and maturity domains.

At the outset, it has to be emphasized that the value differences we observed were small, albeit statistically significant. In this context, one might ask whether the observed initial value differences in 1991 actually reflect the impact of the different political or ideological systems in former Eastern and Western Germany or simply result from relatively trivial differences in sociodemographics between the regions. For instance, persons with lower education place more emphasis on social order and restrictive conformity (Glenn, 1980), that is, they endorse values from the collectivist value domain to a higher degree than well-educated people. As a matter of fact, a smaller proportion of Eastern adolescents attended academically oriented school tracks as compared to the West (Kornadt, 1996). In addition, a higher proportion of the

Eastern population lived in smaller cities or even rural areas as compared to the West, which may have fostered their forming of a collective identity. Furthermore, a higher proportion of Eastern young adults were married and/or had children. These living conditions potentially promote the endorsement of security-related collectivist values, too. Controlling the logistic regressions for education, community size, and marital status, however, provided no evidence that Eastern peculiarities of living conditions, such as an earlier commitment to family roles or the more vocationally oriented school education, accounted for a substantial portion of the initial value differences between East and West in 1991.

Regarding value convergence, one might still ask who among the younger cohorts were especially susceptible to change – highly educated adolescents more than those from vocationally oriented school tracks? Additional analyses showed that the amount of change in value differences between 1991 and 1996 was the same whether members of the younger cohorts came from academically oriented or from vocationally oriented school tracks. However, the absolute levels of East–West value differences appeared more pronounced among young academics as compared to young people with lower education. This finding might indicate that members of academic school tracks in the East represented a privileged elite who were particularly conforming to the prevailing collectivist values. A further exploration of this issue, however, would go beyond the limitations of this chapter.

Turning to the distinctive patterns of value differences in 1991, shortly after unification, Easterners' surprisingly greater enthusiasm for Variety in Life ('filled with challenges, novelty and change') and Authority ('the right to lead and to decide') deserves a comment. Easterners' greater emphasis on these particular values from the individualistic domain did not match with their downgrading of Freedom and Social Power. In 1996, however, their greater subscription to Variety as compared to Westerners had completely levelled, while their previously higher regard for Authority was markedly attenuated. Taking these findings together, it seems unlikely Easterners' initial enthusiasm for Variety and Authority was a harbinger of a broader shift toward individualism after unification. Instead, it seems more plausible that unification opened a valve for young Easterners' accumulated demands for variety, enjoyment of life, and self-direction, which could already be observed before unification (Friedrich and Foerster, 1994; Trommsdorff, 1994). The newly gained freedom in the course of unification led to a short-term over-emphasis on these particular values. This effect, however, was neither accompanied by Eastern youngsters' dissociating themselves from their higher endorsement of collectivist values in 1991; nor had it generalized to other individualistic values in 1996.

Before attempting a detailed interpretation of the cohort-specific changes in value differences, some thought should be given to the question of who the protagonists of these changes are. Because our analytical strategy inherently focused on relative value differences between East and West rather than absolute levels in either part of Germany, it could not reveal whether the greater similarity in 1996 among the younger cohorts resulted from mutual convergence of values or from Easterners' unilateral adoption of Western values. Without any doubt, Easterners were the ones confronted with sudden, massive social change in the course of unification exemplified by reduced job security, a new definition of social roles and, in the case of adolescents, the implementation of the West German educational system (Bovier and Boehnke, 1994; Fischer, 1992). Such fundamental changes are apt to mobilize individuals' adaptational efforts in order to regain control (Elder and Caspi, 1992), including the adoption of new value orientations which seem more adequate and promising than the old ones. From this point of view, it seems more likely that the greater similarity in 1996 was achieved mainly through Eastern adolescents' and young adults' changing their value orientations.

In the natural experiment of unification, however, the Western part of Germany cannot be regarded as the control condition with social change not affecting people's lives and values there. In contrast to the East, social change in the West was less dramatic, less clear-cut, and occurred with slower pace (Zapf, 1996). Nevertheless, the economic constraints after unification, e.g., reductions in social benefits and a continuously high level of unemployment, have produced feelings of uncertainty and economic decline in Westerners (Zapf, p. 323). According to Inglehart (1977, 1990), times of economic uncertainty favour individuals' endorsement of security-related values, whereas unclouded prosperity forms a prerequisite for the emergence of post-materialistic values. Against this backdrop, the levelling of the East–West difference in collectivist values may well have been the result of Easterners' scaling down their collectivism toward Western levels and of Westerners' growing adherence to security-related values.

Although our second hypothesis referred to the concept of 'impressionable years', it would be too simplistic to regard adolescents as the only carriers of social change who grasp the *Zeitgeist* and transport it through time. Members of older cohorts also integrate social change into their value systems, but not to the same degree and less 'feverishly' than their younger counterparts who come into 'fresh contact' with ongoing social changes (Mannheim, 1952; Dowd, 1980). In our data, the overall value differences between Eastern and Western members of the older cohorts also shrank, but not to the same degree as those of the younger cohorts because the similarity achieved in collectivism was counteracted by a pronounced difference concerning individualistic and maturity values.

What could be the reason for the accentuation of differences in the domain of individualism? It does not seem very likely that Western young adults had become more individualistic over time. Instead, an increasing commitment to security-related values among young Westerners would better fit into the scenario of growing economic uncertainty in the West. More likely, Eastern young adults had further refrained from individualism in response to their personal experiences of social change in the course of unification. By 1991, the vast majority of these birth cohorts had completed vocational training and achieved financial self-support, which almost uniformly occurred at age 18 or 19 in former East Germany (Reitzle, Vondracek and Silbereisen, 1998). Another 40 per cent were living with a partner and one fifth had children. The fundamental restructuring of the Eastern economy peaked after 1991 and entailed numerous ruptures of careers and vocational biographies (Minx, 1997). Only a small part of the former work force remained at the same workplace or in the same occupations. Most of these vocational reorientations were not self-initiated. Under these circumstances, many of the Eastern young adults might have perceived social change as a threat to their identity and feelings of control rather than as a challenge (Trommsdorff, 1994), especially if options for individual change were restricted by conflicting responsibilities for a family.

One way to deal with social change in situations of threatened or even eliminated control is 'reactance' (Brehm and Brehm, 1981; Elder and Caspi, 1992), a motivational tendency to resist external influences in order to restore control. At the attitudinal level, reactance is characterized by individuals' not only maintaining, but even accentuating their existing attitudes and values (Karpf, 1978). From the perspective of the reactance concept, it seems plausible that Eastern members of the older cohorts intensified their reluctance to endorse individualistic values in response to social change threatening their identity and control. The fact that reactance manifested itself in their downgrading of individualistic values rather than in emphasizing collectivism, may relate to Easterners' perception of a mismatch between Western ideals of individualism and the freedom they experienced.

It should be mentioned that, while we did not study intraindividual change, our study design allowed for a comparison of equivalent samples of the same birth cohorts in 1991 and 1996. Such a cohort study addresses average change at the cohort level, not at the individual level. Nevertheless, it obviously provides information on stability versus change within cohorts (Jackson and Antonucci, 1994; Alwin, 1994). Furthermore, within the constraints of such a design we learn whether younger, in contrast to older, cohorts are affected by social change to the same or different degrees. A further limitation of the study is that macrolevel change as a potential causal agent of individual value change was inferred from the historical time span and the geographical location of the study, but was not directly measured. One might think of variables representing social change such as unemployment rates at local, regional, and state levels, or forced vocational changes, perceived threats and opportunities affecting values at the individual level.

Despite these limitations, the present findings corroborate the idea that younger cohorts are more susceptible to influences of social change. Most of the questions raised above, however, can be answered only through longitudinal studies. For example, panel data would help to determine the relationship between perceived opportunities and the susceptibility to social change or experienced loss of control and subsequent accentuation of existing value orientations, thereby elucidating the psychological mechanisms of value change at the individual level.

Acknowledgements

We are grateful for the support received from the German Research Council (Si 296/14-1, 2, 3, 4, 5; Principal Investigator: Rainer K. Silbereisen). Special thanks go to the colleagues of our research consortium at the University of Siegen (Principal Investigator: Juergen Zinnecker) and the University of Bamberg (Principal Investigator: Laszlo Vaskovics), and to our colleague Christof Schuster for his help with the S-Plus statistical program package. We also appreciate the thoughtful comments and inspiring suggestions provided by Jacqueline J. Goodnow, Linda Juang, Michael J. Shanahan and Fred W.

Vondracek. Last but not least, we want to thank all the young people who participated in the studies. A previous version of this paper was presented at the Biennial Meeting of the Society for Research in Child Development, 3–6 April 1997, Washington, DC; Symposium 'Social, Cultural, and Developmental Change in Adolescents' Values and Attitudes'.

Appendix

Individualistic values

Freedom (to do and think as one pleases)
Creativity (originality, imagination)
Social power (control or dominance over others)
Authority (the right to lead and to decide)
Wealth (material property, money)
Stimulating life (stimulating experiences)
Variety in life (filled with challenges, novelty and change)

Collectivist values

World at peace (void of war and conflict)
True friendship (close, supportive friends)
Politeness (good manners)
Family safety (security for loved ones)
National security (protection of one's nation against enemies)
Social order (stability of the society)
Respect for tradition (conservation of venerable customs)

Mixed-type maturity values serving individual and collective goals

Inner harmony (a balanced personality)
World of beauty (beauty of nature and arts)
Being one with nature (blending into nature)

Note: Detachment (from worldly wants); could not be categorized into the value types suggested by Schwartz (1990).

Note

1. Although comparing two cross-sectional studies, we use the term 'change' for the description of differences between the 1991 and 1996 results (e.g., changes in the predictive patterns, cohort-specific changes in value differences, etc.) in order to avoid confusion with the term 'difference' which describes East–West differences throughout the paper.

References

Alwin, D. F. (1994) 'Aging, personality, and social change: the stability of individual differences over the adult life span', in D. L. Featherman, R. M. Lerner and M. Perlmutter (eds), *Life-span Development and Behavior,* **12** (pp. 135–85). Hillsdale, NJ: Lawrence Erlbaum.

Bovier, E. and Boehnke, K. (1994) 'Einheit? Ein Vergleich der Werthaltungen von Ost- und Westberliner Lehramtsstudentinnen und -studenten vor der Waehrungsreform' [Unity? A comparison of value orientations of East and West Berlin students of the teaching profession before the monetary union], in P. Dudek and H. E Tenorth (eds), *Transformationen der deutschen Bildungslandschaft* (pp. 245–57). Beltz: Weinheim.

Brehm, S. S. and Brehm, J. W. (1981) *Psychological Reactance: A Theory of Freedom and Control.* New York: Academic Press.

Dowd, J. J. (1980) 'The problems of generations: and generational analysis', *International Journal of Aging and Human Development,* **10**(3): 213–29.

Elder, G. H. (1974) *Children of the Great Depression.* Chicago: University of Chicago Press.

Elder, G. H. (1979) Historical change in life patterns and personality', in P. B. Baltes and O. G. Brim, Jr (eds), *Life-span Development and Behavior,* **2** (pp. 118–59). New York: Academic Press.

Elder, G. H. and Caspi, A. (1992) 'Studying lives in a changing society: sociological and personological explorations', in R. A. Zucker, A. I. Rabin, J. Aronoff and S. J. Frank (eds), *Personality Structure in the Life Course* (pp. 276–322). New York: Springer.

Fijnman, Y. A., Willemsen, M. E. and Poortinga, Y. H. (1996) 'Individualism–collectivism: an empirical study of a conceptual issue', *Journal of Cross-Cultural Psychology,* **27**: 381–402.

Fischer, A. (1992) *Das Bildungswesen der DDR* [The educational system of the GDR]. Darmstadt: Wissenschaftliche Buchgesellschaft.

Friedrich, W. and Foerster, P. (1994) 'Jugendliche in den neuen Bundeslaendern' [Adolescents in the new federal states], in H.-J. Veen (ed.), *Eine Jugend in Deutschland? Orientierungen und Verhaltensweisen der Jugend in Ost und West* (pp. 119–52). Opladen: Leske & Budrich.

Friedrich, W. and Foerster, P. (1997) Politische Orientierungen ostdeutscher Jugendlicher und junger Erwachsener im Transformationsprozess [Political orientations of East German adolescents and young adults in the process of transformation], in H. Sydow (ed.), *Entwicklung und Sozialisation von Jugendlichen vor und nach der Vereinigung Deutschlands* (pp. 17–73). Opladen: Leske & Budrich.

Glenn, N. D. (1974) 'Aging and conservatism', *Annals of the American Academy of Political and Social Science,* **415**: 176–86.

Glenn, N. D. (1980) 'Values, attitudes and beliefs', in O. G. Brim, Jr and J. Kagan (eds), *Constancy and Change in Human Development* (pp. 596–640). Cambridge, MA: Harvard University Press.

Hofstede, G. (1980) *Culture's Consequences: International Differences in Work-related Values.* Beverly Hills, CA: Sage.

Hormuth, S. E. and Heller, P. (1996) 'Erwachsene im Transformationsprozess' [Adults in the process of social and political transformation], in S. E. Hormuth,

W. R. Heinz, H.-J. Kornadt, H. Sydow and G. Trommsdorff (eds), *Individuelle Entwicklung, Bildung und Berufsverlaeufe* (pp. 143–200). Opladen: Leske & Budrich.

Hosmer, D. W. and Lemeshow, S. (1989) *Applied Logistic Regression*. New York: Wiley.

Inglehart, R. (1977) *The Silent Revolution: Changing Values and Political Styles among Western Publics*. Princeton: Princeton University Press.

Inglehart, R. (1990) *Culture Shift in Advanced Industrial Society*. Princeton: Princeton University Press.

Jackson, J. S. and Antonucci, T. C. (1994) 'Survey methodology in life-span human development research', in S. H. Cohen and H. W. Reese (eds), *Life-span Developmental Psychology: Methodological Contributions* (pp. 65–94). Hillsdale, NJ: Lawrence Erlbaum.

Jugendwerk der Deutschen Shell (ed.) (1992) *Jugend '92*, 4 vols. Opladen: Leske & Budrich.

Karpf, R. J. (1978) 'Altering values via psychological reactance and reversal effects', *Journal of Social Psychology*, **106**(1): 131–2.

Kornadt, H.-J. (1996) 'Erziehung und Bildung im Transformationsprozess' [Education in the process of social and political transformation], in S. E. Hormuth, W. R. Heinz, H.-J. Kornadt, H. Sydow and G. Trommsdorff (eds), *Individuelle Entwicklung, Bildung und Berufsverlaeufe* (pp. 201–72). Opladen: Leske & Budrich.

Krebs, D. (1992) 'Werte in den alten und neuen Bundeslaendern' [Values in the old and new federal states of Germany], in Jugendwerk der Deutschen Shell (ed.), *Jugend '92*, **2**: *Im Spiegel der Wissenschaften* (pp. 35–48). Opladen: Leske & Budrich.

Leung, K. and Bond, M. H. (1989) 'On the empirical identification of dimensions for cross-cultural comparisons', *Journal of Cross-Cultural Psychology*, **20**: 133–51.

Mannheim, K. (1952) 'The problem of generations', in P. Kecskemeti (ed.), *Essays on the Sociology of Knowledge* (pp. 276–320). London: Routledge & Kegan Paul.

Marcia, J. E. (1980) 'Identity in adolescence', in J. Adelson (ed.), *Handbook of Adolescent Psychology* (pp. 158–87). New York: Wiley.

Mathsoft Inc. (ed.) (1995) *S-Plus, Version 3.3 for Windows*. Seattle, WA: Mathsoft Inc.

McAdam, D. (1989) 'The biographical consequences of activism', *American Sociological Review*, **54**: 744–60.

Minx, B. (1997) 'Berufsbiographien und Karrierebrueche von qualifizierten Erwerbstaetigen vor und nach der Wende' [Vocational biographies and career ruptures of qualified employees before and after unification], in W. R. Heinz and S. E. Hormuth (eds), *Arbeit und Gerechtigkeit im ostdeutschen Transformationsprozess* (pp. 73–124). Opladen: Leske & Budrich.

Reitzle, M., Vondracek, F. W. and Silbereisen, R. K. (1998) 'Timing of school-to-work transitions: A developmental-contextual perspective', *International Journal of Behavioral Development*, **22**: 7–28.

Resetka, H.-S. (1997) 'Individuelle Erfahrungen mit Qualifizierungs- und Beschaeftigungsprogrammen in verschiedenen Altersgruppen und Lebenslagen in den neuen Bundeslaendern' [Individual experiences with employment programs across different age groups in the new federal states], in W. R. Heinz and

S. E. Hormuth (eds), *Arbeit und Gerechtigkeit im ostdeutschen Transformationsprozess* (pp. 125–230). Opladen: Leske & Budrich.

Rokeach, M. (1973) *The Nature of Human Values*. New York: Free Press.

Sackmann, R. and Wingens, M. (1996) 'Berufsverlaeufe im Transformationsprozess' [Career patterns in the process of social and political transformation], in M. Diewald and& K. U. Mayer (eds), *Zwischenbilanz der Wiedervereinigung* (pp. 11–31). Opladen: Leske & Budrich.

Schaie, K. W. (1965) 'A general model for the study of developmental problems', *Psychological Bulletin*, **64**: 92–107.

Schnabel, K., Baumert,S. and Roeder, P. M. (1994) 'Wertewandel in Ost und West – Ein Vergleich von jugendlichen und Erwachsenen in den neuen und alten Bundeslaendern' [Value change in East and West – A comparison of adolescents and adults in the new and old federal states], in G. Trommsdorff (ed.), *Psychologische Aspekte des soziopolitischen Wandels in Ostdeutschland* (pp. 77–93). Berlin: de Gruyter.

Schulenberg, J., O'Malley, P. M., Bachman, J. G. and Johnston, L. D. (in press) '"Spread your wings and fly": the course of health and well-being during the transition to young adulthood', in L. J. Crockett and R. K. Silbereisen (eds), *Negotiating Adolescence in Times of Social Change*. New York: Cambridge University Press.

Schwartz, S. H. and Bilsky, W. (1987) 'Toward a universal psychological structure of human values', *Journal of Personality and Social Psychology*, **53**: 550–62.

Schwartz, S. H. and Bilsky, W. (1990) 'Toward a theory of the universal content and structure of values: extensions and cross-cultural replications', *Journal of Personality and Social Psychology*, **58**: 878–91.

Schwartz, S. H. (1990) 'Individualism–Collectivism: critique and proposed refinements', *Journal of Cross-Cultural Psychology*, **21**: 139–57.

Shanahan, M. J. and Elder, G. H. (1997) 'Nested comparisons in the study of historical change and individual adaptation', in J. Tudge, M. Shanahan and J. Valsiner (eds), *Comparisons in Human Development: Understanding Time and Context* (pp. 109–36). New York: Cambridge.

Silbereisen, R. K., Schwarz, B. and Rinker, B. (1996) 'The timing of psychosocial transitions in adolescence: commonalities and differences in unified Germany', in J. Youniss (ed.), *After the Wall: Family Adaptation in East and West Germany* (pp. 23–38). San Francisco: Jossey-Bass.

Smith, P. B., Dugan, S. and Trompenaars, F. (1996) 'National culture and the values of organizational employees: a dimensional analysis across 43 nations', *Journal of Cross-Cultural Psychology*, **27**: 231–64.

SPSS Inc. (1994) *SPSS Advanced Statistics 6.1*. Chicago, IL: SPSS Inc.

Strohmeier, K. P. and Schulze, H. S. (1995) 'Die Familienentwicklung der achtziger Jahre in Ost- und Westdeutschland im europaeischen Kontext' [Family development during the Eighties in Eastern and Western Germany in the European context], in B. Nauck, N. Schneider and A. Toelke (eds), *Familie und Lebensverlauf im gesellschaftlichen Umbruch* (pp. 26–38). Stuttgart: Enke.

Trommsdorff, G. (1994) 'Psychologische Probleme bei den Transformationsprozessen in Ostdeutschland' [Psychological problems in the processes of social and political transformation in Eastern Germany], in G. Trommsdorff (ed.), *Psychologische Aspekte des sozio-politischen Wandels in Ostdeutschland* (pp. 19–42). Berlin: de Gruyter.

Van Snippenburg, L. B. and Hendriks Vettehen, P. G. J. (1992) 'Dutch youth in transition to adulthood: Differential changes in their political and socio-cultural values since the 1970s', *Journal of Youth and Adolescence*, **21**: 573–91.

Zapf, W. (1996) 'Zwei Geschwindigkeiten in Ost- und Westdeutschland' [Eastern and Western Germany at a different pace], in M. Diewald and K. U. Mayer (eds), *Zwischenbilanz der Wiedervereinigung* (pp. 317–28). Opladen: Leske & Budrich.

6
Consequences of economic pressure for adolescent xenophobia in East and West Germany[1]

Klaus Boehnke and *Petra Butz*

Social change can be understood as a gradual non-teleological transformation of the social structure. It is a phenomenon all modern societies experience (Beck, 1992). When this 'natural' social change is, however, supplanted by particular social events that accelerate the base rate of transformation, the coping resources of individuals and groups may easily be overstrained.

Elder (1974) studied individual and family consequences of the Great Depression in the 1930s and showed that *economic pressure* was the main criterion of social change during that era. The extent to which families were able to cope with economic pressure during that time was critical in relation to the way young people behaved. In the tradition of Elder's work (and in close cooperation with him) Conger et al. (1992, 1994) are studying the consequences to the family of the farm crisis that hit the American Midwest in the 1980s. That crisis brought about an increasingly problematic financial situation for almost every family in certain farm regions, e.g., in the state of Iowa, where the study is being conducted. Conger's research group again has shown that the quality of human resources in the families was decisive in determining to what extent economic pressure resulted in problem behaviour among the children. The present study examines the extent to which Elder's and Conger's approaches can serve as a theoretical framework for analysing the consequences of the ongoing transformation processes for young people's behavioural problems in Germany. Its focus is on a type of behavioural problem which, for understandable historical reasons, is a particular concern for social research in Germany: xenophobia.

German unification, as an instance of accelerated social change, may be viewed as a unique event, at least in the second half of the twentieth century. The macrosocial change that has taken place in East Germany is very complex in nature. It does not easily compare with either the farm crisis in Iowa, or the Great Depression. Increasing financial uncertainty for the average family, however, is obviously an element of the transformation process. Hundreds of thousands of jobs were lost in the process of transforming a planned economy in East Germany into a market-oriented economy. In contrast with the situation in the farm belt in the United States, however, economic hardship was usually an anticipated state of affairs, not an actual one (Noack et al., 1995). Especially if one compares the economic situation of the average family of the GDR with the economic situation of the same family in a united Germany, it becomes clear that on average there is no objective financial loss. More significantly, East Germans (and even Germans in general) feel that they live in an economically (and otherwise) crisis-laden situation.

Noack et al. (1995) postulate that the ways in which German families cope with this perceived crisis, can be analysed using Elder's theoretical approach. They assume that economic change, as one aspect of the ongoing more complex social change in Germany, will influence the self-esteem, mood, and open-mindedness of adolescents. As in Elder's work, family connectedness is postulated to be a buffering variable: economic loss is assumed to have less negative consequences for young people's behaviour in families that exhibit a high degree of connectedness, i.e., offer strong social relations. In their study, Noack et al. (1995) operationalized social change by eliciting their respondents' subjective assessment of change in the family's purchasing power. They gathered this information *from the parents* of adolescents. Mothers and fathers were asked to estimate whether certain things in everyday life were less affordable or more easily affordable than five years before. Noack et al.'s general hypothesis was that a perceived loss in the purchasing power of families would threaten adolescent self-esteem, general mood, and open-mindedness.

Furthermore they assumed that the relation between economic pressure and individual well-being is moderated by gender and by place of residence (East versus West Germany). Earlier studies had found a differential resilience of girls and boys with regard to family strain. Elder (1974) as well as Rutter (1990) found a higher vulnerability for boys than for girls in early childhood, whereas for the adolescent years the reverse seemed to be the case. Girls were more vulnerable than boys. However, Flanagan and Eccles (1993), as well as Forehand, Neighbors, and Wierson (1991), found no gender difference in stress-related problem behaviours among adolescents (see also Elder and Caspi, 1994).

To assume an influence from the place of residence is, of course, a reflection of vast differences in the socialization experiences of East and West German families in the 40 years before unification. Also, youth in East Germany currently have to cope with more drastic economic adjustment processes than do West German youth.

In a number of studies Conger et al. (1992, 1994) have shown, however, that economic pressure per se has only a few immediate consequences for adolescent problem behavior. They showed that an insecure work situation, or the actual loss of a job, increases the pressure on the parents and worsens *their* general mood. This may then result in marital conflict which in turn puts the parent–child relationship under pressure. Consequently, the strained parent–child relationship is the central source of the adolescent's developmental problems. The psychosocial well-being of the family system, is thus the decisive mediator between macrosocial crises and adolescent behavior (Conger et al., 1992). When the well-being of parents is affected, there is marital discord and the parent–child relationship becomes problematic; the family system can no longer retain its function of being an 'alliance against society' (Youniss and Smollar, 1985).

Within this conceptual framework Noack et al. tested whether the quality of family relations (measured with *mothers, fathers, and young people*) served as a mediator variable between social change and various aspects of the psychological well-being of adolescents. The latter was measured among *adolescents* by employing among others a scale of 'anti-foreigner attitudes'. Noack and his associates showed that indeed strong social relations in the family lowered the impact that losses in a family's purchasing power had on adolescent xenophobia. Xenophobia was higher in families that suffered from a greater loss in purchasing power and less pronounced in families that expressed a high degree of connectedness.

The current study attempts to replicate partially, and at the same time extend, Noack et al.'s model. In doing so, however, it has to rely only on adolescent self-report data.

In accordance with findings of German studies of right-wing extremism and xenophobia (Schnabel, 1994; Oesterreich, 1993), we propose to

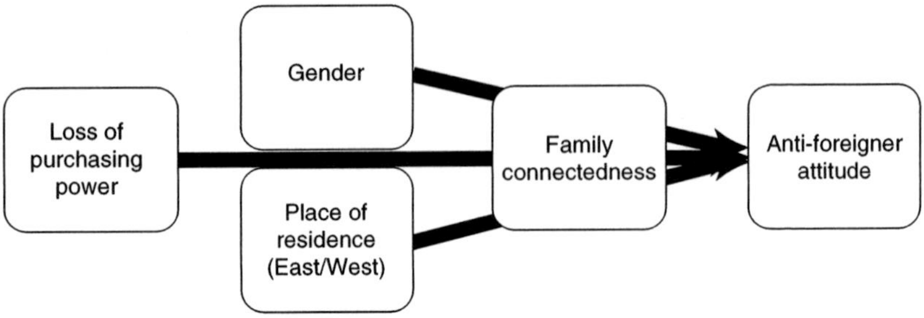

Figure 6.1 Model tested in the investigation by Noack et al. (1995)

include a third exogenous variable in the model. The studies by Schnabel and by Oesterreich (and others) have shown that the school context of adolescents explains considerable variation in xenophobic attitudes of East and West German youth. Those students who go to *Gymnasium*, the university-bound, academic school track, show substantially less xenophobia than do students from other, non-academic school tracks.

Secondly, we propose to decompose the variable of economic change. Noack et al. operationalized their purchasing power variable in the sense of a discrepancy score. They showed that a loss in the purchasing power of a family (as reported by parents) resulted in an increase in adolescent xenophobia. Economic pressure may, however, take different forms. First of all, it should make a difference where a family stands at the beginning of a social change process. Secondly, it should – as proposed by Noack et al. – make a difference what kind of change (loss/gain) and size of change the family experiences. Thirdly, certain aspects of the quality of the change may also make a difference. A gradual change may have other consequences compared with the situation in which drastic change follows or is followed by relative stability. Strong variability in economic resources may increase general feelings of insecurity. We, thus, propose to include three variables of economic pressure in the model, namely *level of economic resources*, *change in economic resources*, and *variability of economic resources*.

In order to minimize the considerable drawback of the present study, viz. its sole reliance on adolescent self-report data, we broaden the meaning of economic pressure. We take into consideration adolescent financial resources from parental allowances (pocket money), financial resources from other sources (e.g., minor jobs), availability of high quality consumer goods in the family, and the subjective quality of the living quarters of the family home.

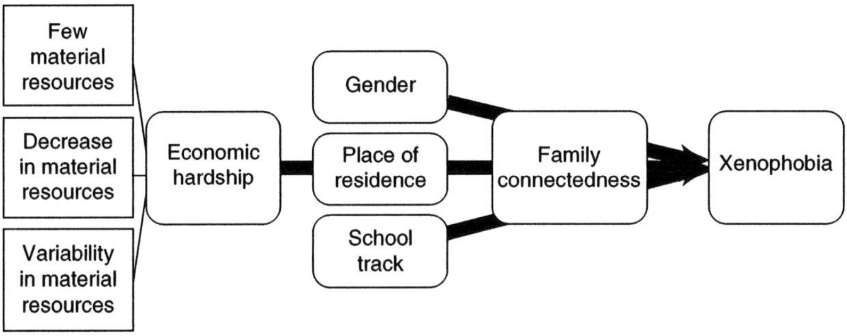

Figure 6.2 Model tested in the present study

As proposed by Elder and by Conger, and in accordance with Noack et al.'s model depicted in Figure 6.1, we also assume a buffering effect of an intact family system. Even if economic pressure is high, we expect xenophobia to be less strong when there are strong social relations in a family, i.e., when there is high family connectedness.

Our model, thus, assumes the relationship depicted in Figure 6.2. Economic pressure is assumed to result in increased xenophobia. The effect can, however, be buffered by a high degree of family connectedness (strong social relations in the family). Gender, place of residence (East/West), and type of school visited are assumed to make a difference with regard to the extent to which adolescents express xenophobic convictions.

Method

Sample

Data were gathered as part of the so-called East–West Youth Study (EWYS). The design of that study followed a cohort-sequential strategy. After a pilot study in 1990, for four years – starting in 1991 – 7th- to 10th-graders from East and West Berlin were surveyed. All participants that were not in the tenth grade in a particular year were followed up in the next wave of data gathering. New 7th-graders were incorporated in the study in each of the four waves. The sample is heterogeneous with regard to its social stratification, though not formally representative of secondary school youth in Berlin. When data collection was started in 1990, less than a year after the Wall had come down, no common statistical indices existed for East and West Berlin. Our decision at that time was to use statistical indicators from the East and West separately, and to sample students from the socially most diverse district of each part of the city on the grounds of these indicators. This led to the selection of the district of Lichtenberg in the East, and of Charlottenburg in the West, both of which can be seen as microcosms of their parts of the city of Berlin.

Data analyses relate only to the panel of seventh graders from 1991, of whom data from all four waves were available. Their average age in 1991 was 12.8 years. Students from all types of school other than special education schools – *Hauptschule, Realschule, Gesamtschule* (comprehensive school), 72 per cent; and *Gymnasium*, 28 per cent, were sampled in proportions that came close to representativeness. In total, 157 boys and girls participated in all four waves of data gathering (55 per cent boys and 45 per cent girls). Of these, 43 per cent came from East Berlin, 57 per cent from West Berlin. The four-year retention rate was 43.5 per cent on average. In East Berlin it was 39 per cent, in West Berlin it was 48 per cent. These retention rates are low, but the reader needs to take into consideration that the study was conducted as a school-based study only. This means that the young people were only followed up when they had remained at the schools they had gone to in 1991. The lower retention rate in East Berlin is due to the fact that there was more student mobility in that part of the city in the early years of our study. This was because 1991 was the first year in which the East Berlin school system was organized according to 'Western' school laws. Until 1990 a one-track (comprehensive) school system up to Grade 10 had existed in East Germany.

Instruments

Instruments used in the study are shown in Table 6.1. Consistency coefficients were above $\alpha = .70$ for all instruments in both subsamples. Details are omitted here.

Scale scores for the *family connectedness scale* were calculated in a two-step procedure. First, average raw scores across the items per wave of measurement were calculated. In a second step the annual (average) scale scores were once again averaged over the four years. This was in order to obtain a variable that depicted the average family connectedness, i.e., the mean strength of social relations in the family over the full period of the study.

Scores for the *xenophobia scale* were calculated as average raw scores across the items shown in Table 6.1. Information was taken from the 1994 wave only.

Table 6.1 Scales on 'economic resources', xenophobia' and 'family connectedness'

Scale	Number of items	Item(s)
Personal resources I	1	How much allowance (pocket money) do you get from your parents per month?
Personal resources II	1	How much money per month do you get or earn on average aside from your allowance?
Family resources I	10	Which of the following things does your family possess? (car, motorcycle, musical instrument, stereo receiver, record player, video recorder, library [more than 50 books], summer house, computer, dish washer)
Family resources II	4	I think the area where I live is beautiful.[a] You can't really do anything decent in the area where I live.[b] I think the area where I live is friendly. In the area where I live a lot of things need to be done (such as cleaning up, painting, refurbishing etc.).[b]

Continued on next page

Table 6.1 Continued

Scale	Number of items	Item(s)
Xenophobia	6	People can only be truly happy in their homeland. Foreigners can be trusted in every respect exactly like Germans.[b] Guest workers have helped us when we needed them, so in case of lack of work they should not be fired before Germans.[b] It is not good to have many foreigners in the country, because they are unpleasant and presumptuous. Developmental aid to foreign countries must primarily be of use for ourselves; otherwise it would be excessive philanthropy and a waste. The most important goal of German politics should be to regain Germany the power and influence it once had.
Family Connectedness	3	How do you evaluate the relationship to your father?[c] How do you evaluate the relationship to your mother?[c] Do you feel at ease at home?[d]

[a]To be answered on a four-point rating scale ranging from completely false (0) to completely true (3).
[b]Reversed for scale calculation.
[c]To be answered on a four-point rating scale ranging from seriously disturbed (0) to excellent (3).
[d]To be answered on a five-point rating scale ranging from no, never (0) to yes, always (4). To add items with a four-point and a five-point rating scale in one indicator means that the five-point item is weighted more strongly in the average score. In our case this is appropriate, because exploratory factor analyses showed that the 'at ease' item had the highest loading on the common factor for the three items.

Scores for the four economic resource variables were calculated as follows: To measure the *level of economic resources in 1991*, scale or item raw scores per person (depending on which variable we dealt with) were converted into standard *z*-scores, i.e., the sample mean was subtracted from the raw score and the difference was divided by the standard deviation from the mean. The transformation was done separately for the East Berlin and West Berlin adolescents, so that the scores stood for the relative economic resources of an adolescent in his or her part of the city in 1991. This takes account of the still grossly different standards of living in East and West Germany. In order to assess the *size of change* in economic resources between 1991 and 1994 discrepancy scores contrasting 1994 and 1991 were treated in the same manner, i.e. first, East/West-specific standard *z*-scores for each year were calculated, then the scores for 1991 were subtracted from the scores for 1994. Numerically high scores stand for an increase in economic resources. In order to assess the *variability of change* in economic resources, one-year discrepancy scores, e.g., pocket money 1992 – pocket money 1991, were calculated. These were contrasted with the average change over the whole time period of four years. This means that the three one-year discrepancy scores were contrasted with the overall discrepancy scores divided by 3. Absolute scores of the three differences were then averaged.

Again, the transformations used East/West-specific standard *z*-scores per year. Overall, we used four variables to measure the level of economic resources at the beginning of the change process (Personal Resources I and II, Family Resources I and II), four variables to measure change in economic resources (in the same four variables) and three variables to measure variability in change. (For Family Resources II data were gathered in Waves 1 and 3 only, so that only level and change of resources could be calculated).

Results

Forced-entry multiple regression analysis was used to test the model depicted in Figure 6.2. In the first step, variance in the dependent variable xenophobia was accounted for in terms of gender (male = 1, female = 2), place (East = 1, West = 2) and school-type (non-academic = 1, academic = 2) effects. In the next step, the variables used to assess the three aspects of economic resources were entered. In the final step, family connectedness was included. Analyses were conducted separately for the four types of economic resources (Personal Resources I and II, and Family Resources I and II). The results are presented in Table 6.2.

Table 6.2 Prediction of xenophobia

Predictor	Personal resources I			Personal resources II			Family resources I			Family resources II		
	Step I	Step II	Step III	Step I	Step II	Step III	Step I	Step II	Step III	Step I	Step II	Step III
Gender	$-.13^{+}$	–.11	–.10	$-.13^{+}$	-13^{+}	–.11	$-.13^{+}$	-13^{+}	–.11	$-.13^{+}$	-12^{+}	–.11
Place	$-.22^{\ddagger}$	$-.22^{\ddagger}$	$-.22^{\ddagger}$	$-.22^{\ddagger}$	$-22^{\S}$	$-.23^{\ddagger}$	$-.22^{*}$	$-22^{\ddagger}$	$-.23^{\ddagger}$	$-.22^{\ddagger}$	$-.22^{\ddagger}$	$-.23^{\ddagger}$
School type	$-.44^{\S}$	$-.45^{\S}$	$-.45^{\ddagger}$	$-.44^{\S}$	–.44	$-.45^{\S}$	$-.44^{\S}$	$-.46^{\S}$	$-.46^{\S}$	$-.44^{\S}$	$-.45^{\S}$	$-.46^{\S}$
Level of economic resources		.04	.04		.05	.06		.08	.08		.04	.00
Increase in economic resources		$.29^{\S}$	$.29^{\S}$		.01	.00		.10	.09		–.03	–.06
Variability of economic resources		–.02	–.02		.07	.06		–.04	–.02		–	–
Family connectedness			.04			.08			.05			.08
Explained variance (R^2)	.24	.31	.32	.24	.25	.26	.24	.25	.26	.24	.25	.26

$^{\dagger}p \le 10$, $^{*}p \le .05$, $^{\ddagger}p \le .01$, $^{\S}p \le .001$

The table shows that there was a very strong influence of school type. Xenophobia was considerably stronger among young people from non-academic than from academic school-tracks. Secondly, the table shows that there was a sizeable influence of place of residence. Xenophobia was higher among East Berlin youth than among West Berlin youth. Thirdly, there was a marginal gender effect. Girls were slightly less xenophobic than boys. The latter difference, however, lost its marginal significance when economic resources (which in all cases were slightly lower for girls) were taken into account.

Furthermore, the table shows that the hypothesis put forward in Figure 6.2, namely that a low level of economic resources, a decrease in economic resources, and/or a high degree of variability in economic resources, would lead to high xenophobia, was not confirmed for any of the four variables. The table does, however, document quite an unexpected finding. An *increase* in pocket money led to an increase in xenophobia. Those young people who, relative to the average young person in their part of the city of Berlin, had an increase in pocket money between 1991 and 1994 were the ones who exhibited more xenophobic attitudes in 1994. The reader should be reminded that the variable depicts a relative increase. It is important to note that by using East/West-specific standard *z*-scores per year, the age-related increase of pocket money between Grade 7 and Grade 10 is controlled.

The degree of family connectedness did not show any buffering influence mediating the relationship between economic pressure and xenophobia. This finding does not necessarily invalidate the assumptions of the 'Elder' model depicted in Figure 6.2, because buffering influences can only come into play when economic pressure and the 'problem variable' exhibit a relationship.

The unexpected finding that a relative increase in the monthly allowance provided by parents in 1994 compared with 1991, was related to a strong xenophobic attitude in 1994, led us to engage in several additional exploratory analyses. Our main interest was directed at the three exogenous variables gender, place of residence, and school type. Including these variables in the regression equation means that the variation that is accounted for by these variables is partialled out. If we want to find out whether these exogenous variables are 'context' variables, we need to compare the relationships of the economic resource variables, family connectedness and xenophobia in distinct groups defined by them. Is the relationship the same for girls and for boys, for East Berliners and West Berliners, and academic and non-academic track students? Optimally we might even want to find out whether the relationship is the same for boys in non-academic schools in East Berlin compared with academic groups, but our sample size was too small to permit this. We thus examine the groups defined by the three exogenous variables. If we find the same relationships between economic resources, family connectedness, and xenophobia in both groups defined by the variable under scrutiny, this means that the variable is *not* a context variable. The reason for its influence on the dependent variable remains unclear. If, however, a difference in the relationships among the variables is found, the exogenous variable in question functions as a context variable. Certain relations only occur in one context, not in the other. Analyses were conducted for the Personal Resources I ('pocket money') variable only.[2] Table 6.3 documents results for girls vs. boys, East Berliners vs. West Berliners, and Gymnasium vs. non-Gymnasium students.

The table shows that for girls and boys the relationship of economic resource variables, family connectedness, and xenophobia was essentially the same. The variables included in our model did, however, explain more variance for boys than they did for girls. In particular, type of school was more decisive in determining boys' xenophobia (higher xenophobia among boys from non-academic track schools) than girls' xenophobia.

In contrast to gender, place of residence *is* a context variable. An increase in pocket money relative to one's peers was a valid predictor of xenophobia in *East Berlin only*. In West Berlin the sign of the relationship was the same, but the size was much smaller and statistically insignificant.

The strongest context effect was found for type of school. Again, the finding that increased personal resources covary with high xenophobia replicated only in one group – namely for *non-academic* track students. For Gymnasium students the relationship did not seem to exist. Given that sample sizes were quite small, a furher breakdown of the sample was not advisable and additionally would have introduced an element of multiple testing into our data analyses. If, however, we compare non-Gymnasium students from *East Berlin* with the rest of the sample, for purely heuristic reasons, we find that none of the predictors (gender, level of economic resources, increase in economic resources, variability in economic resources and family connectedness) were significant in the comparator group. Only 3 per cent of the variance of xenophobia was explained. Among the non-Gymnasium students from East Berlin, however, 20 per cent of the variance was explained. The β-coefficient for the increase in economic resources was $\beta = .43$, ($p = .04$).

Table 6.3 Prediction of xenophobia in distinct groups of youth

Predictors	Personal Resources I																	
	Girls			Boys			East Berliners			West Berliners			Non-academic			Academic		
	I	II	III	I	II	III	I	II	III	I	II	III	I	II	III	I	II	III
Gender	–	–	–	–	–	–	–.10	–.04	–.04	–.16^{+}	–.17^{+}	–.16^{+}	–.22*	–.19*	–.19*	.14	.13	.13
Place	–.24*	–.28*	–.28*	–.22*	–.20*	–.20*	–	–	–	–	–	–	–.24‡	–.24‡	–.24‡	–.30*	–.31*	–.31^{+}
School type	–.30‡	–.33‡	–.33‡	–.56§	–.55§	–.55§	–.43§	–.42§	–.42§	–.47§	–.48§	–.48§	–	–	–	–	–	–
Level of economic resources		.10	.10		.07	.07		.10	.11		–.01	–.03		.08	.09		–.13	–.13
Increase in economic resources		.40*	.39*		.28‡	.28*		.41*	.41*		.18	.18		.37‡	.36‡		–.02	–.02
Variability of economic resources		–.04	–.04		–.04	–.04		–.03	–.03		.01	.01		–.07	–.07		.02	.02
Family connectedness			.02			.01			.02			.08			.03			–.04
Explained Variance (R^2)	.14	.25	.25	.33	.39	.39	.19	.30	.30	.25	.29	.29	.09	.20	.20	.11	.13	.13

$^{†}p \leq .10$, $^{*}p \leq .05$, $^{‡}p \leq .01$, $^{§}p \leq .001$

With considerable caution one may say that a *relative increase in pocket money* is a risk for xenophobia among students from *non-academic school tracks in East Berlin.*

Discussion

To discuss the results of the current study is a difficult task, particularly in interpreting the finding that economic pressure was not related to increased adolescent 'problems' in any of our analyses. Secondly, the discussion has to offer explanations for the finding that – at least in a certain context – improved economic resources 'cause' youth problems.

Let us first summarize the most important findings. (1) Xenophobia was much higher among students from non-academic schools than it was among students from the Gymnasium. (2) Xenophobia was higher among East Berlin youth than among West Berlin youth. (3) The quality of social relations in the family, as reported by young people, was unrelated to xenophobia. (4) In no case was economic pressure positively related to xenophobia. (5) In certain social contexts a relative increase in personal economic resources of adolescents (pocket money) seemed to be a 'risk factor' for adolescent xenophobia.

Let us first consider why no relation of the kind predicted from Elder's theory was found. Why, regardless of which economic pressure variable was under scrutiny, was no increased xenophobia found for adolescents who reported economic strain? One reason could be the phenomenon we investigated. Xenophobia, as we measured it, is not typical of behaviour problems. It is a self-reported attitude, an ideological or value orientation. In Conger et al. (1994) terminology, however, it may be seen as an 'adolescent externalizing symptom'. Conger et al. measure hostility as a personality feature. Noack et al. (1995) see 'anti-foreigner attitudes' reflecting a lack of open-mindedness, which they interpret as part of an externalizing symptom that may result from 'unbuffered' economic pressure. In contrast, they see a personality characteristic such as a depressive mood, as an internalizing symptom.

If we can reject the idea that Elder's model does not 'work', because the phenomenon to be explained is not one which can be explained in that theoretical framework, what other explanations can be found for the conclusion that economic pressure does not have any impact on adolescent xenophobia? We see the main reason lying in the source of information on economic pressure. We had information only on adolescent-perceived economic change. On the one hand, adolescents may be biased reporters of such change: what they see is what they themselves have, not what happens to their family or in their immediate or broader context. On the other hand, adolescents may very well be unbiased reporters of economic change, but their perceptions may already have been buffered in Elder's sense. To take the point to the extreme, one could argue that asking adolescents for an evaluation of economic pressure does not give a measure of the independent variable in Elder's model, but documents a dependent variable, namely the degree to which their family has been unable to buffer economic pressure.

Which of the arguments outlined above is true, and which of the two is more plausible, cannot be tested in the current study. We need data from parents to decide between them. The project has in fact gathered parent data, but these were not available for analyses reported here, so we have to remain in the realm of speculation.

The second issue to be resolved here, is to find a post hoc explanation for the finding that a relative increase in personal resources is related to stronger xenophobia. A hypothesis that might explain the finding is that of *Wohlstandschauvinismus* – a phenomenon that literally translates into English as 'welfare chauvinism'. The term comes from political science and refers to the idea that people in rich countries are strongly against sharing their wealth with poorer parts of the world. The term plays a role, among others, in the refugee debate. The proportion of refugees in different populations is correlated negatively with per capita gross national product (UNHCR, 1997, Table 6.2). On the individual level this means that those who enjoy relative wealth should be the ones who voice the most xenophobic attitudes. First and foremost, the level of wealth should play a role. That, however, was not what we found. In no single case was the *level* of economic resources related to xenophobic attitudes. What showed an effect, and supports the 'welfare chauvanism' hypothesis, was the disproportionate increase in allowances an adolescent got from his or her parents. And the effect was strongest for those who 'quickly' acquired relative 'wealth' in an otherwise disadvantaged context – lower school tracks in East Berlin. Adolescents in such a life context, may indeed be the ones who see themselves in competition with foreigners, e.g., for jobs, giving their xenophobia a pseudo-rational basis.

Certainly, even though our study was longitudinal and therefore offers a certain basis for causal inference, our sample was small and its representativeness is difficult to assess. This means that replication of our findings is essential, before we can advocate with confidence the use of the concept, 'welfare chauvinism', in explanatory models of xenophobia.

Overall, our study showed that xenophobia among adolescents could not be attributed to mere economic hardship, buffered or unbuffered by strong versus poor social relations in the family. Xenophobia seems to have a cultural basis: it is strong in certain environments (East Berlin, lower school tracks) only. Additionally, there is preliminary evidence that welfare chauvinism, as identified with a strong inclination not to share newly acquired wealth with the less well-to-do, is a driving force behind xenophobia in youth.

Notes

1. The study reported here was supported by repeated grants of the German Research Council (DFG) to the first author and to Hans Merkens from the Free University of Berlin
2. In principle, it is certainly possible that context influences could be found for the other economic resource variables as well, but as their influence on xenophobia was very low, this is highly improbable.

References

Beck, U. (1992) *Risk Society*. London: Sage.

Conger, R. D., Conger, K., Elder, G. H., Lorenz, F. O., Simons, R. L. and Withbeck, L. B. (1992) 'A family process model of economic hardship and adjustment of early adolescent boys', *Child Development*, **63**: 526–41.

Conger, R. D., Ge, X., Elder, G. H., Lorenz, F. O. and Simons, R. L. (1994) 'Economic stress, coercive family process, and developmental problems of adolescents', *Child Development*, **65**: 541–61.

Elder, G. H. and Caspi, A. (1990) 'Persönliche Entwicklung und sozialer Wandel. Die Entstehung der Lebensverlaufsforschung' [Personal development and social change. The origin of life course research], in K.-U. Mayer (ed.), *Lebensverläufe und sozialer Wandel. Kölner Zeitschrift für Soziologie und Sozialpsychologie* (special issue): 22–57.

Elder, G.H. (1974) *Children of the Great Depression*. Chicago: University of Chicago Press.

Flanagan, C. A. and Eccles, J.S . (1993) 'Changes in parents' work status and adolescents' adjustment at school', *Child Development*, **64**: 246–57.

Forehand, R., Neighbors, B. and Wierson, M. (1991) 'The transition to adolescence: The role of gender and stress in problem behavior and competence', *Journal of Child Psychology and Psychiatry*, **32**: 929–37.

Noack, P., Hofer, M., Kracke, B. and Klein-Allermann, E. (1995) 'Adolescents and their parents facing social change: families in East and West Germany after unification', in P. Noack, M. Hofer and J. Youniss, (eds), *Psychological Responses to Social Change*, (pp. 129–48). Berlin: de Gruyter.

Oesterreich, D. (1993) 'Autoritäre Persönlichkeit und Gesellschaftsordnung' [Authoritarian personality and the structure of society]. Weinheim: Juventa.

Rutter, M. (1990) 'Psychosocial resilience and protective mechanisms', in J. Rolf et al. (eds), *Risk and Protective Factors in the Development of Psychopathology* (pp. 181–214). New York: Cambridge University Press.

Schnabel, K. (1994) 'Zur Fremdenfeindlichkeit bei Jugendlichen in Ost- und Westdeutschland' [On xenophobia among adolescents from East and West Germany], in D. Hartung (ed.), *Ausländerfeindlichkeit, Rechtsradikalismus, Gewalt* (pp. 66–87). Berlin: Max Planck Institute.

United Nations High Commissioner for Refugees (UNHCR) (1997) *Populations of Concern to UNHCR. Statistics 1997*. Geneva: UNHCR.

Youniss, J. and Smollar, J. (1985) *Adolescent Relations with Mothers, Fathers, and Friends*. Chicago: Chicago University Press.

7
On the realization of scientific talent[1]

Ingrid Schoon

In modern society there is an increasing demand for young talented scientists. Recruitment statistics for University courses in science and technology show a continuous decline in student uptake, and in the UK the entry requirements for these courses have been lowered considerably in the recent few years. Governments try to respond to this situation by introducing and enhancing science training in all types of secondary schools in order to foster the development of scientific ability. The need to build a strong pool of highly-qualified and motivated scientists, and to attract young, high quality applicants to science courses in higher education, had been stressed in the UK government publication *Realising our Potential: Strategy for Science, Engineering and Technology* (HSMO, 1993). The shortage of young women in science and engineering has been noted in particular, not only in the UK but throughout Europe. For example, a recent European Parliament/Commission meeting (held in May 1998 in Brussels) proposed a European observatory for women in science as part of the Fifth Framework research programme.

How can young scientifically talented individuals be attracted to a career in science and have their interest fostered and maintained? A child, or young adolescent with the skills of a superior scientist cannot be recognized as talented except in a culture where scientific domains are well developed and where so-called 'gatekeepers' are actively looking for talent (Csikszentmihalyi, 1988). Talent has to be understood as a social construction, constructed with reference to the particular needs and values of a culture (or in this case a discipline). It is a label of approval in the particular context in which we live, and consists of an exceptional ability or endowment to perform by the rules of a recognized domain according to criteria set up by a relevant field[2] (Czikszentmihalyi et al., 1993; Gagné, 1993). Thus the study of talent cannot isolate individuals from the social and historical context in which their actions are carried out. In particular, questions regarding how budding talent is transformed and developed into adult achievement, and which factors stimulate and foster this development, require more than cross-sectional status diagnosis. When an individual is identified as talented, we should ask: 'Does the identification have an effect on the individual and if so, how? Does it enable predictions to be made about the future?' It is not only the size of the initial ability that counts, but what each person can make of it. Studies have shown that interest in a scientific career is formed quite early in life compared to interest in other professional careers (Roe, 1952; Zuckermann, 1977; Simonton, 1988). Only some young people, however, become committed to the cultivation and realization of their interests and abilities by taking up a professional career in the sciences, while other equally gifted teenagers lose interest and never develop their skills, settling for careers that require other competencies (Hanson and Neujahr, 1976; O'Donnel and Andersen, 1977; Csikszentmihalyi et al., 1993).

Factors linking promise to fulfilment

In this paper the transition of scientifically talented teenagers from school to work is investigated, exploring factors associated with the realization of scientific talent. By taking a longitudinal perspective the relative impact of social structural forces, cognitive abilities, personality characteristics and individual motivation on their career trajectories can be analysed. Since gender seems to be a universally important variable in patterns of talent development (Subotnik and Arnold, 1993), particular emphasis will be given to the different patterns of encouragement experienced by male and female individuals who show scientific talent at age 16. Considerably more males than females take natural science classes in school and later in college, and are more likely to enter scientific professions in later life (Weinreich-Haste, 1979; Steinkamp and Maehr, 1983; Golombok and Fivush, 1994; Colley, 1995). Scientific interests are crystallized in boys by the time they are between 10 to 14 years old, while for girls they form a bit later (Eiduson and Beckman, 1973). Females were found to show lower self-confidence and aspirations, even when matched with males of equivalent talent or test scores (Eccles, 1987; Subotnik and Arnold, 1993).

Furthermore, there is evidence that certain scientific professions, for example physics and engineering, are dominated by males, while women opt for the 'softer disciplines', such as biology and medicine. Women choose domains that are perceived as more person-oriented, affectionate and compassionate, involving interaction with people, while males prefer areas that have an image of being forceful, analytic, ambitious, individualistic and competitive, dealing with things rather than people (Weinreich-Haste, 1979; Colley, 1995). Besides gender, previous studies revealed a number of variables that have been found to provide the structure and support for talent development.

Socio-economic background

The notion of social determination or 'occupational inheritance' has been tested in numerous studies on scientists, with Galton's study on the inheritability of eminence (1874) as a prominent predecessor, or in more recent times the study of Bourdieu (1988) on the *homo academicus*. A positive relationship between professional background and occupational attainment has been generally found (Oden, 1968; Zuckerman, 1977), particularly for males. There is, however, evidence that natural scientists are more likely to come from a middle-class background, while social scientists seem to be more upper class (Roe, 1953; Knapp, 1963). Educational background of the parents, a closely related area, has been shown to be a good indicator for the kind of intellectual interests encouraged in the child (Getzels and Jackson, 1961) as well as for educational achievement and occupational attainment (Tomlinson-Keasy and Little, 1990; Trost and Sieglen, 1992). Parental orientation, their attitudes toward the child and their interest in the child's education have been identified as critical dimensions influencing the kinds of occupations to which the child then turns (Roe, 1953; Bloom, 1985; Trost and Sieglen, 1992).

Role models

In a number of studies the importance of the mother as a role model has been demonstrated, where mothers of scientists were identified more with achievement than were fathers, who were often absent from the home (Eiduson and Beckman, 1973). Maternal employment, in particular, has been identified as an important moderator in female career development (Vondracek, Lerner, and Schulenberg, 1986). Daughters of employed mothers formulate higher prestige vocational aspirations, often in more traditionally masculine professions (Almquist and Angrist, 1970). Not only the mother but also the father can play an important role in determining vocational outcomes for females. For example, fathers can be influential in exposing their daughters to career fields, sometimes their own, or indirectly provide a counter-model to a more stereotypical 'male attitude' (Weitz, 1977; Schulenberg, Vondracek and Crouter, 1984). There is evidence that fathers, not mothers, encourage independence in scientifically talented girls (Rossi, 1965; Hackett, Esposito and O'Halloran, 1989).

Intellectual resources and capabilities

Eminent scientists with outstanding achievements show a fairly wide range of ability extending from average levels to very superior scores on standard intelligence tests (Barron, 1969; MacKinnon and Hall, 1971). These findings lead to the conclusion that high level intelligence certainly is an advantage for later achievement in science, yet it is not a necessary prerequisite. Rather, the importance of a number of non-intellectual factors, such as intellectual curiosity, or the ability to restructure problems are considered as important predictors (Terman and Oden, 1959; Eiduson, 1962; Roe, 1953; Heller, 1993). Likewise, the Nobel laureate Peter Medawar (1979) stresses that the importance of intellectual skill in science (as measured by standard intelligence tests) should not be overrated, since different branches of science call for rather different abilities. Mathematical ability, however, has been identified as a 'critical filter' for later occupational success (Sells, 1973), and underpins achievement in science, technology, as well as many other professional fields (Stanley, 1990).

Personality and motivation

Scientists have consistently been described as independent and self-sufficient producers who are autonomous and enthusiastic with regard to their work: they show interest in things rather than in people or interpersonal relationships, easily accept challenges, have an unusual drive and task commitment, high aspirations, and a high self-esteem (Galton, 1874; Roe, 1953; Eiduson and Beckman, 1973; Zuckerman, 1977; Simonton, 1988; Wilson and Jackson, 1994). Scientists themselves, however, are keen to ward off any stereotyping. Yet, in giving advice about how to tell if one is cut out to be a successful scientist Medawar (1979:7) stresses that a potential scientist can be characterized by diligence, a sense of purpose, the power to concentrate, and the ability to persevere and not be cast down by adversity. Motivation and perseverance have been identified as powerful long-range predictors of professional success in science, and are generally considered to play a mediating role in achievement outcomes (Gagné, 1993; Subotnik and Arnold, 1993).

In summary it can be said, that the realization of scientific potential does not have one cause but depends on the combined impact of contextual and person-related variables. Which of these factors is the most important in predicting success in realization of scientific talent? Only time can show. In this chapter I report an investigation of the transition from school to work in a longitudinal cohort study, following the progress of scientifically talented 16-year-old teenagers into adulthood. A longitudinal approach has a number of methodological advantages for this research question: reports of early life events are not influenced by knowledge of the subsequent personal history; the cohort contains normal controls, and the conjoint impact of different factors can be analysed in a multivariate model.

Method

The study draws on data collected for the National Child Development Study (NCDS), one of Britain's richest research resources for the study of human development. NCDS takes as its subjects all persons living in Great Britain who were born between 3 and 9 March 1958. In five follow-up studies data were collected on the physical, psycho-social and educational development of the cohort at age 7, 11, 16, 23 and 33 years. In this study data collected in 1974, when the sample subjects were 16 years old, are linked with data collected in 1991. In 1991 the subjects participating in the study were aged 33 and it can be assumed that most subjects will have completed their education and training and will have established their occupational career. The information collected in 1991 provides a comprehensive picture of where earlier experiences, expectations and characteristics of the cohort have led them.

Sample

The sample is a subgroup of the National Child Development Study (NCDS) for whom data were collected in both 1974 and 1991. In 1974, at age 16, about 11,000 children, their teachers and parents completed a number of questionnaires and interviews related to the purpose of this study. Due to sample attrition and exclusion of cases with incomplete data in 1991, this analysis was limited to 8376 cases (50 per cent males and 50 per cent females) and further reduced especially for multivariate analyses due to missing values. Generally satisfactory response rates have been achieved at each time point. An analysis of response bias shows that the achieved sample does not differ from the target sample, although the most disadvantaged groups are slightly underrepresented in 1991 (Shepherd, 1995).

Identification of scientific talent

In the present study scientific talent has been identified through teacher- and self-assessments of scientific aptitude. Teachers are generally assumed to be the experts in the field who can adequately evaluate the student's performance. There has been conflicting evidence regarding the usefulness of teacher nominations on various sets of abilities (Pegnato and Birch, 1959; Gear, 1976). Yet recent reviews and reanalyses of the literature suggest that teachers can indeed reliably assess outstanding talent in various domains (Hoge and Cudmore, 1986; Trost, 1993; Gagné, 1995). Within NCDS teachers' ratings of scientific ability were collected in 1974 when the study child was aged 16. The ratings were assessed on a five-point scale ranging from 1 (capable of A-level and above) to 5 (below average ability).

Although teachers' ratings are an important indicator of the child's scientific ability, they do not reflect how committed the teenagers themselves feel about their abilities. Studies have shown that self-evaluation of school performance is crucial for the prediction of high professional achievement in science (Trost and Sieglen, 1992). To get at this aspect, the teenagers themselves were asked how good they thought they were in science compared with other children of their age, using a four-point scale ranging from 1 (below average) to 4 (above average). To get a single measure of scientific talent identification, teachers' ratings and self-evaluations were combined into a composite dichotomized score. This differentiated between individuals identified as above average in science (by either teacher-rating or self-rating) and normal teenagers.

Realization of scientific talent

In 1991 the subjects participating in the study were asked to indicate their profession. Professions were coded following the Standard

Occupational Classification (SOC). In 1991 the subjects were aged 33 and it can be assumed that they represent the settled and stable features of mature adulthood. Most subjects had completed their education and training and had established their occupational career. The degree to which the children with scientific talent were able to realize their potential is reflected in a dichotomous talent realization score ranging from 0 (no realization), 1 (realization). A score of 1 is given to individuals who became either natural scientists, engineers, or medical practitioners at age 33. Linking this outcome data with the data from previous information at age 16 allows us to investigate the different factors that stimulate the continuous cultivation of scientific talent in male and female individuals.

Assessing the predictor variables

Family background factors

These are indicated through social class, parents' education, and parents' interest in child's education. *Social class* was assessed at birth, based on the father's occupation. Where there was no father the mother's occupation was substituted. Social class is defined by the job status and the associated education or prestige (OPCS, 1980). For further analysis we will differentiate between professionals (including managers and administrators) and others (including skilled and unskilled occupations). *Parental education* was coded for both father and mother separately, indicating the age band at which the parents left full-time education. For later analysis we differentiate between parents who continued full-time education after the age of 18 years and parents who left education earlier. *Parental interest in the child's education* was assessed on a 5-point scale by the child's teacher. We have separate scores for both father and mother which were dichotomized to differentiate between parents who were very interested in their child's education versus others. *Maternal employment* is indicated by a question differentiating between mothers who were in paid employment ('does the mother [or mother figure] do paid work') versus mothers not in (paid) employment.

Academic abilities

Mathematical ability was assessed by using the Mathematical ability test which was devised at the University of Manchester and originally intended for use in the National Foundation for Educational Research (NFER) study of comprehensive schools in England and Wales. Reading ability was measured with the Reading comprehension test – which was constructed by NFER specifically for use in the NCDS study.

Personality factors

Personality characteristics were assessed by teacher-rating, and self-description. The teachers evaluated the behaviour of their pupils on a 5-point Osgood scale contrasting, among others, the following attribute pairs: moody versus even-tempered, timid versus aggressive, and lazy versus hardworking. Self reports of the teenagers themselves covered leisure interests, to obtain some insight into how the 16-year-olds spend their time. They were asked to indicate for various activities whether this was something they did 'often', 'sometimes', 'never or hardly ever'. The replies are subjective – an indication of the time they felt they spent in relation to their peers rather than of the absolute time given. The activity that we used in our analysis is the 'boogie' factor, indicating whether the students spend their time going to discos and parties, socialising with others.

Occupational aspirations

The pupils were furthermore asked about their concrete job aspiration ('What would you like to be your first full-time-job?') and the coding of the answers identifies individuals who aspire to become a scientist, an engineer, or a health professional.

Results

Identification of scientific talent

Overall 19.2 per cent of the total sample, the majority of whom were boys, were identified as scientifically talented (Table 7.1). The combination of both teacher- and self-rating places the identified individuals

Table 7.1 Identification of scientific talent differentiated by gender

	All		Male		Female	
	n	%	n	%	n	%
Total sample	8376	100.0	4174	49.8	4202	50.2
Overall talent	1612	19.2	1024	24.5	588	14.0
Teacher rating	919	11.0	552	13.2	367	8.7
Self rating	1164	13.9	793	19.0	371	8.8

within the top 15–20 per cent threshold zone of their age peers (Gagné, 1993).[3] Clearly fewer girls than boys were identified as scientifically talented – both by their teachers and by themselves. Moreover, the girls themselves seemed to be less convinced of their scientific abilities then the boys were, since a higher proportion of male teenagers described themselves as talented than did their teachers. For females we find the same proportions of self- and teacher-rating.

Generally, teachers and students did not agree with one another in their rating of scientific ability. The Kappa coefficient was 0.38, indicating poor agreement (Fleiss, 1981). So the lack of overlap is quite substantial, suggesting that students whom the teachers thought highly of did not necessarily think of themselves as being talented, and vice versa. In fact, only 471 of the teenagers (40.5 per cent) who described themselves as scientifically talented were also identified as such by their teachers, and nearly half of the students who were described as talented by their teachers did not see their ability in science as above average compared with their peers.

In order to test whether the recognition of scientific talent has a correspondence in objective test performance the mean scores of two academic achievement tests were compared for the talented and the average teenagers.

In Table 7.2 it can be seen that the talented teenagers outperformed the 'average' teenagers in both mathematical and reading ability. This means that the students who had been identified as scientifically talented by their teachers, or who perceived themselves as having above average aptitude for science did indeed have good mathematical ability and reading ability. There were no significant gender differences between scientifically talented male and female teenagers regarding their academic abilities. There were, however, significant differences between teacher- and self-assessment: students (both male and female) who were identified as talented by their teachers had higher test scores than students who described themselves as scientifically talented.

Table 7.2 t-test comparing the mean ability test scores between scientifically talented and average students

	Average		Talented			
	Mean	std	Mean	std	t-value	P
Maths at 16	11.9	6.0	19.6	6.9	44.5	0.00
Reading at 16	25.2	6.5	30.1	4.7	28.3	0.00

Outcome: career moves

What became of our scientifically talented teenagers? What professions did they finally end up with? Table 7.3 shows that the scientifically talented teenagers, both male and female, did quite well in adult life compared to the average teenagers. Generally, a considerable higher proportion of talented teenagers moved into managerial and professional occupations, and very few took up unskilled professions.

There were, however, notable gender differences in occupational development. Scientifically talented females were much more likely to enter a professional career than average individuals, but their chances of becoming managers or administrators in a leading position were less than for either talented or average males. There was, furthermore, a female preponderance in the associate professional and technical occupations, and in the clerical and secretarial occupations, while males dominated the skilled crafts.

But how many of the scientifically talented individuals realised their potential directly and took up a career in science? Table 7.4 shows that only very few individuals entered a career in the sciences (that is they became either natural scientists, engineers or health professionals): just 3 per cent of the total sample (including the talented teenagers),[4] or about 13 per cent of the talented males, and 8 per cent of the talented females. Yet, the majority of individuals who took up a career in the sciences had shown scientific talent at age 16: 88 per cent of all natural scientists had been identified as scientifically talented at age 16, as had

Table 7.3 Career moves differentiated for talented and average teenagers

	Average teenagers			Talented teenagers		
		Male %	Female %		Male %	Female %
Managers and administrators		18.8	10.5		27.2	13.9
Professionals	5.5	6.8		23.6	22.6	
Associate professionals	7.9	10.9		14.8	23.3	
Clerical and secretarial	5.4	27.1		5.3	21.8	
Skilled craftsperson	29.5	3.0		13.9	1.4	
Personal and protective service	6.6	17.3		4.1	6.8	
Sales		4.1	10.1		3.9	5.6
Plant and machine operators	14.5	5.7		5.0	1.9	
Other (Agriculture, forestry and fishing)	7.7	8.5		2.1	2.7	
All (100%)		3150	3614		1024	588

Table 7.4 Career moves into scientific and technological professions differentiated by gender

	Total sample (n = 8376)		Talented teenagers: Male (n = 1024)		Talented teenagers: Female (n = 588)	
	n	%	n	%	n	%
Scientists	42	0.5	27	2.6	10	1.7
Engineers	134	1.6	73	7.1	7.0	1.2
Medical practitioner	67	0.8	32	3.1	31	5.3
All	243	2.9	132	12.8	48	8.2

60 per cent of all engineers, and 94 per cent of all medical professionals. Contrasting the 'hit rate' of teacher-versus self-rating, it becomes apparent that self-rating is the better predictor of occupational attainment: 81 versus 70 per cent matches for the scientists (for female scientists we even find a 100 per cent match: all female scientists described themselves as scientifically talented at age 16), 77 versus 64 per cent for engineers, and 92 versus 89 per cent for the health professions.

From Table 7.4 we can furthermore see that the question 'What sex is science?', which had been posed by Weinreich-Haste (1979), can only be answered in reference to the specific scientific discipline: engineering was clearly dominated by males, as were the natural sciences (to a lesser extent). Medicine, on the other hand, was clearly the preferred option for scientifically talented females, and we find parity in the distribution of the sexes.

Predicting professional attainment

Why do some talented teenagers enter a career in the sciences and others not? The combined impact of the contextual and person-related factors on the development of scientific talent was analysed using a logistic regression analysis. This allows us to predict a binary dependent variable from a set of independent variables. The logistic model calculates the relative odds of an event (becoming a scientist) occurring or not. The baseline for the occurrence of an event is 1. If the risk of its occurrence is raised, the estimated risk value is greater than 1; if the risk is lower, the estimated risk value is smaller than 1 (a detailed description of the procedure can be found in Norusius, 1990). For this analysis the method of forward stepwise logistic regression was chosen, and separate models were run for scientists, engineers, and medical professionals, differentiated for males and females. The results of the analysis are shown in Table 7.5.

Table 7.5 Logistic regression predicting which of the talented teenagers enters a scientific profession

	Scientists		Health profs		Engineers	
	Male Odds Ratio	Female Odds Ratio	Male Odds Ratio	Female Odds Ratio	Male Odds Ratio	Female Odds Ratio
Family background						
Professional (yes)	ns	ns	ns	3.58*	ns	.11†
Parents' interest in child's education						
Father (very)	ns	ns	ns	ns	ns	ns
Mother (very)	ns	ns	ns	ns	ns	ns
Parents in higher education						
Father (yes)	.00*	ns	2.27†	ns	ns	ns
Mother (yes)	ns	ns	ns	ns	ns	ns
Mother working (yes)	ns	ns	ns	ns	ns	.11†
Ability in Maths	ns	1.19†	1.25*	1.27*	ns	1.30*
Personality						
Even-tempered	ns	ns	ns	ns	ns	ns
Aggressive	ns	ns	ns	ns	ns	ns
Hard working	1.81†	ns	ns	2.40†	1.52*	ns
No teenage social life	1.48†	ns	ns	ns	ns	ns
Job aspiration						
Become a scientist (yes)	3.61*	5.09†				
Become a doctor (yes)			16.4*	14.71*		
Become an engineer (yes)					ns	ns

* <.001
† <.05

Different patterns emerged for the three different scientific disciplines, and there were crucial gender differences within each discipline. Scientifically talented males had increased chances of becoming scientists if they had the aspiration to do so, if they were hard working, and did not like to go to discos and parties. Talented males with a father who went into further education were less likely to become a scientist than sons of fathers who left school before the age of 18. For talented females the chances were increased, if they had the aspiration, and if they were good in mathematics. Talented males with the aspiration to become a doctor, who had a well-educated father, and who were good in mathematics were most likely to become a health professional. For females the most important predictors for entering the domain of medicine were: occupational aspiration, professional family background, mathematical ability, and willingness to work hard. The only factor influencing the career path of talented males into engineering, was the willingness to work hard. For females the predictors were: good mathematical abilities, a non-professional family background, and a non-working mother. Parental interest in the child's education, and mothers level of education had no direct influence on the occupational development of the talented teenagers.

Summary and discussion

Before interpreting the findings a number of aspects have to be considered: a particular cohort was used as a sample and this may limit the generalizability of the results. There is a slight under representation of the most disadvantaged groups (low social class), so the estimates are possibly slightly optimistic. All cohort members entered the labour market in the 1980s where possibilities and prospects were good compared with later years. Also in recent years we have seen dramatic changes in science education, and in the labour market, enhancing, particularly, the creation of equal opportunities for women. Thus, a comparison of the present data with a later cohort, and/or in a different national context, would provide additional insights on the influence of structural forces on talent development. We should also keep in mind that the data were not collected for their potential in investigating the identification and realization of scientific talent, and stronger associations might have been obtained by using different independent variables. Nonetheless, the data offers a unique opportunity to investigate the development of scientifically talented teenagers from school age to adulthood.

The identification of scientific talent was based on both teacher- and self-assessment of outstanding scientific ability. About 19 per cent of the 16-year-old cohort members – the majority boys – were identified as scientifically talented. The combination of both ratings allows us to identify as many talented individuals as possible, without leaving the top 15–20 per cent threshold specified by Gagné (1993). There is a considerable disagreement between teachers and students, indicating that students whom the teachers thought highly of did not necessarily think of themselves as being talented, and vice versa. Yet, both ratings corresponded with objective test performance, indicating that the teenagers who had been identified as scientifically talented either by their teachers or by themselves, outperformed the 'average' teenagers in both mathematical and reading ability. Comparing the test scores of students identified by teacher-versus self-rating, it seems that the teachers based their evaluation of scientific talent more on test performance than the students, who seemed to rely on other factors as well, as for example their interest in science, or their aspiration to become a scientist.

Clearly fewer girls than boys were identified as scientifically talented. There were no gender differences among the talented teenagers regarding their test scores. Yet, it seems that girls, in contrast to the boys, tend to underestimate or to downplay their scientific aptitude. This finding supports earlier studies that emphasize the lack of self-confidence of talented women (Subotnik and Arnold, 1993). However, once identified as scientifically talented, the females seem to be at least as dedicated to the discipline (if not more so) as the males. Considering that the subsample of talented teenagers is already dominated by males with a 2/1 ratio, and excluding the highly gender-stereotyped domain of engineering, a higher proportion of talented females than males (7 versus 5.7 per cent) realized their potential in a direct way and became either medical professionals or natural scientists. Furthermore, all females in the sample who became natural scientists in adult life described themselves as scientifically talented at age 16, indicating that belief in one's own capacities is a major force linking promise to fulfilment, especially for women.

The field of science itself, offers only very few openings: merely 3 per cent of the total sample (including the talented individuals) took up a career in the sciences, a figure comparable to the national Census data. Most of the professional scientists in the cohort, however, had been identified as scientifically talented at age 16, and the proportion of scientifically talented teenagers taking up a scientific profession was about ten times higher than the proportion of average individuals doing so. Generally, the scientifically talented teenagers did well professionally, and were more likely to enter prestigious administrative or professional occupations than the average teenagers. There is, however, a remarkable gender bias insofar as talented women were succeeding in professional occupations, but were less likely than males in general to get into the more prestigious administrative and managerial positions. Thus, the talented young women had not fully realized their talents in the occupational world, and were excluded from the top echelons. Nevertheless, it can be concluded that being identified as scientifically talented at age 16 not only increases the chances to do well professionally in general (especially for the males), but also the likelihood of entering a scientific profession.

But why do some individuals pursue the development of their abilities, while others loose interest? The factors influencing the pathways of the scientifically talented individuals differed for males and females, and across the scientific disciplines, indicating not only gendertyping, or differences in ability, personality and motivation, but different selective mechanisms across the professions. Being identified as scientifically talented, women were more likely than men to become health professionals, but were less likely to become natural scientists, or engineers. Thus, the female preference for the more person-oriented, affectionate and compassionate professions (Weinreich-Haste, 1979; Colley, 1995) has been reaffirmed by this analysis. Young women from a professional family background had a higher chance to become a health professional, but were less likely to become an engineer. This result points to the higher social prestige of medicine in comparison to engineering. Yet, it can be assumed that this difference is culturally determined. For example, in Germany engineering has a higher social standing than in the UK, and in the former East Germany the engineering professions were less gender stereotyped. We also see that talented women with a working mother were less likely to become engineers. This is a surprising finding, since previous studies showed that working mothers encourage less traditional occupational choices in their daughters. It was pointed out by Schulenberg, Vondracek and Crouter (1984) that having an employed mother is not enough to explain career orientation of the daughters and departure from traditional feminine roles; only if the mother is satisfied with her role as a employee, is the daughter likely to follow her example. Thus, more research in different cultural contexts is necessary to clarify the relationship between family background, maternal employment and career development of women.

The realization of talent in the domain of science is not only influenced by structural forces, but also by intra-individual differences. The chances of entering any of the scientific disciplines were increased for talented women with good mathematical ability. For men this link only existed for the domain of medicine. Thus, mathematical ability seems to be a critical filter for occupational attainment, especially for women. Possibly, talented females need the additional feedback and encouragement, implied in good test scores, to pursue their careers in the domains of science. This underlines the importance of self-evaluation of school performance for the prediction of high professional achievement in science (Trost and Sieglen, 1992), especially for women. A complementary explanation would be that women have to achieve an even higher level of mathematical ability than men to succeed in the sciences, except for medicine, where the opportunities of achievement are equally distributed between men and women. It seems that women professionals in science, medicine, and engineering require superior credentials and outstanding performance. For a talented woman to succeed in the health professions, she needs not only professional aspirations, a privileged family background, and good mathematical ability, she also has to be willing to work hard. These findings underline, as already stressed by Eccles (1985), the important role of diligence and effort in the career development of women. This does not mean that talented men have an easy ride into the professions: they too have to prove their credentials, and they have to be prepared to work hard in order to realize their potential to the fullest.

For both males and females, a key predictor of occupational attainment in the health professions at age 33 was teenage occupational choice. The same applied to attainment in science, but to a lesser extent, while for the domain of engineering occupational aspirations had no significant impact. It seems that at the age of 16 interest in a particular scientific career seems to be firmly rooted. The anticipation of becoming a medical practitioner, in particular, but also to become a natural scientist helps the young person to persist through the strenuous training and career establishment periods (Bloom, 1985). Engineering, on the other hand, appears to have a less salient profile (at least in the UK), and the anticipation of becoming an engineer does not predict entry into a career in engineering. This finding indicates that what teenagers say about their career aspirations has predictive value for specific career attainment in adulthood, and that adolescence is a crucial period in terms of career commitment. To win new recruits to the professions, the sciences, and especially engineering, are advised to promote themselves to the young and to explain, by examples, possible career paths for both males and females.

The development of scientific talent from early manifestations in the school environment to adult achievement is mediated by both intra-personal and contextual catalysts. Individual characteristics undoubtedly determine whether a person will or will not develop their talent. Those individuals who have the ability, the motivation, persistence, and the belief in their own capacity will take advantage of the few openings available in that field. Yet, the question why so few talented individuals realise their potential cannot be answered by looking at personal traits only, but depends as much on the social realities that constrain fields of accomplishment. This study has identified different selective mechanisms across the professions and across the sexes. For a better understanding of the factors linking promise to fulfilment in the domain of science, comparative studies across countries would provide useful insights into the relative contributions of either individual or contextual variables.

Notes

1. This project is funded by a Leverhulme Personal Research Fellowship (RG&G/2/9699474).
2. Csikszentmihalyi (1988:325) differentiates between the field, a set of social institutions that select from the variations produced by individuals those that are worth preserving, and the domain that preserves and transmits the selected new ideas or forms for the following generations.
3. Gagné (1993) specifies the top 15–20 per cent as an appropriate threshold zone between the gifted and talented and the average population, arguing that a threshold zone similar to a confidence interval should be used instead of a cut of point.
4. The proportion of these three professional groups in the NCDS sample was similar to the proportion of these professions in the 1991 Census data, comparing individuals in the same age band.

References

Almquist, E. and Angrist, S. S. (1970) 'Career salience and atypicality of occupational choice among college women', *Journal of Marriage and the Family*, **32**: 242–9.

Barron, F. (1969) *Creative Persons and Creative Process*. New York: Holt, Rinehart & Winston.

Bloom, B. S. (ed.) (1985) *Developing Talent in Young People*. New York: Ballantine.

Bourdieu, P. (1988) *Homus Academicus*. Cambridge: Polity Press.

HMSO (1993) *Realising our Potential: A Strategy for Science, Engineering and Technology* (White Paper, Cmnd. 2250). London: HSMO.

Colley, A. (1995) 'Psychology, Science and women', *Psychologist*, **8**: 346–52.
Csikszentmihalyi, M. (1988) 'Society, culture and person: a systems view of creativity', in R. J. Sternberg (ed.), *The Nature of Creativity* (pp. 325–39). Cambridge: Cambridge University Press.
Csikszentmihalyi, M., Rathunde, K. and Whalen, S. (1993) *Talented Teenagers. The Roots of Success and Failure*. Cambridge: Cambridge University Press.
Eccles, J. S. (1985) 'Why doesn't Jane run? Sex differences in educational and occupational patterns', in F. D Horrowitz and M. O'Brien (eds), *The Gifted and Talented: Developmental Perspectives* (pp. 251–95). Hyatsville, MD: American Psychological Association.
Eccles, J. S. (1987) 'Gender roles and women's achievement-related decisions', *Psychology of Women Quarterly*, **11**: 135–71.
Eiduson, B. T. (1962) *Scientists: Their Psychological World*. New York: Basic Books.
Eiduson, B. T. and Beckman, L. (eds) (1973) *Science as a Career Choice: Theoretical and Empirical Studies*. New York: Basic Books.
Fleiss, J. L. (1981) *Statistical Methods for Rates and Proportions*, 2nd edn. Chichester:Wiley.
Gagné, F. (1993) 'Constructs and models pertaining to exceptional human abilities', in K. A. Heller, F. J. Mönks and A. H. Passow(eds), *International Handbook of Research and Development of Giftedness and Talent* (pp. 69–87). Oxford: Pergamon Press.
Gagné, F. (1995) 'Learning about the nature of gifts and talents through peer and teacher nominations', in M. W. Katzko and F. J. Mönks (eds), *Nurturing Talent: Individual Needs and Social Ability* (pp. 20–30). Assen: Van Gorcum.
Galton, F. (1874) *English Men of Science*. London: Macmillan.
Gear, G. H. (1976) 'Accuracy of teacher judgment in identifying intellectually gifted children: A review of the literature', *Gifted Child Quarterly*, **20**: 478–89
Getzels, J. and Jackson, P. (1961) 'Family environment and cognitive style: a study of the sources of highly intelligent and of highly creative individuals', *American Sociological Review*, **26**: 351–9.
Golombok, S. and Fivush, R. (1994) *Gender Development*. Cambridge: Cambridge University Press.
Hackett, G., Esposito, D. and O'Halloran, M. S. (1989) 'The relationship of role model influences to the career saliance and educational and career plans of college women', *Journal of Vocational Behavior*, **35**: 164–80
Hanson, R. A. and Neujahr, J. (1976) 'Career development of high school students talented in science', *Science Education*, **60**: 453–62.
Heller, K. A. (1993) 'Scientific ability', in *Ciba Foundation Symposium 178: The Origins and Development of High Ability* (pp. 139–59). Chicester:John Wiley.
Hoge, R. D. and Cudmore, L. (1986) 'The use of teacher-judgement measures in the identifiction of gifted pupils', *Teaching & Teacher Education*, **2**: 181–96.
Knapp, R. H. (1963) 'Demographic, cultural and personality attributes of scientists', in C. W. Taylor and F. Barron (eds), *Scientific Creativity: Its Recognition and Development* (pp. 205–16). New York: Wiley.
MacKinnon, D. W. and Hall, W. B. (1971) 'Intelligence and Creativity', in B. T. Eiduson and L. Beckman (eds) (1973), *Science as a Career Choice: Theoretical and Empirical Studies*. New York: Basic Books.
Medawar, P. B. (1979) *Advice to a Young Scientist*. London: Pan Books.
Norusius, M. J. (1990) *SPSS/PC+ Advanced Statistics 4.0*. Chicago: SPSS.

Oden, M. (1968) 'A 40-year follow-up of giftedness: fulfillment and unfulfillment', *Genetic Psychological Monographs*, **77**: 3–93.

O'Donnell, J. and Andersen, D. G. (1977) 'Decision factors among women talented in math and science', *College Student Journal*, **11**: 165–8.

OPCS (Office of Population Censuses and Surveys) *Classification of Occupations 1980*. London: HMSO.

Pegnato, C. W. and Birch, J. W. (1959) 'Locating gifted children in junior high schools: a comparison of methods', *Exceptional Children*, **25**: 300–04.

Roe, A. (1952) *The Making of a Scientist*. New York: Dodd, Mead.

Roe, A. (1953) 'Early background of eminent scientists', *Psychologcal Monographs*, **67**: 27–54

Rossi,, A. S. (1965) 'Barriers to the career choice of engineering, medicine or science among American Women', in J. A. Mattfeld and C. G. Van Aken (eds), *Women and the Scientific Professions* (pp. 51–113). Cambridge, MA: MIT Press.

Schulenberg, J., Vondracek, F. W. and Crouter, A. C. (1984) 'The influence of the family on vocational development', *Journal of Marriage and the Family*, **10**: 129–43

Sells, L. W. (1973) 'High school mathematics as the critical filter in the job market', in R. T. Thomas (ed.),_*Developing Opportunities for Minorities in Graduate Education* (pp. 37–9). Berkeley, CA: University of California Press.

Shepherd, P. (1995) *The National Child Development Study. An Introduction, its Origins and the Methods of Data Collection*, Working Paper 1. London: City University, SSRU.

Simonton, D. K. (1988) *Scientific Genius: A Psychology of Science*. Cambridge: Cambridge University Press.

Stanley, J. C. (1990) 'Finding and helping young people with exceptional mathematical reasoning ability', in M. J. A. Howe (ed.), *Encouraging the Development of Exceptional Skills and Talents* (pp. 211–21). Leicester: British Psychological Society.

Steinkamp, M. W and Maehr, M. L. (1983) 'Affect, ability and science achievement: a quantitative synthesis of correlational research', *Review of Educational Research*, **53**: 369–96

Subotnik, R. F. and Arnold, K. D. (1993)' Longitudinal studies of giftedness: investigating the fulfillment of promise', in K. A. Heller, F. J. Mönks and A. H. Passow (eds), *International Handbook of Research and Development of Giftedness and Talent*, pp. 149–59. Oxford: Pergamon Press.

Terman, L. M. and Oden, M. H. (1959) *Genetic Studies of Genius*, Vol. 5: *The Gifted Group in Mid-life: Thirty-five Years' Follow-up of the Superior Child*. Stanford, CA: Stanford University Press.

Tomlinson-Keasey, C. and Little, T. D. (1990) 'Predicting educational attainment, occupational achievement, intellectual skill, and personal adjustment among gifted men and women', *Journal of Educational Psychology*, **82**: 442–55.

Trost, G. (1993) 'Prediction of excellence in school, university and work', in K. A. Heller, F. J. Mönks and A. H. Passow (eds), *International Handbook of Research and Development of Giftedness and Talent*, pp. 325–36. Oxford: Pergamon Press.

Trost G. and Sieglen, J. (1992) 'Biographische Frühindikatoren herausragender beruflicher Leistungen', in E. A. Hany and H. Nickel (eds), *Begabung und Hochbegabung*, pp. 95–104. Bern: Huber.

Vondraceck, F. W., Lerner, R. M. and Schulenberg, J. E. (1986) *Career Development: A Life-span Developmental Approach*. Hillsdale, NJ: Erlbaum.
Weinreich-Haste, H. (1979) 'What sex is science?', in O. Harnett, G. Boden and M. Fuller (eds), *Women: Sex Role Stereotyping*. London: Tavistock.
Weitz, S. (1977) *Sex Roles*. New York: Oxford University Press.
Wilson, G. D. and Jackson, C. (1994) 'The personality of physicists', *Journal of Personality and Individual Differences*, **16**: 187–9.
Zuckerman, H. (1977) *Scientific Elite*. New York: Free Press.

Part 3

Social change and social exclusion

8
Moral obligations and values in an individualized society

Hans Bertram

Introductory remarks

Currently the 'generation contract', which comprises the solidarity between the older generation, the adult generation and children and young people, is being called into question, not only in politics but also in the media and by scholars. For a long time services for the younger generation were regarded as an investment in the future, which was to be made jointly by parents, communities, and the state. This was considered to be the only basis for the future development of a society. Today, however, people in these different areas of society are increasingly inclined to view these services as a burden for Germany. In so far as these services (kindergarten, child allowances, schools, universities and grants for students) are not paid for by parents, they are increasingly subject to any savings policy adopted by the political parties. This change in values, in both the political and economic spheres, is also prevalent in academic circles. It is repeatedly alleged that the parents of today's young people are shouldering their own responsibilities less and less. They are criticized with respect to the number of children they have, or for failing to impart moral obligations to the younger generation. In view of this radical change in the assessment of the services for the younger generation, it makes sense to investigate how the generations themselves interpret their relationship with each other. This can be achieved using data from about 16,000 interviewees of all age groups in East and West Germany, based on three large empirical surveys (Bertram, 1995). The surveys focus explicitly on the issue of moral obligations between the generations.

Utilitarian and co-operative individualism

In modern society, personal freedom, equality, scepticism towards authority and belief in having an environment worth living in, have become more important than economic growth and security. Family values concerning the mutual obligations between partners, parents and children, as well as grandchildren and grandparents, are being interpreted differently from the way they were interpreted in the past. Actions are becoming more self-directed even within the family context. According to many social scientists, this change in values is leading to a situation where we are living in a more and more atomized, adult-centred society: expressive individualism is the cultural ideal, where only the self is emphasized. Political movements, such as communitarianism, for example, which want to revive the traditional family among other things, are based on such interpretations of current social developments. For their advocates, the procreation of children is a moral act – a position which is also prominent in current German theoretical debates. At the same time, society is obliged to support parents in taking on the responsibilities involved. Not only Etzioni (1994), but also other authors, such as Coleman (1995), allege that today, parents are not living up to their responsibilities to the full extent. Reasons cited include the increased involvement of women in paid employment and parents wanting to live their own lives even at the expense of their children.

One questionable aspect of this debate is that it focuses exclusively on the obligations of parents towards their young children. In contrast, obligations between other family members, stemming from the lasting relationships of childhood, are never discussed. Skolnick (1994) has interpreted criticisms of family life in the United States as possibly projecting onto society the critics' experiences of their own lives, which they now regard as having been inadequate. He questions whether these personal experiences really reflect those of society as a whole. Bellah (1991), among others, and Gans (1988) show that the concept of modern individualism is open to two theoretical interpretations, at least since Durkheim (Bertram, 1995). *Utilitarian individualism* is really a form of individualism which puts the individual's career and convenience before all else. The alternative attitude, according to Bellah is *co-operative individualism*. In terms of the theoretical tradition stemming from Durkheim, the latter is based on the individual realization that the development of ideas about life goals and personal autonomy, are necessarily linked to co-operation and mutual support. In a highly differentiated society, exhibiting a wide range of expectations, individuals are no longer able to meet adequately the differing demands placed on them, unless they attempt to fulfil them in co-operation with others. Individualism as independence, and the pursuit of personal aims in co-operation with and support from others, requires recognition of the necessity for a high degree of reciprocity, ie mutual obligation and mutual support. According to this line of thought, mutual support is one of the most important prerequisites for individual moral autonomy.

This distinction between utilitarian individualism and co-operative individualism is overlooked in the current debate about moral obligations within the family and between the generations. Instead it is argued that the change in values has destroyed the significance and binding nature of mutual obligations within and between the generations and within the family. Moreover, the communitarian position investigates only the moral obligations of parents towards young children. In this chapter, we shall investigate the values and orientations existing across all generations. Societal trends point to a situation in which such values and orientations will be of decisive significance for the family relations of the future. It may become as important for the future family to accept that they have to support and look after their own parents, as it is for parents to look after and rear their young children.

Because of their theoretically backward views, rooted in a conservative idealization of the past, the communitarians and sociological theorists overlook one of the main future tasks of our society. Co-operation between the generations cannot be controlled through values concerned exclusively with rearing children, but rather through values and orientations concerned with mutual obligations among adults.

Individualism and age

In the debate about individualist values which embraces Inglehart's (1990) 'post-materialism' thesis, attention also focuses on the so-called secondary virtues, such as a sense of duty, obedience, orientation towards performance and diligence. Regardless of whether one favours Inglehart's post-materialist views or the disappearance of the secondary virtues, both concepts assume that society's expectations of the individual have declined, with a consequent increase in personal freedom. Such a shift, from acceptance of societal standards and values as a basis for action, to acting in accordance with one's own predilections, is regretted by the one side but welcomed by the other side, who see it as an expression of liberation.

The comparison of age groups (Figure 8.1), which deals with the relationship between post-materialism and materialism for different educational levels, shows two clear effects. In all age groups, the *gymnasium* leavers show a much lower materialism and a higher degree of post-materialism than those with extended elementary schooling (*Hauptschule*). The extended elementary school leavers, born between 1913 and 1928, show more or less exclusively materialist values. This pattern of values decreases considerably among those born in 1933 and later, and in the youngest age group of those investigated, almost drops to the level of the *gymnasium* leavers. The point needs to be made here, that the *gymnasium* leavers born in 1913 display more or less the same extent of materialist or post-materialist value orientations as the extended elementary school leavers born in 1938. For that generation, the materialist orientations among the *gymnasium* leavers decreased to a low level, which, according to this investigation, has not changed much up to the present day.

This is, of course, a comparison of age groups so we cannot exclude the possibility that young adults born in 1968, and later, might have a different set of values when they reach the age of 80. We need to acknowledge an ongoing process, which Inglehart (1990) quite rightly

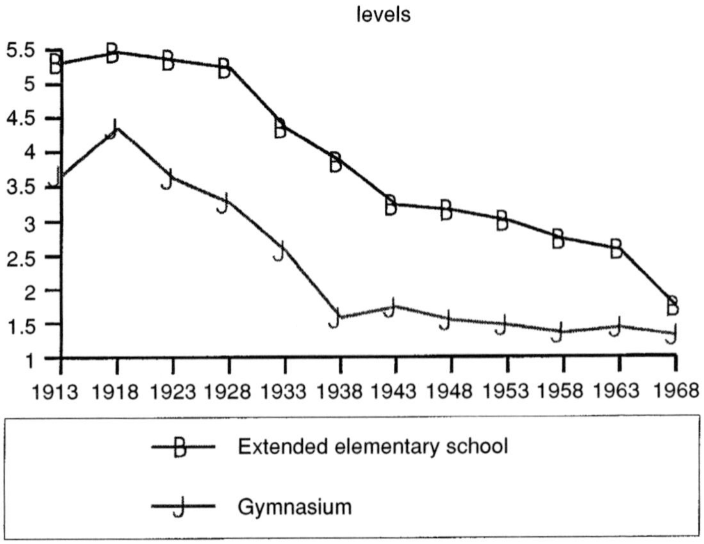

Figure 8.1 Age, post-materialism and educational levels

described as a 'quiet revolution'. The generations born from 1938 onwards showed very low levels of materialism. Thus it is possible with this investigation to identify a change in values across the generations, which is linked to the generation of 1968. The changes in sense of duty, obedience and performance, between the age groups, occur in the same way, but again, are differentiated according to educational levels (Figure 8.2). The sense of *duty* among the extended elementary school leavers born up until about 1928 is at a very high level, expressed as approximately +0.8 on a scale of between −1 to +1. In the younger age groups it drops slowly but consistently to a level of about −0.4 among those born in 1968. The *gymnasium* leavers have much lower values of about +0.4 throughout. The difference in their values across cohorts between those born between 1913 and 1923, and those born after 1938, is considerably larger among them than among the extended elementary school leavers.

There is a far-reaching parallel between the attitude patterns associated with post-materialism as well as the sense of duty and performance orientation in these different age groups. This may be interpreted as showing that those *gymnasium* leavers educated after the Second World War displayed a clearly different value consciousness to those whose up-bringing, educational and vocational training dated from before that

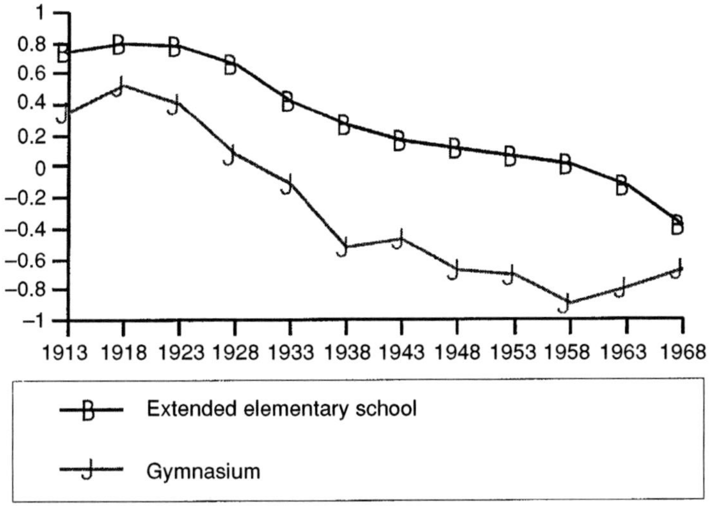

Figure 8.2 **Age, duty obedience and performance and educational level**

time. The difference in the orientation is not as blatant across the age groups for those with extended elementary schooling. But between those born in 1913 and those born in 1968 a consistent and clear liberalization of attitudes and values can be identified. However, on the basis of multivariate analyses, these trends need to be explained in terms of age group affiliation. Of the 26 per cent of variance in post-materialism explained by other factors, a large part can be attributed to age; but educational level plays an even more decisive role. Apart from the educational level and age, regional identity is also of considerable significance. Possibly the different rates of change in values are also influenced by regional factors, over and above societal change.

In the case of the secondary virtues – duty, and obedience performance – the multivariate analysis shows a relatively high proportion of explained variance (21 per cent), which can be attributed to educational level, age and region, i.e. more or less in parallel with the findings for post-materialism. The explanatory power of all other factors is dwarfed by these three variables. It is important to mention here, that indicators such as living alone, partnership, marital status, household membership, size of household and children did not play any significant role.

The increasing individualism of the interviewees and the growing rejection of the secondary virtues of duty, obedience, performance and subordination also find their parallel in attitudes towards marriage. 25 per cent of the variance was explained as being mainly made up of age, religion, and marital status as well as educational level and regional identity (Figure 8.3).

The difference between the age groups is less strongly marked than for post-materialism and the secondary virtues, and the difference between the two levels of schooling (extended elementary school and *gymnasium*) is also smaller. The significance of marital status is, of course, plausible as the married and widowed interviewees would articulate a more positive assessment of marriage than divorced or single people. The influence of religion, measured by the frequency of church attendance, also identifies the role of cultural traditions in attitudes towards marriage and family.

It needs to be stressed, that the assessment of marital values contains only attitude statements which attach a positive meaning to marriage. Examples of these statements are: 'When you love one another, you should marry'; 'Marriage means readiness to take on obligations towards each other'; 'Only when the parents are married, do the children really have a home'; 'Marriage means safety and security'. These

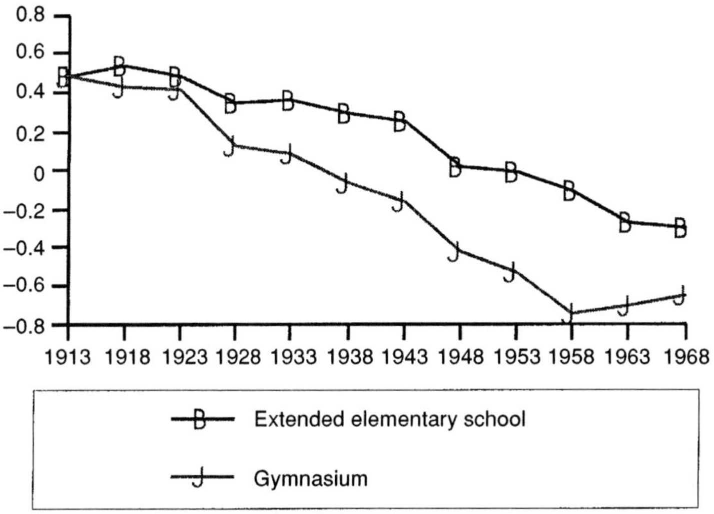

Figure 8.3 Marriage as a sense in life, age and schooling

statements correspond well to the positive bourgeois ideal of marriage; today they are regarded as less important or are less frequently endorsed by the average interviewee. The institution of marriage is not given the same positive emotional significance among the younger interviewees in our survey. The strongly positive attitude to it, especially among the older interviewees, impressively refutes the hypothesis that marriage in earlier times was a mere union born of necessity, while today's partnership is rather a union of choice. This would predict that the older interviewees would stress the usefulness of marriage more – i.e. security and being cared for in marriage – not those bourgeois ideals of love and personal obligation which are actually expressed by the interviewees.

The fact that all interviewees in the oldest age groups, regardless of their marital status, drew such a positive picture of marriage, shows how deeply and firmly rooted the bourgeois ideal was of a marriage based on love for the generations born up to 1928. It has gradually lost such significance among those born later – sooner among the *gymnasium* leavers than the extended elementary school leavers. This change in attitude signalled less of a transition from a union of necessity to a union of choice, but more the possibility that these positive emotional aspects are no longer attributed exclusively to the institution of marriage. Nowadays, they may be experienced in other forms of partnership as well.

Parental responsibility in an individualized society

The idea of being able to implement one's own life perspective independently of social patterns, a growing scepticism towards secondary virtues and the fading of the bourgeois ideal of marriage have been documented in numerous ways but have also been interpreted very differently. Etzioni (1994) regards these trends as pointing to the destruction of the bourgeois family. Like Coleman (1995), he believes that parents concentrate more and more on goals outside the family and thus neglect the rearing of their children, passing this responsibility on to other institutions. Mothers taking up jobs outside their homes when their children are under the ages of 3 or 6, for example, are seen as exemplitying parents' weakened sense of responsibility towards their own children.

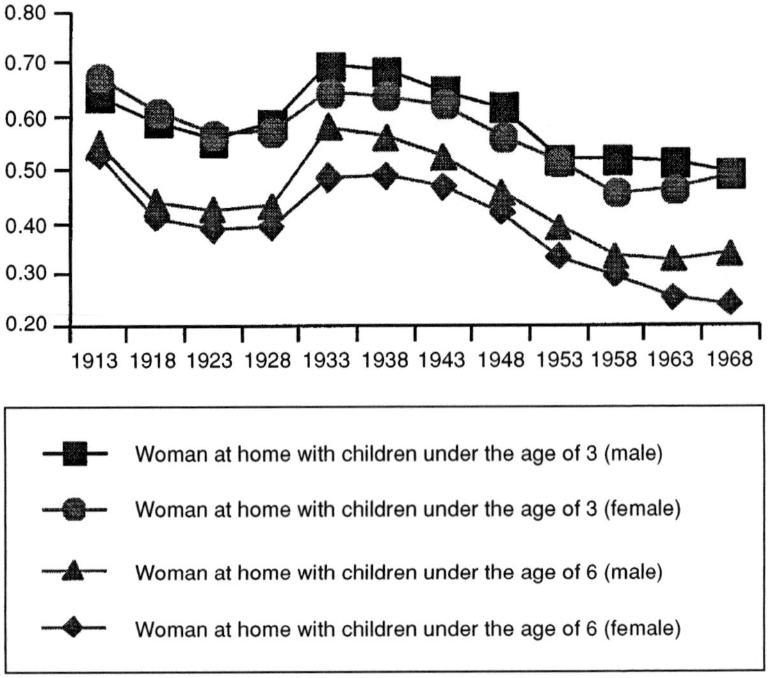

Figure 8.4 Compatibility of family and job, children between 3 and 6 years of age

With respect to the idea that the woman should remain at home with children under the age of three, comparisons across age-groups for the whole of Germany show that 65 per cent of the oldest interviewees believe that the woman should be only a housewife and mother. This idea was considerably less popular among those born in the 1920s among whom it was advocated by some 55 per cent. There was, then, a 70 per cent increase between those born in 1933 and 1943 of respondents favouring women remaining in the home. Among those born after 1948, the idea met with markedly less approval – only 50 per cent among the youngest age group interviewed.

This curvilinear course was also evident in attitudes to whether a woman should dedicate herself completely to rearing a child up to the age of 6. In the oldest age group, some 50 per cent voted for such a model of incompatibility between family and job. Among those born between 1933 and 1943, advocacy of a child-centred model without women working outside the home was especially high at 60 per cent. Endorsement dropped to 20 per cent among the youngest women interviewed. The trend among men is generally more conservative on this issue than among women.

Analysis of the main determinants of this viewpoint show that age is of less relevance for attitudes towards compatibility of a family and a job for women with children under the age of 3, than regional identity. This is the case for both East and West Germany, but there are considerable regional differences, particularly between urban and rural areas. Furthermore, educational level has a strong effect: the higher the level, the higher the rejection of the conservative model. A similar result occurs with regard to whether the mother should remain at home with children between the ages of 3 and 6. In the multivariate analysis, 13 per cent of the variance is explained in terms of region, educational level and gender.

However, full-time employment of women is not the only alternative, as Etzioni and Coleman assume. Part-time employment is an option in the case of parents with children under the age of 3. This is currently an option taken mainly by women, but it is becoming increasingly common for men to consider part-time employment. There was no significant proportion in any group who advocated the full-time employment of both men and women when the children were under the ages of 3 or 6. In the case of children under the age of 6, it was less than 1 per cent and even in the case of school children it was as low as 10 per cent. Also, in a situation where social standards are not binding on individuals, this finding points to a responsible approach by parents towards their children, regardless of whether they hold post-materialistic values.

Given these attitude patterns, we can exclude the possibility for all age groups in Germany of parents not wanting to look after their children. This appears to run counter to the situation described by Etzioni and Coleman, who maintain that people increasingly gain fulfilment through their jobs. The analysis of other attitudes towards childrearing makes clear that the change in values in this area, has played a lesser role than in other areas identified with post-materialism. Growing up to adopt responsibility towards others as well as oneself, an understanding for others, and the ability to bear criticism, can be characterized as co-operative individualism. In this case it proves to be totally invariant with regard to the age groups.

In the multivariate analysis, which could explain only 5 per cent of the variance in this variable, educational level turns out to be the main and most important explanatory factor, followed to a much lesser extent by occupation, gender and family size. The orientation towards co-operative individualism thus depends, as Melvin L. Kohn (1969) has frequently demonstrated, particularly on the educational level reached and partly on occupation. This is not only plausible from a theoretical point of view, as higher educational level is usually associated with an increasing degree of autonomy in the work place, but also because in a highly differentiated industrial society, a sense of personal responsibility and the readiness to work in a group and thus orient oneself towards others and to bear criticism, are part of modern working life. In so far as schooling and work promote these attitude patterns, they develop independently of the age of the interviewees.

In the analysis of attitudes towards children, three dimensions were identified: 'children as giving meaning to life', 'children as an asset', and 'children as a burden'. Especially on the scale of 'children as giving meaning to life', the age of the interviewees played more or less no role; the 14 per cent explained variance was mainly accounted for by the gender of the interviewees. 'Children as giving meaning to life' was measured with such items as: 'It is fun to see children grow up'; 'Life gains its full meaning from children'. This attitude pattern was not specific to any one age, but varied according to gender, and at the same time co-varied with the number of children. Women attached greater significance to children as part of their own lives than did men, and parents of several children tended to rate these items higher than parents with only one child or people without children at all. The assessment that children may become a burden in one's own life, because they may curtail personal freedom, varied by gender: men typically did not hold such a view.

In view of the significance gender has for the two scales of 'children as giving meaning to life' and 'children as a burden', it is not surprising that for the scale of 'children as an asset' with items such as 'children are important for old age', 'children are important for emergencies', and 'children can render support', it was gender again which was by far the most important variable. It explained 19 per cent of the variance. Men saw children as more of an asset, whereas women stressed the meaningfulness of having children. This result was independent of age. The orientation towards children seems to be less influenced by age than by gender roles or the life plans of men and women.

The results introduced here lead us to conclude that even at a time of changing values, in which the binding nature of social expectations and institutional regulations is dwindling in favour of larger scope for individual freedom, and the pattern of standards for the individual is declining, this is not necessarily leading to a lack of responsibility on the part of individuals. Possibly, the control exercised over individuals by social patterns is being replaced by an internal, more subjective control. In the case of children, for instance, who depend on their parents, responsibility is controlled from inside and not by the standards of the whole society. This interpretation is based on the people concerned being able to differentiate between the different spheres of life, such as marriage and family, whether they should act in accordance with the dictates of society, or on the basis of personal decisions. As the interviewees in the West and in the East make the compatibility of family and job, of child care and emancipation in the job more or less dependent on the age of the children, this also reflects cultural standards in relation to rearing children in Germany.

The thesis by Etzioni (1994) that the self-fulfilment of parents inevitably results in the needs of the children taking a back seat, is not substantiated by the research presented here. It would probably make more sense to assume that changes in the values of a society are on the one hand inconsistent but that on the one hand, the decline in the binding nature of certain social standards is stimulating responsible actions by the subjects on the basis of their own insights, (cf. Durkheim). It is arguable that the authors, who are greatly concerned about marriage and family because of the evidence of changes in values, have too mechanistic a perspective. Individuals do not only act on the basis of predetermined social standards, but also on the basis of personal judgements. The positive consequences that may result from the dissolution of traditionally predetermined standards and understandings of roles is illustrated by an examination of the division of labour between men and women across age groups (Figure 8.5).

In Figure 8.5, the answers given about certain household chores are compared for men and women and yield relatively clear trends across the various age groups. For activities which are typically regarded as women's jobs, such as cleaning, cooking or looking after the children, men usually enter somewhat higher values with regard to shared work than do women. In contrast, women quote slightly higher values for shared work than men do for jobs such as repairs, which are typically regarded as the man's domain.

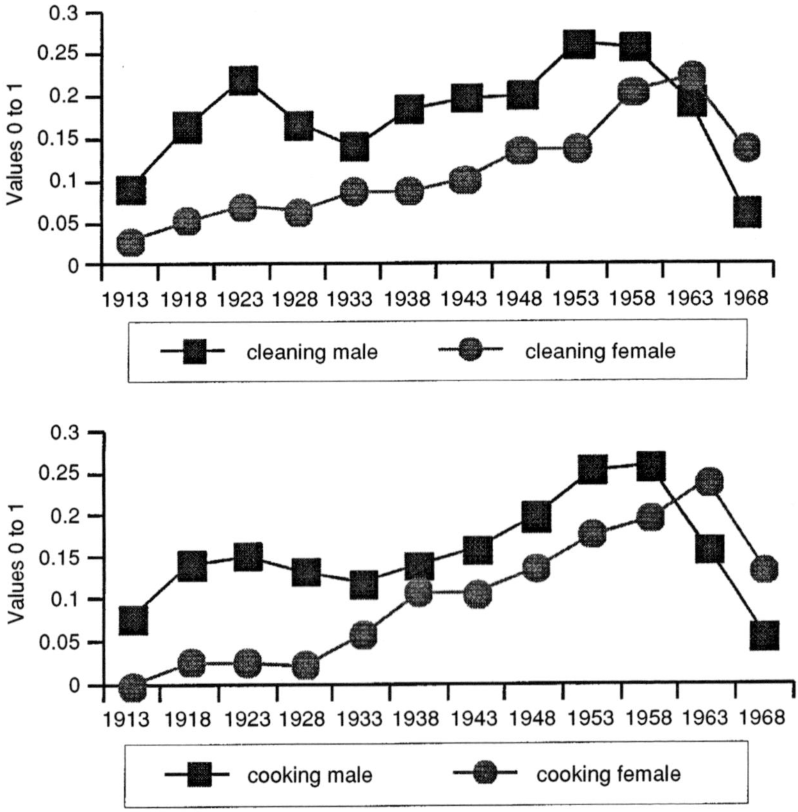

Figure 8.5 Division of labour between men and women: sharing household chores

This typical man–woman difference must not obscure the fact that in the younger age group 40 per cent of the men and nearly as many women stated that they shared the work of looking after the children. This was expressed very rarely by the older interviewees regarding their own participation in childcare. A similar change was evident for looking after the sick, spending money and shopping. In these cases, too, the proportion of men and women who said that they did this has clearly risen. In the case of cleaning, cooking and repairing, the differences in perceptions between men and women were dominant. It is reasonable to assume that for activities regarded as typical woman's jobs such as cleaning and cooking, the answers given by the women

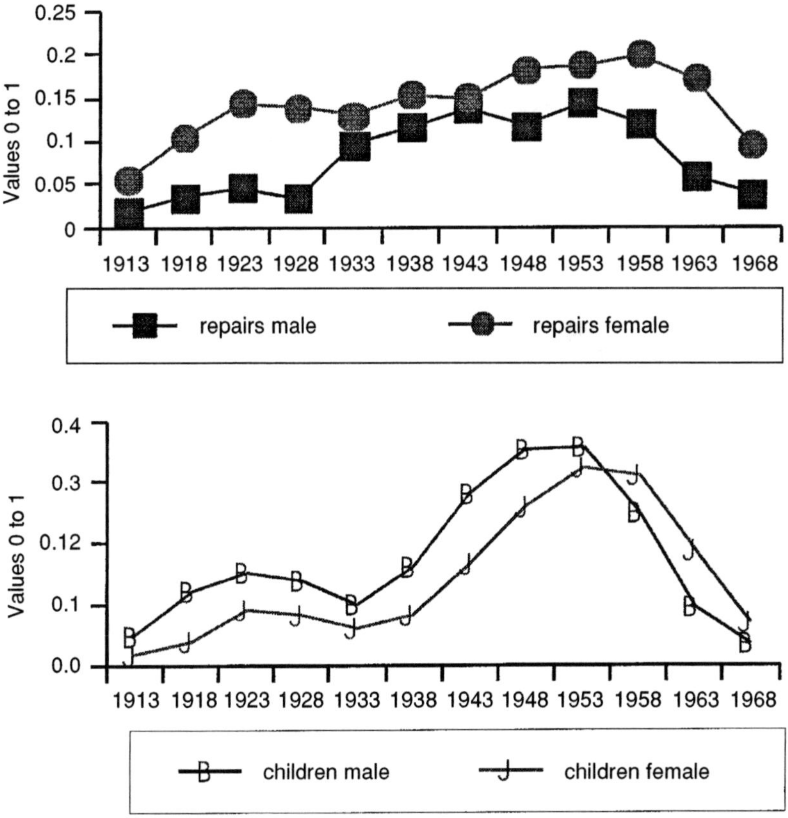

Figure 8.5 Continued

would be more realistic than those given by the men. But it is still clear that in the younger age-groups, a larger proportion of the men were prepared to share the household chores with women. These results suggest that there may well be positive consequences resulting from the less binding nature of socially determined standards – namely, the dissolution of classical gender role divisions in the area of marriage and family life.

Social duties and social support

For the oldest group in the survey, the 55- to 80-year olds, it has been possible to investigate their expectations with regard to support when in need of care. Within the framework of a network analysis, this oldest group was asked from which individuals they would expect care and support should they become incapacitated. Thus, a moral obligation – one of the most binding forms of obligation the younger generation has towards the older one – was investigated from the perspective of the interviewees. General support and help in old age was experienced less bindingly than the expectation of care. This only referred to situations in which the person was not able to care for themselves any longer.

The 4,130 people surveyed between the ages of 55 and 80, identified as providers of care just under a quarter of the 32,141 mentioned as their partners in social interaction, that is a total of 7,500. This is evidence once more of the fact that even at the age of 80 there was still a relatively high percentage of people who were able to cope with their lives more or less without any support.

Because of the very low number of cases mentioned, the experience of care will not be discussed in detail here. Rather, the aim is simply to establish whether this perceived moral obligation imposed by the older generation on the younger, varies with the values and orientations of the older generation. An analysis of variance, including the most important values, as discussed in the previous section, was conducted in order to establish which values and attitudes were of greatest significance. It comes as no surprise that children were identified as providing help by 40 per cent, and partners by almost 20 per cent. It is also more or less self-evident that the expectations of care relate nearly exclusively (80 per cent of all cases) to members of the family. Friends (11 per cent), neighbours (7 per cent) and other people (just under 1 per cent) play a subordinate role.

The analyses of variance showed clearly that the values and orientations investigated shared little common variance with the expectations of care. The explanatory weight of all values and attitudes considered can only explain the variance in one case – friends – a mere 6 per cent. Despite the relative insignificance of the values in relation to the expectation of care, there were certain systematic effects. When we assess children as to whether they promised to help and support their parents in old age, that is to say we attach the value of usefulness to them, then we expect to be cared for by them. This attitude towards the children's usefulness is also transferred to the children-in-law, the partner and in a weaker form to the grandchildren. In contrast, the values of materialism and post-materialism, individualist concepts of child-rearing and attitudes to duty and performance that feature so strongly in debates about the change of values, played little or no role in the interviewees' expectations regarding care. Regardless of which attitudes and values older people hold, their idea of who is going to care for them and look after them in the case of incapacity, does not depend on these same attitudes. This result allows us to conclude that the expectations of care, as found among the older generation, have developed irrespectively of value change. Thus, to explain where these expectations come from, further indicators have to be included in the analysis.

The next stage of the analysis included living alone, forms of partnership, marital status and the number of children as predictors. The explanatory value of these variables in relation to the expectations about care is somewhat greater than for values and attitudes, at least in relation to the subject's own children (8 per cent variance explained) and also for friends (8 per cent variance explained). The expectation of care from children depends mainly on the number of children. So, for example, if you have several children, the expectation of care from them grows. The marital status of the interviewees had a weaker effect. Age influenced the expectation of care with regard to the grandchildren and the number of children. The expectation of care from friends was determined by marital status, the number of children, the type of religion and living alone. Finally, the expectation was also related to social status as measured by occupation. People from the upper occupational groups more often directed their expectation of care towards friends than to the own families.

The multivariate analyses were not able to explain this form of moral obligation imposed by the older generation on the younger one, in terms of values and attitudes or social indicators. It becomes clear, therefore, that the expectation of care is more or less exclusively controlled through the social relations of the older generation to the younger one. Judging by the results of the analysis, the explanatory value of social relations regarding the expectations of care from children is quite considerable with 21 per cent accounted for by spouses, 53 per cent by neighbours, 24 per cent by friends. Studying the individual results, emotional relations and the leisure time spent together were the best predictors of the expectation of care from children. The other indicators taken into consideration here, such as frequency of contact, distance and shared meals, were of less significance. The expectations of care from the partner were more weakly related to emotional attachment and personal exchanges than to being together, joint meals, shared leisure time, and distance. Thus, when the partner lived with the interviewee or close to him or her, spending their leisure time together and sharing meals, the expectations of care were directed exclusively towards the partner. In this case it was not the emotional attachment which was decisive but the spatial proximity and time spent together.

In the case of friends, emotional attachment – that is to say the close feelings developed towards a friend and distance from them – plays a decisive role, so that the expectations of care from friends were held especially when the respondent was together with them often and a genuine close emotional bond had grown. This pattern also emerged with regard to neighbours. Of the 24 per cent explained co-variance, the largest part was explained similarly by feelings, attachment, shared meals and distance. Neighbours with whom there were emotional bonds, people with whom the interviewee also shared meals and who really lived in the same house, were less likely to be mentioned in the expectations of who was going to help in the case of incapacity than children and partners were. However, they were perceived in the same way as friends once personal bonds had been developed. Help and support in old age, and especially when unable to look after oneself alone anymore, was not seen as controlled through values but more or less exclusively through personal relations.

These results remind us in many respects of the early childhood theories of bonding, which proposed that the values and attitudes voiced by the parents are usually far less important for the development of children than the personal relationships which the parents develop with the children. The results reported here indicate, perhaps, that expected help and support in old age are less controlled by the values and attitudes of society and the individuals concerned than through emotional bonds, personal relationships and jointly spent leisure time. These, in turn, do not necessarily depend on attitudes and values. A person with "individualised" ideas about life and corresponding values does not necessarily have to call into question traditional social relationships and design his life without any bonds.

Possibly, the people who attribute the alleged lack of support of the younger generation for the older generation to the change in values, or who believe that the change in values is coupled with a breakdown of relationships between the generations, simply have too mechanistic an idea of the development of personal relations. If personal relations are determined only to a small degree by values and attitudes, then the moral obligations and expectations of the kind investigated here have little to do with the changes in them, nor the reduced significance in people's lives of such institutions as marriage.

Analyses of variance were conducted for the individual indicators of relations, the personal exchanges, the close personal feelings, the shared meals, the jointly spent leisure time as well as contact frequency, in order to find an answer to the question of what influences these personal relations.

Altogether 18 variables were included in this study; apart from the values and attitudes, including frequency of church visits, as an indicator of religious affiliation, and the gender of the interviewees. The relations of the elderly, and the expectations of care towards certain people, were found to be almost totally unrelated to values and attitudes. The explained variance was usually between 1 and 2 per cent, which even though statistically significant was otherwise negligible. Neither postmaterialism, nor secondary virtues, played any great role in the analysis of variance. So we have to conclude that these values and attitudes do not substantially influence the relationships between people.

Conclusion

The conclusion, therefore, appears justified that the thrust of individualization in our society is more or less irrelevant with regard to the expectations of care, which are among the main moral obligations imposed by the older generation on the younger generation. Thus we can advance the thesis that social relationships develop just as strongly in an open society with less binding social standards relating to such institutions as marriage and family, and that these relationships remain stable to a large extent throughout the life span. With regard to the children and the grandchildren, these relationships also withstand divorce or death of a partner. The idea of who is going to help in the case of an emergency, is based on these life-long patterns of relationships.

Thus the thesis put forward time and again by Zapf and his colleagues that individuals in an individualized society place more and more demands on the state, because of the dissolution of family bonds, has to be called into question (Zapf and Habich, 1995). The results presented here permit a totally different conclusion: it is the family which is regarded first and foremost as a guarantor in emergencies, and it is expected from the family, or from individual family members that they provide support. Unfortunately there is no data for comparison on such expectations of care from the 1950s or the beginning of this century. Thus, we can only speculate how earlier generations formulated their own security requirements in old age.

The stable expectations directed towards the family should not obscure the fact, however, that those who do not live in such familial relationships have no opportunity to voice such expectations towards their family. In view of the growing proportion of old people and a dwindling share of younger people, we should also raise the critical question as to whether not only families, children, grandchildren, but also neighbours and friends, are really able to live up to these expectations, as they were formulated by the interviewees. The consequences of such a change, for how expectations of care are expressed in the different groups, and especially, how they are actually implemented, will have to remain the subject of further analyses.

References

Bellah, Robert N. (1991) *The Good Society*. New York: Vintage Books.

Bertram, Hans (ed.) (1995) *Das Individuum und seine Familie. Lebensformen, Familienbeziehungen und Lebensereignisse im Erwachsenenalter.* Opladen: Laske & Budrick.

Coleman, James S. (1995) *Grundlagen der Sozialtheorie: Körperschaften und die moderne Gesellschaft*, 3 vols. München: R. Oldenburry Verlag München.

Durkheim, Emile (1986) 'Der Individualismus und die Intellektuellen', in Hans Bertram (ed.), *Gesellschaftlicher Zwang und moralische Autonomie*. Frankfurtam Main: Suhrkanto.

Etzioni, Amitai (1994) *Jenseits des Egoismus-Prinzips: Ein neues Bild von Wirtschaft, Politik und Gesellschaft.* Stuttgart: Schäfter-Poeschel.

Gans, Herbert J. (1998) *Middle American Individualism: The Future of Liberal Democracy*. New York: The Free Press.

Inglehart, Ronald (1990) *Culture Shift in Advanced Industrialized Society*. Princeton: Princeton University Press.

Kohn, Melvin L. (1969) *Class and Conformity: A Study in Values*. Chicago: Chicago University Press.

Skolnick, Arlene S. (1994) *The Intimate Environment: Exploring Marriage and the Family*. New York: Harper Collins.

Zapf, W. and Habich, R. (1995) 'Die sich stabilisierende Transformation – ein deutscher Sonderweg?' [Stabilising transformation – a specific German way?] in H. Rudolph (ed.), *Geplanter Wandel, ungeplante Wirkungen. Handlungslogiken und –ressourcen im Prozess der Transformation* (pp. 137–59). Berlin: Sigma.

9

Social capital and intergenerational transmission of cultural capital within a regional context

Bernhard Nauck

Introduction

German social reports identify astonishing regional differences in children's living conditions. For example, official statistics show considerable regional variations among birthrates as well as among sociodemographic characteristics of children (Bertram, Bayer and Bauereiss 1993; Bauereiss, Bayer and Bien, 1997). Regional social reporting also shows that not all of the differences between West and East Germany are the result of belonging to one or other political system for decades. Time series of childrens' legal position in relation to their parents show, for example, that the illegitimate birth ratio was already higher in East Germany than in West Germany during the immediate post-war period (Hullen and Schulz, 1993); regional analyses show additionally that the regional boundaries for high proportions of illegitimate children do not correspond with the former borders between the German Democratic Republic (GDR) and the Federal Republic of Germany (FRG), but also include large parts of northwest Germany (Nauck 1993a and 1993b). In addition, the regional distribution of the proportions of pre-school children subsidized through state welfare provision in no way corresponds to political borders, especially not to the former borders between the GDR and the FRG. Rather the picture that emerges is one of two structural principles: a regional concentration of high welfare rates within northern Germany, and a concentration of high welfare rates in urban metropolitan areas. Deeper aggregate data analyses show additionally, that children profit quite differently in the respective regions from welfare support (Nauck, 1995a, 1995b). The central result of these analyses in West Germany, as well as in East Germany, is the existence of a clear north–south divide, concerning take-up of welfare benefits for children – independent of political borders. In the northern regions, the take-up is below average. In the southern regions, take-up is above average.

Reports containing such descriptive information regularly attract much public attention. But the existence of empirical regularities tells us nothing about their explanation. Connections between 'region', on the one hand, and measures like 'birthrate', 'illegitimate birth ratio', 'secondary school graduate ratio', or 'proportion of under-aged welfare recipients', on the other hand, represent aggregate-phenomena, which can be related to many different behavioural characteristics. Accordingly, explanations of regional differences cannot be made without assumptions about actors and their individual actions, nor can they be made without assumptions about the existence and the effects of special contextual conditions. The development of an explanatory model will thus have to relate the connections on the macro-level to an explicit micro-model.

A specific micro-model that is concerned with the production of human capital will be employed in this chapter. Coleman's ideas (Coleman, 1988) set out in his article 'social capital in the creation of human capital' will be used, as extended to the question of how contextual factors influence the transmission of cultural capital within families. This leads to a fundamental consideration of how regional contexts affect individual behaviour, i.e. the mechanisms have to be elucidated: how do contextual characteristics drive the actions from which the aggregated regional behavioural differences emerge? Only in this way can the characteristics of actors be separated analytically from contextual characteristics. Following Coleman's argument (1988; 1990) we can hypothesize that these regional variations are traceable back to the differential supply of internal and external social capital acquired by children from their families. Social capital represents a set of social relations, which do not usually have the character of an individual attribute. Therefore, whether 'social capital', the production of and the investment in the collective good, optimizes the welfare of a given family depends specifically on contextual conditions. Accordingly, for our purposes, it is assumed that the social capital of families depends on regional–cultural contextual factors, and correspondingly, that high levels of social capital are an important key to understanding regional differences.

Towards a micro-model of regional differences in the production of human capital

Coleman (1988; 1990) developed his theoretical concept of social capital in attempting to explain American high school dropouts. He distinguishes social capital from physical capital and human capital according to their respective availability:

> Just as physical capital is created by changes in materials to form tools that facilitate production, human capital is created by changes in persons that bring about skills and capabilities that make them able to act in new ways. Social capital, however, comes about through changes in the relations among persons that facilitate action. If physical capital is wholly tangible, being embodied in observable material form, and human capital is less tangible, being embodied in the skills and knowledge acquired by an individual, social capital is less tangible yet, for it exists in the relations among persons. The function identified by the concept of social capital is the value of these aspects of social structure to actors as resources that they can use to achieve their interests (Coleman, 1988).

Social capital is created through entering into social relations and it generates mutual obligations, expectations, and trust, through which social goods are exchanged and controlled collectively. Coleman assumes that individuals *within dense, multiplex networks accumulate social capital with higher probability than individuals within loose, monofunctional networks*. This is because social capital is relatively unstable, needing to be renewed and confirmed continously through permanent interaction. This can be achieved at lower expense within multiplex networks. Coleman drew from these assumptions immediate consequences for the development of human capital in children (Nauck, Kohlmann and Diefenbach, 1997):

> The higher the density of the mutual relationship between parents and the stronger their physical presence for their children, the higher the investments into jointly spent time and joint activities with children, and the more help and control in schooling tasks are given, the more probable is the educational success of the children.

Coleman applies his analysis of the transformation of social capital into human capital not only to family specific social capital, but to the ecological context (in an analogous way):

> Closure is present only when there is a relation between adults who themselves have a relation to the child. The adults are able to observe the child's actions in different circumstances, talk to each other about the child, compare notes, and establish norms. The closure of the network can provide the child with support and rewards from additional adults that reinforce those received from the primary adults and can bring about norms and sanctions that could not be instituted by a single adult alone. (Coleman, 1990).

Two influences are important for the creation of human capital in children : the human capital of the individuals connected with the child ('nodes') *and* the closure of the social network ('links'). Within the family context the 'links' between *parents and their children* are constituted by intergenerational bonds or transgenerational closures. Within the extrafamilial context of 'links' between parents and childrens, other *extrafamilial closely related persons* constitute closures in the children's social control.

However, there is an astonishing contrast between the richness of Coleman's explanation on the one hand and his application of it to the empirical analysis of the influence of familial social capital on high school dropouts on the other. In the latter, he uses a number of comparatively dubious proxy-variables. An unanswered question is, for instance, whether the social capital produced within families can compensate for the costs originating from the loss of 'exogenous' social capital (Diefenbach and Nauck, 1997). Follow-up studies, therefore, have raised the question whether specific forms of social capital are necessary to the coping capabilities in completing the developmental tasks of the life course (Furstenberg and Hughes, 1995). The question has also been raised as to whether intrafamilial and extrafamilial forms of social capital work as additive influential factors in the creation of human capital within the succeeding generation (Teachman, Paasch and Carver, 1996).

Moreover, it is questionable whether Coleman's indicators are useful to depict both the complex relationships between different types of capital as well as the transformation process, which is nessesary to transform one type of capital into the other (Diefenbach and Nauck, 1997). Bourdieu (1983:186) is surely right in his criticism: 'human capital theorists condemn themselves to disregard the best hidden and socially most effective educational investment, namely the *transmission of cultural capital within families.*' They overlook the fact that the outcome of educational investments 'depends on the cultural capital, which was invested by the family beforehand and that the economic and social value of educational qualifications is also dependent on the inherited social capital, which can be used to support them.' Thus, with regard to intrafamilial relations, a clear distinction between the types of capital is unavoidable. Otherwise, if we focus only on social capital, the means by which useable capital is passed on from one generation to the next is overlooked. For example, 'the transformation of economic capital into cultural capital demands an expenditure of time...which is made possible through the disposal of economic capital. Or, more precisely, the cultural capital, which is actually passed on within the family, depends not only on the value of the cultural capital to the family, which accumulates over time; it also depends on how much useable time (especially in the form of the mothers' spare time) is available within the family. This latter resource makes the passing on of cultural capital possible and encourages the extension of education and the corresponding delay in entry to the labour market' (Bourdieu, 1983).

We can thus conclude that the analytical differentiation of types of capital is fundamental to the explanation of educational transmission processes in families. Because the explanation only refers to 'education' it seems to be better to use the narrow term 'cultural capital' (cf. Bourdieu) whenever educational transmission and success are under consideration. The broader term 'human capital' (cf. Coleman) includes additionally other characteristics of actors, such as health, physical strength and youthfulness, for example.

With Coleman's model, which imputes a linear-additive effect of intrafamilial and extrafamilial social capital, it is not possible to specify the differential effects of these forms of social capital, which arise for instance out of the time constraints on the family members or from the social context. For example, families with high investments in extrafamilial occupational activities will have to make as hard uncompromising choices as families living in culturally or ethnically very heterogeneous environments (in both cases probably in favour of investments into intrafamilial social capital). Additionally, Coleman's model misses out theoretical assumptions, which specify the relations between economic, social and human capital (except for somewhat derogatory remarks concerning the harmfulness of mothers being gainfully employed). For example, economic capital might be used to create and maintain social capital by making 'spare' time available through exempting household members from employment. In this expanded theoretical perspective the transmitted social capital accruing to the next generation is conceptualized as resulting from the total parental investment in their children. These social location processes are thus decisively determined by the capital available to the parents for their investments. It can therefore be assumed that the respective constellation of economic, social, and cultural capital within the parental generation is a determining factor for childrens' success within the educational system.

The major advantage of such an expanded model is that – unlike Coleman's empirical analysis – all the factors need not be introduced as being exogenous. Rather, through the introduction of assumptions about the relations between the types of capital an extensive endogenization of the theoretical model can be achieved, and the interdependence of the predictors can be investigated empirically. With this endogenization, the model can be related directly to models and results from socialization research (Bertram, 1981). Such a micro-model, takeing up, expanding and endogenizing Coleman's theoretical concepts, is summarized in Figure 9.1 (the diagram, especially with regard to the impact of contextual effects, uses the notation of Burr et al., 1979).

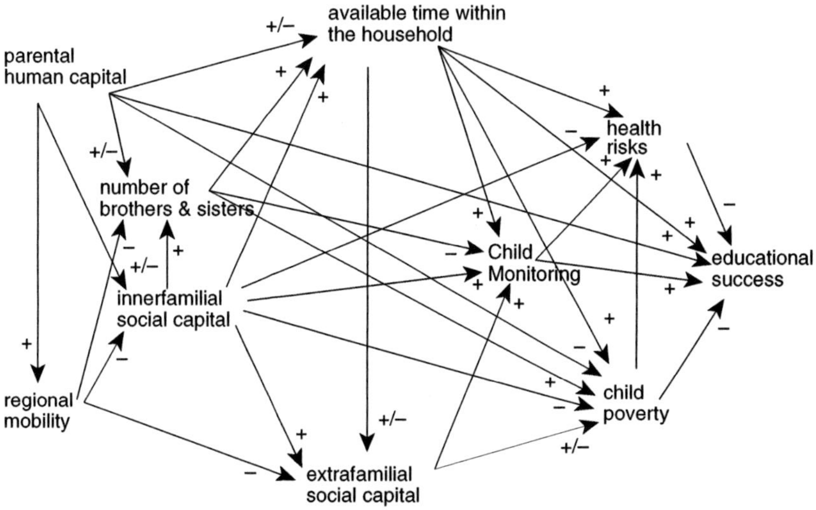

Figure 9.1 A Micro-model of intergenerative transmission

The model's only exogenous factor is (1) *parental human capital.* Because economic gains can be maximized more effectively by mobility in the case of high human capital – social costs remaining constant – a positive correlation between parental human capital and (2) *regional mobility* is expected (Esser, 1985; Wagner, 1989; Kalter, 1997). According to Coleman (1988), regional mobility destroys social capital – directly (in the case of extra-familial social capital) and indirectly, by weakening links between family members and extrafamilial nodes – (3) the *intrafamilial social capital.* Additionally, it is assumed that regional mobility lowers the willingness to invest in a high number of children (Nauck, 1997) and that accordingly a negative correlation between mobiltity and (4) the *number of brothers and sisters* exists. There is no endogenous relationship between parental human capital and intrafamilial social capital on the one hand and the number of brothers and sisters on the other resulting from the theoretical model. Rather it is assumed that – depending on whether the regional cultural context tends to individualism or collectivism – positive as well as negative relations may exist. Within *individualistic* contexts a negative correlation between parental human capital, on the one hand, and intrafamilial social capital and the number of brothers and sisters on the other, is assumed. But in *family-oriented* contexts a positive correlation is assumed.

Analogous assumptions need to be made about the correlation between parental human capital and (5) *available time within the family's household* for the care, support, and control of children. Because of the rising price of family work with increased human capital (especially for mothers), a negative correlation between human capital and available time in the household has to be assumed (Becker, 1991). But this correlation should be stronger in individualistic contexts than in family-oriented contexts. Independently of social context, a positive correlation between intrafamilial social capital and the number of brothers and sisters on the one hand, and the available time for the family on the other, is assumed. Whilst regional mobility destroys (6) *extrafamilial social capital,* its production requires available time and it is promoted by the existence of close familial bonds. Therefore, single parent families can mobilize less social capital than dual parent families. Accordingly, a positive correlation between the available time within the family household and intrafamilial social capital on the one hand and extrafamilial social capital on the other is assumed.

(7) *Child monitoring* takes a key position in Coleman's model, i.e. the supervision and control of children in the intrafamilial and extrafamilial context. This is the way in which parental investments are trans-

formed into children's human capital. According to his assumptions, the more perfect the monitoring, the higher the investment of available time, and the higher the social capital. Accordingly, a negative correlation between the number of brothers and sisters (being a limiting factor for time investment in each child) and intrafamilial and extrafamilial social capital is assumed together with a positive correlation for the available time within the family household.

With respect to the effects of the constellation of capital amongst parents on the creation of human capital in their offspring we expect the following. The risk of (8) *child poverty* (as an indication of low provision of economical capital) rises, the lower the parents' human capital and their social capital, and the higher the number of household members, among whom the economic capital has to be distributed, i.e. the poverty risk for each child rises with the number of siblings (Nauck and Joos, 1996a, 1996a; Joos, 1997; Joos and Nauck, 1998). But as the poverty risk is mainly an indication of the absence of gainful employment, the available time for child care also rises, i.e. a positive correlation between available time within households and child poverty is assumed. The correlation between external social capital and child poverty remains an open question. The theoretical assumption is that no (or only a low) correlation between economic and social capital exists in family-oriented cultural contexts, whilst in individualistic environments there will be a positive correlation. Accordingly, in family-oriented environments, child poverty should lead to a mobilization of external social capital, whilst in individualistic environments a negative correlation is to be expected: extrafamilial social capital should decrease with the increase of child poverty risks.

(9) *Health risks of children* are expected to be dependent on economic provision, and intrafamilial social capital is a protective factor against health risks. Additionally, health risks of children should lead to increased care and control of children, i.e. positive correlations between the available time within the household, child monitoring, and health risks are expected.

(10) *Children's success at school* as an indication of the transmission of cultural capital within the family is influenced negatively by child poverty and by health risks. Coleman's assumptions suggest, furthermore, a positive correlation between child monitoring (as an indication of social control) and available time within the family household (as an additional indication of parental support) and a negative correlation between these family factors and school dropout. Finally, a direct human capital transfer effect between the generations is assumed.

In specifying the model, I have already indicated where the influence of regional contexts on it is to be expected. Such effects, which alter the relationships between the factors within the model, need to be distinguished from the non-specific effects of regional contexts. For example, clear differences between regions with respect to health risks or child poverty can be taken for granted, as the result of, for example, health endangering pollution or generally low purchasing power in a given region. Such differences are of no importance for the model, as long as they affect all children in the same way. (This should, of course, not be mixed up with the neglect of such differences in the regional life chances of children in real life.) But such contextual effects become extremely relevant for the model construction, if they selectively influence particular groups of children, or if the model's mechanisms operate differently in the different social contexts. They may intensify or reduce the relationship between the elements of the micro-model or even reverse it. For example:

1. the correlation between the human capital of parents and the educational success of children may vary. Social contexts where the educational system is stratified by the amount of school fees will result in higher correlations than in those with an educational system without school fees or without stratification of school tracks;
2. the positive correlations between parental human capital, available time within the household and child monitoring, may change if parents are rewarded by the occupational system. For example, if special institutional care is provided for the children of employed parents, this may then affect the allocation of the children to particular educational tracks.

As was made clear when the model was specified, such contextual effects also affect strategies of investment in intrafamilial and extrafamilial capital, and thereby also the theoretical core of the model. The closure of social contexts increases the expectation of mutual obligations and of the reliability of social relations. Accordingly, incentives for long-term investment into social relations are prevalent only in such contexts. For these reasons it is necessary to extend the model with explicit assumptions about the effects of social contexts (Nauck, 1995b). Social contexts are related to individual behaviour through the following mechanisms: they work as (1) *opportunity structures* for the realization of individual action preferences, as (2) places of *social control*, as (3) places of *cultural transmission* of life styles and traditions, as (4) goals of selective *migration*, and as (5) objects of *identification*.

Opportunity structures for our purposes comprise the differently distributed opportunities for earning, childcare and participation in the educational system according to urban and rural settings in East and West Germany.

Regionally distributed opportunity structures are especially important for the following analysis, as are regional patterns of cultural transmission, e.g. regional milieus. The latter effect works especially through the socialization of basic normative concepts through which central life goals are taken on and through the intermediate 'goods' that have strategically to be achieved to reach these goals. In terms of this perspective, regional differences are first of all a spatial concentration of population groups with different cultural patterns.

A central hypothesis related to regional milieus is that Germany is placed at the interface of two large regional cultures impacting differently on the institutions of marriage and family. The northern part of East Germany, together with large parts of northern West Germany, follows the pattern of Denmark and Sweden, in maintaining a strong separation between marriage and family. This results in high illegitimate birth rates. Whereas in southern and western Germany – rather in the mediterranean pattern – marriage and family maintain a very close institutional connection (Strohmeier and Schulze, 1995; Nauck, 1995b). One can assume that such family cultures have far-reaching consequences for the intermediate goods, 'children' and 'social capital'.

Accordingly, we can assume that different optimizing strategies are prevalent in the respective cultural milieus. In family-oriented environments, actors pay more attention to marriage and close social relations, whilst within individualistic environments, strategy will concentrate more exclusively on the accumulation of human capital and (if possible) on its intergenerational transfer. These different optimizing strategies in the respective environments would then aggregate to systematic, region-specific action preferences, so that within the family-oriented culture of southern Germany, extrafamilial social capital becomes of far greater importance for the intergenerational transmission of cultural capital than within the individualistic family culture of northern Germany. The first empirical evidence for this distinction come from aggregate data analyses, according to which wealth within southern Germany seems to be closely connected with family orientations. Within northern Germany, it is connected more with individualistic action strategies. Moreover, the prevailing differences in the poverty risks for children, after controlling for the general welfare level in northern and southern Germany, are probably not explicable without regard to regional cultural environments. Two specific mechanisms are of significance for the explanation of these regional constellations. A direct mechanism is the disproportionate use of family income for the benefit of children (probably accompanied by additional income transfers within social networks). An indirect mechanism may be the degree to which parents choose to have children depending on their own welfare level; i.e. the degree to which only relatively well situated adults decide to become parents and the degree to which economic deprivation 'acts' as an obstacle to parenthood (According to the available empirical results, the idea that poverty acts as an incentive for parenthood has to be rejected).

This strategy for deepening sociological explanations, using a micro-model as a starting-point, enlarged by the inclusion of contextual effects, tries to overcome the shortcomings of conventional social ecology with the formulation of specific bridging hypotheses within a multi-level model (Esser, 1988). Accordingly, the additional contribution of the development of such multi-level models to the classification of regions is that it not only identifies regional differences in the distribution of characteristics (as is usually done in social reporting), but that it reveals (1) regional differences in the relationships between model-factors and (2) variations within regions.

Data source and operationalization of constructs

The basis of the following empirical analysis is the data set 'Values and Lifestyles', which was based on a regional survey in 1996 and covers an adult-sample (N = 4,216) from the following seven urban and rural counties (N ≥ 600, each); relevant indicators from official statistics of the respective counties are shown in Table 9.1 of the appendix:

- urban county of Hamburg (in the north of West Germany)
- rural county of Regensburg (in the south of West Germany)
- urban county of Leipzig (in the centre of East Germany)
- urban county of Halle (in the centre of East Germany)
- rural county of Bitterfeld (in the centre of East Germany)
- rural county of Ücker-Randow (in the north of East Germany)
- rural county of Eichsfeld (in the south of East Germany)

The questionnaire contained an extended version of instruments already used in the family survey West Germany (1988 and 1994), the family survey East Germany (1990 and 1994), and some additional

Table 9.1 Social statistical indicators for the counties

	Raw birth rates[1]	Illegitimate births[2]	In higher education[3]	Unemployed[4]	Purchasing power[5]	Housing subsidy[6]	Welfare dependency[7]	Welfare under 7[8]
Hamburg	45	21.4 %	78.6 %	8.6 %	119.70	13.6 %	21.5 %	23 %
Regensburg	54	7.5 %	31.6 %	6.1 %	96.60	3.0 %	2.9 %	3 %
Leipzig	26	45.9 %	*	12.6 %	83.40	22.0 %	14.1 %	9 %
Halle	25	47.1 %	68.6 %	12.8 %	74.40	21.5 %	14.8 %	10 %
Bitterfeld	25	45.2 %	68.5 %	16.9 %	71.90	20.3 %	12.8 %	8 %
Ücker-Randow	23	49.1 %	67.6 %	25.2 %	58.25	20.3 %	10.5 %	5 %
Eichsfeld	33	13.7 %	31.2 %	16.9 %	64.85	21.8 %	4.6 %	3 %

The indicators for Ückermünde und Eichsfeld are means of the former counties Ückermünde and Pasewalck, and of Worbis and Heiligenstadt, respectively, before the regional reorganization in 1993.

*information not available.

[1]Births per 1000 women aged between 15 and 44 (1993)

[2]Births-out-of-wedlock per 100 births (1993)

[3]Percentage of secondary level students in *Realschulen*, *Gymasien*, *Waldorf schulen* and *Gesamtschulen* in the schooling period 1992–93

[4]Unemployment rate (1993)

[5]Purchasing power (1994) relative to the mean of the Federal Republic = 100

[6]Housing subsidy per 100 appartments

[7]Persons receiving permanent welfare subsidies (1993)

[8]Persons under the age of 7 years receiving permanent welfare subsidies (1993)

regional surveys in Bavaria (1989), East Germany (1993), and Leipzig, Erfurt and Worbis (1992), which included a detailed questionnaire for each child of the interviewed adults. For the following analysis, a data set was needed, in which the respective child is the statistical unit of analysis. Accordingly, a data set was generated according to following rules:

First, people were selected out of the 4.216 interviews, who stated that they had children of their own. This included all biological children, but also foster and adopted children, as well as step-children from a marriage or partnership, who were living in the same household with the interviewee. Subsequently, a data record was established for each named child with the information given by the parent, so that it was the particular child, rather than the parent, who represented the unit of analysis. In this respect, the parents, with their distinctive attitudes and values, were treated as part of the social context for the child, as were the child's brothers and sisters. Depending on the number of children, the same parent could be part of the social context for more than one child and was therefore included in the analysis more than once. Families with more than one child were thus weighted according to their quantitative importance in providing socialization opportunities. From this child related data set (N = 5.717) subsequently all minor children were selected. They form the empirical base of the following analyses (N = 1,882).

The empirical analysis was based on the following operationalizations of the theoretical constructs:

(1) The *parents' human capital* was measured by the level of schooling of the interviewed parent. The level of schooling itself was measured by the addition of the numbers of years necessary for the qualifications obtained in general education and vocational training (Blossfeld, 1989).

(2) The effects of *regional mobility* of the interviewed parent on the destruction of social capital in connection with the particular child was measured through a four-point index. The lowest value was given to the persons who had lived in the same place their whole life, followed by those who had moved before the birth of the target child for the last time, and then those, who had moved during the child's preschool time; the highest value was given to those for whom the last move took place after the child started school.

(3) Following Coleman the index of *intrafamilial social capital* was based on the availability of adult household members. The lowest value was given to household constellations with single parents; a

middle-value was given to constellations, where there were step- or foster-children in the household; the highest value was given to constellations with two biological parents, whether married or not. The basis of this operationalization was the assumption, that – because of the legal position of the step parent in Germany, social capital could not be accumulated from step- or fosterchild relations in the same way as it could from relations with biological parents.

(4) The *number of brothers and sisters* was determined by the number of children living together with the target child within one household.

(5) *The time available within the household* was recorded by a four-point index. Within households with single parents it was given the lowest value, if this person was gainfully employed for more than 25 hours a week. A respectively higher value was given, if he or she was employed between 10 and 25 hours, and up to 10 hours, respectively. The highest value was given, if he or she was not employed at all. For households with two adult people, corresponding values were assigned: if one of the parents was gainfully employed for at least 40 hours a week and the other for at least 25 hours, for between 10 and 25 hours respectively, and less than 10 hours (with an analogous scoring for the – very few – cases, where both parents were employed part-time); the highest value was also given to household constellations, where at least one parent was not employed.

(6) *Extrafamilial social capital* we attempted to operationalize theory as closely as possible by means of an ambitious network generator. For theoretical reasons the analysis was based exclusively on the social capital within kinship relations (Nauck and Kohlmann, 1998). According to Coleman's assumptions, social capital is highest in such relations, which are characterized by the highest possible spatial *availability*, by the highest frequency of *social contacts,* and by the multiplicity of *activities* (doing different things with the same person). As only kinship relations are considered, one can assume that high *density* is an additional characteristic of this relationship *closure* (network members not only interact with the respective parent, but maintain dense relationships with each other). According to this approach social capital consists of a product, i.e. the multiplication of the dimensions of network properties. These dimensions were captured in the following way. A named person was classified as being available if he or she was living in the immediate neighborhood; frequent contact was taken to be at least one interaction a week. Complex activities were recognized, if at least one expressive activity took place with this person (having a close personal bond, having meals together, spending spare time

together), and at least one instrumental activity (discussing personal things, giving or getting financial help). Accordingly, the family's social capital consisted of the sum of the products of 'availability', 'contacts', and 'activities' over all the people involved in the relationships and who were named as part of the individual's network.

(7) *Child Monitoring* was determined for all school age children negatively, when the respective child was 'yesterday' neither in an institution (visiting an institution such as day care, school, leisure centre and so on) nor personally cared for (by relatives or friends), but rather, was either 'caring for himself/herself', or the interviewed parent 'did not know where the child was'. This dichotomous measure indicated the threshold value of minimal control of the child's activities by its social context.

(8) As for the control of the child's activities, the economic support for the child was measured by a threshhold value, defined as 'relative *child poverty*'. Following standard procedures in poverty research, relative poverty was determined by the availability of less than 50 per cent of the household equivalent median income of a given population. The household equivalent income was weighed differently for children and adults in the respective household: the first adult person was weighted 100 per cent; every other household member over 16 years, 80 per cent; and every household member under 16, 50 per cent. Because of its regional limitations, the sample was inappropriate for the estimation of median income in East and West Germany. As an alternative, the respective household income medians were derived from separate calculations based on the family survey West and East (Joos and Nauck, 1998).

(9) The *health risks of children* were covered by a list of symptoms, presented to the parents of pre-school and school children in different form. The symptom list for pre-school children included language problems, wetting, skin diseases, asthma and frequent diarrhoea; for school children it comprised frequent appearances of headaches, dizziness, sleeplessness, stomach troubles, poor concentration, sickness, no appetite and sleeping difficulties. The threshhold value was reached if one symptom was named.

(10) In order to investigate the implications of the micro-model it was necessary to restrict the analysis to the educational achievements of children who were still at school, because for those who had already left, no information about (past) health risks and child monitoring was available. School achievement was measured in the following way. For primary school children it was based on information supplied by the

parents about whether the child enjoyed going to school, had no learning difficulties and had no examination fears; for secondary school children the respective school track was also included, e.g. the highest index points were given to those, who were having none of the named problems in the *Gymnasium*-track, and the lowest were given to those, having all of the named problems in the *Hauptschule*-track. The index was standardized for primary and secondary schools.

Intergenerational transmission of cultural capital within regional context

One possibilty for the empirical investigation of the effect of regional contexts on the intergenerational transmission of cultural capital is to analyse the micro-model separately for each context. If the theoretical assumptions hold, then there should not only be *level differences* between regions for the respective model-variables, but also clear differences in the *strength of correlations* within the causal-model. According to the theoretical assumptions about the effect of family oriented versus individualistic regional environments even *reversals in the direction*, i.e. (sign), of correlations are possible. An appropriate method for the empirical testing of causal models is multiple stepwise regression analysis. To keep the empirical results comparable the same statistical model (blockwise introduction of the predictors shown in Figure 9.1) was estimated separately for all regions, to compare the direction and the intensity of the effects between them (figures 9.2 to 9.6). As neither a bivariate analysis nor the regression analysis revealed significant differences for the three counties in central East Germany (Leipzig; Halle; Bitterfeld), they were combined into one regional sample in order to increase the stability of the results.

Clear differences are evident for the correlation between parental human capital and *regional mobility* for the two West German regions on the one hand and the three East German regions on the other. While there was no correlation between parents' educational level and parental mobility in East Germany (at least with regard to parents who *stayed* in these regions), in Regensburg (b = +.20) as well as in Hamburg (+.24) the expected positive correlation showed up. On the other hand, the more far-reaching assumptions about mobility hindering the effect on human capital transmission in corporate contexts, were not confirmed.

With regard to the formation of *intrafamilial social capital* a negative correlation with regional mobility occurred. This correlation was,

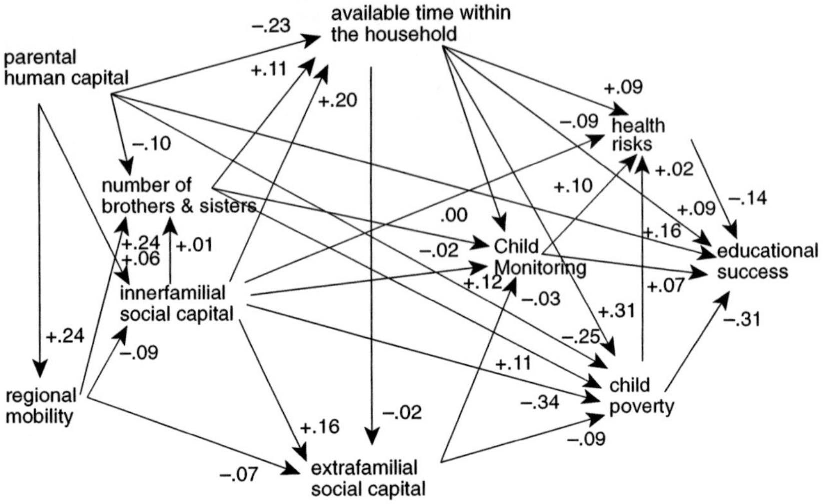

Figure 9.2 Intergenerative transmission of cultural capital: Hamburg

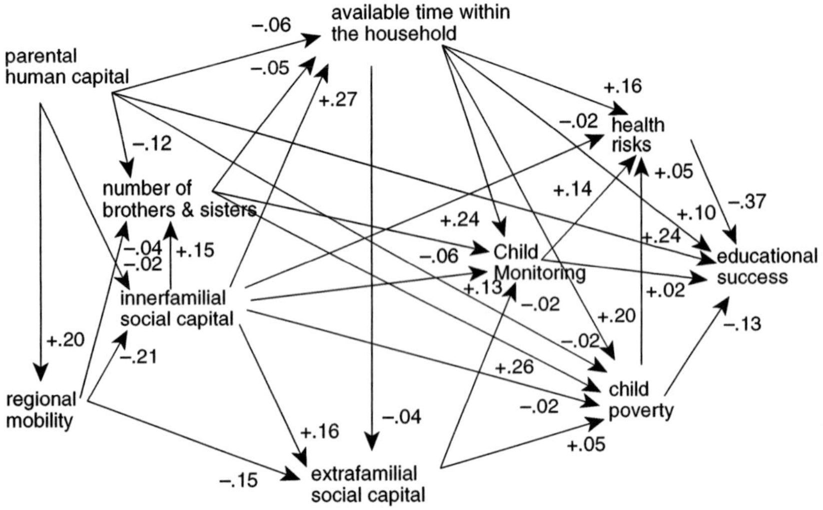

Figure 9.3 Intergenerative transmission of cultural capital: Regensburg

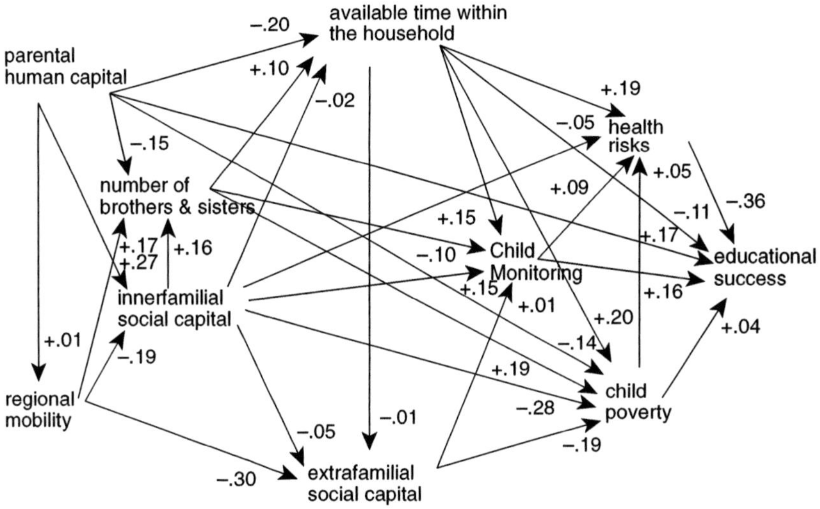

Figure 9.4 Intergenerative transmission of cultural capital: Ücker-Randow

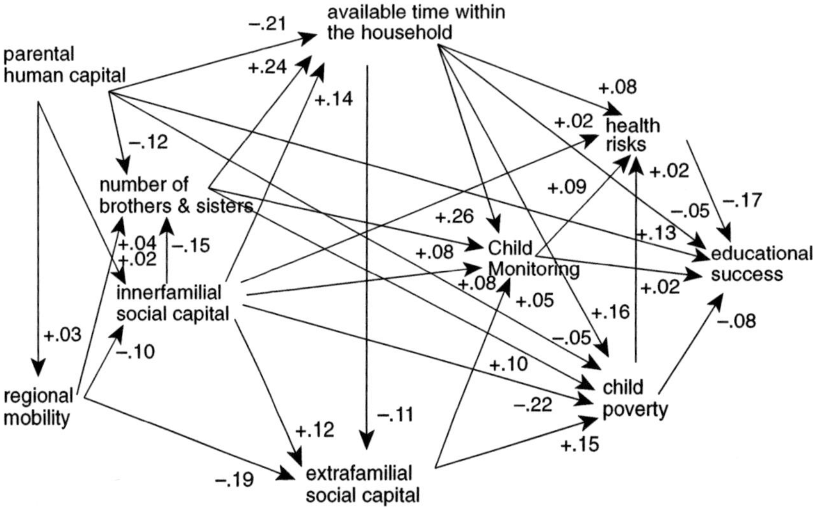

Figure 9.5 Intergenerative transmission of cultural capital: Halle, Leipzig, Bitterfeld

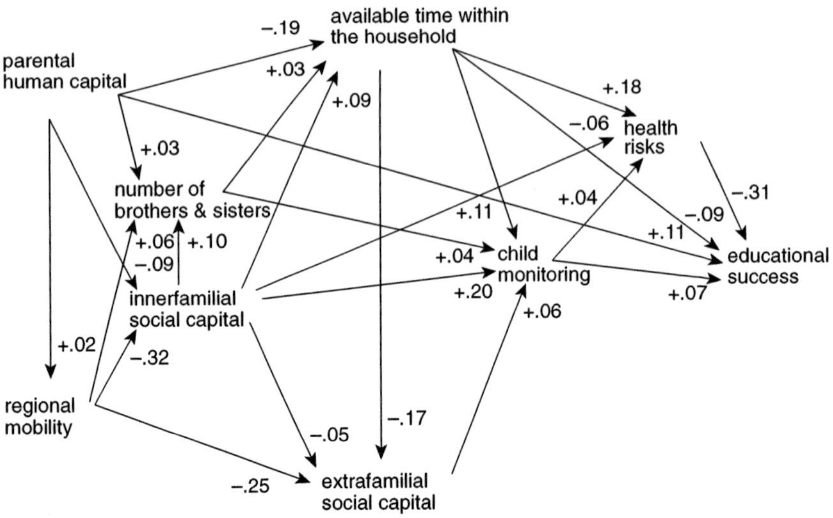

Figure 9.6 Intergenerative transmission of cultural capital: Eichsfeld

however, strongest within the corporate environments of the rural districts Regensburg (b = –.21) and Eichsfeld (–.32). At the same time, in these districts a weak *negative* correlation between parental human capital and intrafamilial social capital occurred, whereas in the individualistic districts the correlation was positive (Ücker-Randow: b = +.21).

Regional differences were large for the effects of the *number of brothers and sisters*; however, they turned out to be not very homogeneous and therefore did not conform to theoretical assumptions. The correlation between parental educational level and number of children was in fact generally negative, but the expected modification of the intermediate good, 'children', for a given level of human capital only showed up in Eichsfeld (b = +.03), not in Regensburg. The correlation between the number of brothers and sisters and regional mobility was clearly positive in the individualistic environments of northern Germany (Hamburg: b = +.24; Ücker-Randow: b = +.17) – which indicates a mobility related to the nuclear family, whereas this correlation was not given within the family oriented environments (Regensburg: b = –.04; Eichsfeld: b = +.06) and in central East Germany (+.04). The correlation between intrafamilial social capital and number of brothers and sisters was positive within the rural districts Eichsfeld (+.10), Regensburg (+.15) and Ücker-Randow (+.16) in contrast with the urban regions of northern and central Germany (Hamburg: b = +.01; Halle – Leipzig – Bitterfeld: b = –.15).

The correlation between parental human capital and the allocation of time for having children (as predicted by the New Home Economy) was generally negative. The expected modifications for family oriented regional cultures, with their higher evaluation of the intermediate good, 'child', were found only in Regensburg (b = +.06), not however in Eichsfeld (b = –.19). According to our theory, (many) children within individualistic environments act as a constraint on the employment of (both) parents. Actually, the correlation between the number of children and *the available time within the household* was strongest in Leipzig – Halle – Bitterfeld (b = +.24; Hamburg: b = +.11; Ücker-Randow: b = +.10), while such a correlation did not occur in Eichsfeld (b = +.03) and Regensburg (b = –.05). The relationship between parental social capital and the allocation of time for work (besides labour market opportunity effects) was especially strongly mediated through opportunity structures for institutional child care. Accordingly, the correlation was considerably lower in all regions of East Germany as compared to both West German regions Hamburg (b = +.20) and Regensburg (b = +.27).

Regional mobility appeared to destroy *extrafamilial social capital* in all regions. This effect was strongest in the rural regions of East Germany (Ücker-Randow: b = –.30; Eichsfeld: b = –.25) and weakest in the West German regions (Regensburg: b = –.15; Hamburg: b = –.07). On the other hand, in those West German regions, intrafamilial social capital clearly increased, as shown by the availability, contact frequency, and multiplicity of kinship relations. In contrast, in the rural regions of East Germany a substitution effect seemed to prevail, as single parents and step-families tended to use intense kinship relations more frequently than families with both biological parents. Surprisingly, in none of the districts was higher disposable time within the family household used to build or maintain extrafamilial social capital. Rather a substitution-relation seemed to exist (especially within the rural regions of East Germany). Kinship relations increased in importance (within families with children), if the parents' own time was scarce.

Contrary to Coleman's assumptions, in none of the regions was there a direct correlation between extrafamilial social capital and the *supervision and control of children* of school age. Such effects only appeared for the intrafamilial social capital and the disposable time for looking after children within the household. The extent to which this disposable time was really used to supervise the children, varied strongly, however, between the regions. The correlation was strongest within the 'family oriented' Regensburg (b = +.24) and weakest within the 'individualistic' Hamburg (.00).

Child poverty was related quite differently to parental human capital in the different regions. While the correlation was relatively strong within the north German regions Hamburg (b = –.25) and Ücker-Randow (b = –.14), this effect disappeared completely within the south German regions (in Eichsfeld no child poverty was found; accordingly, correlation-analyses were not applicable). The same was true for the correlation between intrafamilial social capital and child poverty. While it was the strongest predictor for child poverty in the county of Hamburg (b = –.34), Ücker-Randow (–.28) and Halle – Leipzig – Bitterfeld (–.22), this effect faded away in south Germany (Regensburg: b = –.02), and the number of brothers and sisters became the strongest predictor instead (b = +.26). Also the correlation between extrafamilial social capital and child poverty differed between the regions. While families with child poverty showed *reduced* contact with relatives in the north German regions (Hamburg (b = –.09) and Ücker-Randow (b = –.19)), this contact increased in Regensburg and Halle – Leipzig – Bitterfeld, i.e. economic deprivation and weakened social relations seemed to accumulate within individualistic environments, whereas poverty was compensated for by social capital within family oriented environments. A side effect of child poverty was that when it was the result of unemployment, this increased the available time within the household. (The only exception was Hamburg.)

Health risks of children had practically no endogenous causes in the model. Such risks neither depended to any noticeable extent on the household composition on the related intrafamilial social capital, nor did they increase with economic deprivation – the respective correlations were close to zero in all investigated regions. However, health-impaired children had perceptible consequences for household organization. They were supervised and controlled more rigorously than healthy children and they lived more frequently within households with at least one parent being mainly engaged with household tasks. This might signify two different things. First, in many cases, children's sickness was being responded to by a reduction in the working time (of mothers); secondly, despite the absence of any direct pointers to endogenous protective factors (social and economical capital of families) against health risks of children, it cannot be entirely ruled out that parental unemployment might have been increasing the health risks of the children.

Of decisive importance for the educational success of the child was his or her health status. Particularly in rural regions, poor health could lead to reduced educational chances (Regensburg: b = –.37; Ücker-Randow: b = –.36; Eichsfeld: b = –.31). Considerable regional differences occurred in the intergenerational transmission of cultural capital. While in Eichsfeld (b = +.11) and in Halle – Leipzig – Bitterfeld (b = +.13) the effect of educational inheritance was rather low, it became more apparent in Regensburg (with its retrictive educational opportunities) (b = +.24). The effect of child poverty on educational success was restricted to West Germany. Whereas in the East German regions economic deprivation did not reduce educational chances, it was of major importance in two West German regions, Regensburg (b = –.13) and especially Hamburg (b = –.31).

The remaining differences between Hamburg and Regensburg clarify the effects of individualistic versus family oriented environments. In Hamburg, lack of human capital on the part of parents immediately affected the economic resources of the family and increased directly the child's poverty risk. This in turn lowered his or her educational opportunities. In contrast, the direct effect of human capital on the poverty risk of the child was not apparent in Regensburg, nor was its effect on educational opportunities. Thus, in Regensburg a direct effect of parental human capital on the educational outcome was observed, whereas in Hamburg this effect was mediated by the poverty risk. *Against Coleman's propositions, therefore, the influence of social capital, as compared to the influence of cultural and economic capital on the child's educational success, remained rather low*. With little variations, neither the available time within the family (as potential support for the children in gaining educational qualifications), nor the actual supervision and control of the child, appeared to have any decisive influence on the child's educational success.

Discussion

This analysis was based on empirical data, which allowed a much more appropriate test of Coleman's theoretical propositions than was possible with the data which were available to Coleman himself. At the same time these data allow for a more precise model specification, including the interdependence of predictors in a stronger endogenized model, than was the case in Coleman's simple regression model. However, the empirical analysis was still affected by some theoretical and technical deficiencies, which demand more refinement. First, to keep the theoretical argument and empirical analysis relatively close to Coleman's initial propositions, the model incorporated some dichotomous predictors (child monitoring; health risks; child poverty). As these variables were dependent variables within stepwise multiple regression analyses, the statistical estimates lack robustness, because the size of the coefficients depended strongly on the marginal distributions of these variables. As these predictors targetted deviant conditions (lack of parental or institutional control, poor health, lack of economic provision), they had to be distributed obliquely, which increased the robustness problem even more. Secondly, a causal model based on the relations among constructs measured from cross-sectional data (as always) runs into problems, if the dynamics of the process have no equivalent within the model itself. The construction of an intergenerational transmission model demands on the one hand, that 'child outcomes' have to be ordered causally after the contextual conditions. On the other hand, as the presentation of the results has already made clear, 'child outcomes', at an early point in time, have significant repercussions on the situative-contextual conditions within the family. For example, a child's poor health can lead to alterations within the family's allocation of time. A more accurate modeling of such processes requires a different (longitudinal) data-structure.

The micro-model used here manages without such refinements, because its main aim was not to reproduce intergenerational transmission processes precisely, but to demonstrate empirically the impact of regional differences on these processes and how they relate to the use of social and cultural capital. If the theoretical assumptions are right, one can expect that *not only will regional differences be revealed in the statistical indices* (as is routinely done in social reporting and social ecology), *but that the correlations in the micro-model will also change systematically between regions.*

The comparative empirical analyses for the respective regions on the basis of the micro-model show that such correlation differences exist to a considerable extent. A number of correlations only occurred within special contexts. Moreover, in some specific cases, even a context specific reversal of effects was found. Within one society, with a very uniform institutional structure and a comparable high cultural conformity, this is an unlikely empirical result. It challenges many sociological models based on the stability of mechanisms in different social strata and cultural milieus.

The empirical results show in principle that the strength of the correlations varies in the theoretically expected way according to the differently distributed (institutional) opportunity structures for employment, educational qualifications and child care, and according to differently distributed family oriented versus individualistic family cultures. Nevertheless, the present results show no uniform tendencies, i.e. often effects could not be found for all the regions, for which they had been expected theoretically. But at present this can not be looked at as a severe challenge or refutation of the theoretical assumptions. This is because the design of the regional analysis imposes restrictions on the evaluation. Because of the relatively low number of urban and rural districts included in the analysis, a number of factors were confounded and, thus, could not be statistically controlled. Additionally, an exact matching of data to important theoretical dimensions of the analysis, for instance for urbanity and regional culture, was not possible. Thus West Germany is represented only by one urban metropolitan area in the north and one rural county in the south, and the relation between the Central German region of Halle – Leipzig – Bitterfeld and the other two rural counties of Ücker-Randow and Eichsfeld is questionable, too. Additionally, the characteristics of the regional contexts, which are important for the theoretically derived modification of the micro-model, were not measured directly. Therefore, all the conclusions relate only to the consistency of results for the hypothetically grouped counties (according to opportunity structures and regional family cultures). This makes further in-depth analyses necessary, controlling systematically for the mediating mechanisms of social contexts on the micro-model within a multi-level model. Such a multi-level model can make use of the results presented here in reducing the complexity of the micro-model. As the results have shown that *health risks* do not depend on any of the variables included in the model, this construct can be ignored in further analyses of the transmission of cultural capital.

Especially with regard to social capital the empirical analysis goes beyond Coleman's empirical work, as not only intrafamilial and extrafamilial capital were included simultaneously, but also the latter was measured very precisely within a network approach. However, a main result of this analysis is that – against Coleman's theory – the influence of social capital on the educational success of children was rather low, when compared to the influence of cultural and economic capital.

Is this result a refutation of Coleman's theory for the German case? Or are Coleman's contradictory conclusions from his own North American results to be taken as confirming further the institutional anchorage of intermediate goods in a particular social-cultural context? These questions can only be answered if we reformulate the problem into the different question: why is social capital of greater importance for the intergenerational transmission of cultural capital in the United States than in Germany? A covering explanation can embrace two factors, which have decisive impact on the use of social capital: the heterogeneity of cultural aims and the heterogeneity of institutional means. If the proposition is true that *the more the necessity for the use of social capital increases, the more heterogeneous the cultural aims and the institutional means are,* then the differences between both societies become more understandable. Germany (being the far more family-oriented social system) has, with its stratified uniform schooling system, and its system of governmentally controlled child care provisions, the more homogeneous institutional means. But it should also have, because of its very low ethnic differentiation, more homogeneous cultural aims, so that the *synergetic effects of social control of children become effective, even if no social capital exists or is used on the parents' part.* Accordingly, we have to assume that this effect should be (even) stronger in East Germany than in West Germany and it is plausible, that within such a homogeneous context members of the majority culture are far more successful in the intergenerational transmission of human capital than members of immigrant minorities (Nauck, Diefenbach and Petri, 1998). This effect of cultural heterogeneity has to be separated systematically from the institutional anchorage of social capital (and its legitimate use). It is plausible to assume a higher family mindedness in Germany, as compared to the United States. The analysis also indicates relatively small differences between south and north Germany. But the real test for the context dependent effects of cultural milieus on the relationships between elements of the micro-model would be a cross-cultural comparative research design. This would include societies with much clearer differences concerning the intermediate goods, 'children' and 'social capital', for welfare support. If the general assumptions are right, then the 'small' effects of difference in regional milieus should turn into 'big' reversals in the coefficients cross-culturally. This, in turn, should also have important theoretical consequences. The principles of the New Home Economy have to be reformulated within the framework of a general individualistic-structural theoretical model (Lindenberg, 1990).

References

Bauereiss, R., Bayer, H. and Bien, W. (1997) *Familien-Atlas II. Lebenslagen und Regionen in Deutschland. Karten und Zahlen.* Opladen: Leske & Budrich.

Becker, G. S. (1991) *A Treatise on the Family*, 2nd edn. Cambridge, MA/London: Harvard University Press.
Bertram, H. (1981) *Sozialstruktur und Sozialisation. Zur mikrosoziologischen Analyse von Chancenungleichheit.* Darmstadt/Neuwied: Luchterhand.
Bertram, H., Bayer, H. and Bauereiss, R. (1993) *Familien-Atlas: Lebenslagen und Regionen in Deutschland.* Opladen: Leske & Budrich.
Blossfeld, H. P. (1989) *Kohortendifferenzierung und Karriereprozess. Eine Längsschnittstudie über die Veränderung der Bildungs- und Berufschancen im Lebenslauf.* Frankfurt/New York: Campus.
Bourdieu, P. (1983) 'Ökonomisches Kapital, kulturelles Kapital, soziales Kapital', in R. Kreckel (ed.), *Soziale Ungleichheiten* (Vol. 2, Sonderband der Sozialen Welt, pp. 183–98). Göttingen: O. Schwartz.
Burr, W. R., Hill, R., Nye, F. I. and Reiss, I. L. (1979) "Metatheory and Diagramming Conventions', in W. R. Burr, R. Hill, F. I. Nye and I. L. Reiss (eds), *Contemporary Theories about the Family*, Vol. 1: *Research-Based Theories* (pp. 17–24). New York/London: Free Press.
Coleman, J. S. (1988) 'Social capital in the creation of human capital', *American Journal of Sociology*, **94** (Supplement 95): S95–S120.
Coleman, J. S. (1990) *Foundations of Social Theory.* Cambridge: Harvard University Press.
Diefenbach, H. and Nauck, B. (1997) 'Bildungsverhalten als "strategische Praxis": Ein Modell zur Erklärung der Reproduktion von Humankapital in Migrantenfamilien', in L. Pries (ed.), *Transnationale Migration*, Vol. 12: *Sonderband der Sozialen Welt* (pp. 277–91). Baden-Baden: Nomos.
Esser, H. (1985) 'Soziale Differenzierung als ungeplante Folge absichtsvollen Handelns: Der Fall der ethnischen Segmentation', *Zeitschrift für Soziologie*, **14**: 435–49.
Esser, H. (1988) 'Sozialökologische Stadtforschung und Mehr-Ebenen-Analyse', in J. Friedrichs (ed.), *Soziologische Stadtforschung*, Vol. 29: *Sonderheft der Kölner Zeitschrift für Soziologie und Sozialpsychologie* (pp. 35–55). Opladen: Westdeutscher.
Furstenberg, F. F. and Hughes, M. E. (1995) 'Social capital and successful development among at-risk youth', *Journal of Marriage and the Family*, **57**: 580–92.
Hullen, G. and Schulz, R. (1993) 'Bericht 1993 zur demographischen Lage in Deutschland', *Zeitschrift für Bevölkerungswissenschaft*, **19**: 3–70.
Joos, M. (1997) 'Armutsentwicklung und familiale Armutsrisiken von Kindern in den neuen und alten Bundesländern', in U. Otto (ed.), *Aufwachsen in Armut. Erfahrungswelten und soziale Lagen von Kindern armer Familien* (pp. 47–78). Opladen: Leske & Budrich.
Joos, M. and Nauck, B. (1998) 'Sozialberichterstattung und Kinderarmut in Ost- und Westdeutschland', in H. Oswald (ed.), *Socialisation und Entwicklunginden neuen Bundesländern*, Vol. 2: *Sonderheft der Zeitschrift für Sozialisationsforschung und Erziehungssoziologie* (pp. 248–64). Weinheim/München: Juventa.
Kalter, F. (1997) *Wohnortwechsel in Deutschland.* Opladen: Leske & Budrich.
Lindenberg, S. (1990) 'Rationalität und Kultur. Die verhaltenstheoretische Basis des Einflusses von Kultur auf Transaktionen', in H. Haferkamp (ed.), *Sozialstruktur und Kultur* (pp. 249–87). Frankfurt: Suhrkamp.
Nauck, B. (1993a) 'Regionale und sozialstrukturelle Differenzierung der Kindschaftsverhältnisse in Deutschland', *Zeitschrift für Pädagogik*, **39**: 353–69.

Nauck, B. (1993b) 'Sozialstrukturelle Differenzierung der Lebensbedingungen von Kindern in West- und Ostdeutschland', in M. Markefka and B. Nauck (eds), *Handbuch der Kindheitsforschung* (pp. 143–63). Neuwied: Luchterhand.

Nauck, B. (1995a) 'Regionale Milieus von Familien in Deutschland nach der politischen Vereinigung', in B. Nauck and C. Onnen-Isemann (eds), *Familie im Brennpunkt von Wissenschaft und Forschung* (pp. 91–122). Neuwied/Kriftel: Luchterhand.

Nauck, B. (1995b) 'Sozialräumliche Differenzierung der Lebensverhältnisse von Kindern in Deutschland', in W. Glatzer and H. H. Noll (eds), *Getrennt vereint. Lebensverhältnisse in Deutschland seit der Wiedervereinigung* (pp. 164–202). Frankfurt/New York: Campus.

Nauck, B. (1997) 'Sozialer Wandel, Migration und Familienbildung bei türkischen Frauen', in B. Nauck and U. Schönpflug (eds), *Familien in verschiedenen Kulturen* (pp. 162–99). Stuttgart: Enke.

Nauck, B., Diefenbach, H. and Petri, K. (1998) 'Intergenerationale Transmission von kulturellem Kapital unter Migrationsbedingungen: Zum Bildungserfolg von Kindern und Jugendlichen aus Migrantenfamilien in Deutschland', *Zeitschrift für Pädagogik*, **44**: 701–22.

Nauck, B. and Joos, M. (1996a) 'Kinderarmut in Ostdeutschland – zum Zusammenwirken von Institutionentransfer und familialer Lebensform im Transformationsprozess', in H. P. Buba and N. Schneider (eds), *Familie zwischen gesellschaftlicher Formung und individuellem Design* (pp. 165–81). Opladen: Westdeutscher.

Nauck, B. and Joos, M. (1996b) 'Wandel der familiären Lebensverhältnisse von Kindern in Ostdeutschland', in G. Trommsdorff (ed.), *Sozialisation und Entwicklung von Kindern vor und nach der Vereinigung* (pp. 243–98). Opladen: Leske & Budrich.

Nauck, B. and Kohlmann, A. (1998)'Verwandtschaft als soziales Kapital: Netzwerkbeziehungen in türkischen Migrantenfamilien', in M. Wagner and Y. Schütze (eds), *Verwandtschaft* (pp. 203–35). Stuttgart: Enke.

Nauck, B., Kohlmann, A. and Diefenbach, H. (1997) 'Familiäre Netzwerke, intergenerative Transmission und Assimilationsprozesse bei türkischen Migrantenfamilien', *Kölner Zeitschrift für Soziologie und Sozialpsychologie*, **49**: 477–99.

Strohmeier, K. P. and Schulze, H. J. (1995) 'Die Familienentwicklung der achtziger Jahre in Ost- und Westdeutschland im europäischen Kontext', in B. Nauck, N. Schneider and A. Tölke (eds), *Familie und Lebensverlauf im gesellschaftlichen Umbruch* (pp. 26–38). Stuttgart: Enke.

Teachman, J. D., Paasch, K. and Carver, K. (1996) 'Social capital and dropping out of school early', *Journal of Marriage and the Family*, **58**: 773–83.

Wagner, M. (1989) *Räumliche Mobilität im Lebensverlauf.* Stuttgart: Enke.

10
Continuities and breaks in occupational careers and subjective control: the case of the East German transformation

Martin Diewald

Introduction

The German unification process since 1989 has led to a massive restructuring of East German society and the economy. People in East Germany found themselves within a very short time in a radically changed societal order. The former certainties and security of the old system, as well as its hindrances and blockades, became obsolete, and new opportunities for action emerged. Quite suddenly, the East Germans had to cope with new, unfamiliar, living conditions; they had to abandon old ways of doing things and to invent new ones. 'Normal' expectations of continuity in the life course and everyday life were called into question.

In this chapter, I will deal with the topic of continuities and breaks in individual life courses by focusing on East German occupational careers before and after 1989. How were people re-located in the new labour market, and what impact did structural as well as individual factors have in this context? How well did competences acquired before 1989 fit the new requirements after 1989? What did this mean for continuities and discontinuities in East German occupational careers after 1989?

To study life course dynamics, I adopt the assumption that individual life courses are the product of the mutual interplay between societies and individual personalities. This is demonstrated in the next section of the chapter in two ways: the moulding of personalities by institutionalized life courses; the role of subjective control at the time of a societal break. These general theoretical arguments are then exemplified in the specific context of the East German transformation process, leading to hypotheses concerning its impact on the life course in the GDR, as well as the unique conditions of the transformation as pan-German unification. After describing the data base and methods available, empirical results about continuities and breaks in individual life courses and the role of subjective control are presented.

Life course dynamics, control cognitions and social change

Life course dynamics can be conceptualized as the interplay between societies and individual personalities (e.g., Elder and O'Rand, 1995, Kohn, 1989). The case of a rapid and far-reaching transformation of a society provides a unique opportunity to study the interplay between societies and personalities. Four aspects can be distinguished.

First, when the old institutions are abolished, or considerably reshaped, this leads automatically to a loss of relevance of former knowledge and patterns of behaviour. Much more than under stable conditions attributes like gender, vocational qualifications or occupational position reveal their character as social constructions. This is because they may mean something different under the new circumstances. People's resources, and the advantages and disadvantages linked to them, may change and therefore may force changes in people's perceptions and their perspectives on action. The aspects of the self which are incorporated into, or provided by, the previous life course, and its ascribed and achieved roles or positions, are therefore, more or less, called into question. Thus, even formal continuity (in the sense of life history spells) may, in reality, be discontinuity.

Secondly, prospects of upward and of downward moves are therefore stronger in times of transition than at times of stability. There are high risks of losses from former investments, but insofar as former constraints and barriers get weakened or abolished, there are potentially good prospects, too. The balance of opportunities and risks can be quite different between individuals and depends on resources accumulated beforehand, on personal competencies, and on the specific institutional rules and basic conditions of the transformation process.

Thirdly, because in the more open situation of a society undergoing transformation the chances of gains or losses are higher than in stable societies, the impact of motivation and subjective control should be higher, too. The more the former system blocked such subjective resources, the higher the impact should be. The new situation since 1989 is much more burdened with tasks of reorientation and coping from which people are normally protected by stable institutions. As Elder and Caspi (1990) have argued, 'accentuation' of individual inequalities is likely to occur in such a situation.

Fourthly, a factor having an impact on the extent of continuities and breaks is the degree to which both institutional systems – the 'society of origin' and the 'society of destination' – differ from one another with respect to the qualifications and skills required. The assumption of large-scale discontinuities assumes that these requirements are discrepant, but this is by no means necessarily the case.

The self as 'an originating agent seems crucial to the fundamental experience of self' (Gecas, 1982:17). Gurin and Brim (1984) define the striving for control as 'a central aspect of the self', and according to Inkeles (1983:38), is one of the core elements of modern individual identity. Rothbaum, Weisz, and Snyder (1982) even go so far as to refer to control as a quasi-anthropological need. Beliefs about control 'may be defined as a person's generalized expectancies that he or she is capable of producing intended outcomes. In contrast, beliefs about causality represent generalized expectancies that particular causes or conditions result in particular outcomes. Finally, beliefs about agency refer to generalized expectancies regarding the availability of the antecedent conditions to the particular agent' (Skinner, 1985:130). The enormous interest in control beliefs in psychological research is based on the hope of explaining and predicting actual behaviour and problem-solving. Control beliefs are a product of prior experiences in society as well as a psychological resource leading to more active and persistent problem solving behaviour when confronted with stresses. As learning theory suggests, this expectation should be confirmed mostly for unknown and ambiguous situations, where no situation-specific experiences and expectations are available.

The context of the East German transformation process

The GDR as a point of departure

'Unmodern' personalities formed by the 'unmodern' institutions of the GDR, are often seen as serious impediments to a successful transformation process in East Germany (e.g., Engler, 1993, Andretta and Baethge, 1995). The most criticized in this respect are what could be termed, in

Melvin Kohn's (1989) words, lags in 'occupational self-direction' and less developed occupation-oriented achievement strivings, conformism and traditionalism. There is a lack of personal autonomy, a low level of primary control, and a 'niche' mentality. In contrast, other authors state that there are also mentalities, dispositions and habits acquired under the specific circumstances in the GDR, which can now have potential for muddling through and building up a new, partly 'post-modern', service economy. These also fit into 'new production concepts' in industry, such as communitarian orientations, solidarity, communication abilities, and the ability to improvise creatively, combined with tenacity (e.g., Senghaas-Knobloch, 1992; Hradil, 1995). A third position, combining the two assumptions, asserts that there were different social milieus in the GDR characterized by different ways of behaving. These now underpin success and failure in response to the transformation process (Vester, Hofmann and Zierke, 1995).

The main debate in this field concerns the question of how deeply working life and occupational careers did indeed follow the autonomous logic ('Eigenlogik') of a highly differentiated, achievement-oriented and competence-oriented occupational system. Were they also steered or 'overridden' by the primacy of a political regime mainly interested in loyalty and equality (instead of achievement) in the labour market and in industrial relations? The more this political imperative applies, the more the class-specific and occupation-specific crucial distinction of 'differential opportunities for occupational self-direction' ('the use of initiative, thought, and independent judgement in work', Kohn et al., 1990), as in market societies, is supposed to disappear, or at least to level off, and the lower the general level of occupational self-direction should be. The following arguments to support this hypothesis can be found in the literature:

- The Party kept control over the means of production, so that even managers at a middle and a higher level (with the exception of the Party elite positions) had few opportunities to plan and decide actively. This was part of the monopoly of power and control in East German society which made all other differentiations more or less meaningless (cf. Adler, 1991).
- Due to a 'pampering of the working class' ('Hofierung der Arbeiterklasse', Lötsch, 1990) in the GDR, workers had much more control over their work than in market economies, and their relationship to supervisors and managers was less one of subordination than one of bargaining (Voskamp and Wittke, 1990; Rottenburg, 1992).

- For the same reason as above, the GDR had a more egalitarian distribution of material and cultural living conditions irrespective of occupational position or class membership (Meuschel, 1991; Geissler, 1993; Engler, 1993). Additionally, the comprehensive welfare state of the GDR provided an encompassing system of social security and subsidies. Incentives for achievement therefore should have been considerably lower.
- The daily hassles and conditions at work places were so demotivating that they led to a far-reaching withdrawal or disengagement from responsibilities and commitment to work and occupation itself.

Taken together, workplace and occupation, and especially the firm, seemed to play a major role in the lives and selves of people in the GDR, but it was not so much dedicated to the ethics of occupational commitment and performance as to work as 'the centre of daily life' (Voskamp and Wittke, 1990; Kohli 1994). Under such conditions, occupational upward mobility and higher occupational positions generally did not signal the same competences and orientations as in market economies: i.e. striving for achievement and internal subjective control. Thus it is argued by some authors that occupational mobility in the GDR was undertaken mainly for private, rather than for occupational or career, reasons (Andretta and Baethge, 1995; Grünert and Lutz, 1995). Mobility processes contradicting this picture – such as job shifts to obtain a more interesting job – were therefore the exception, not the rule.

There is, however, some counter-evidence:

- Differences in material rewards for different jobs were less pronounced than in market economies but still considerable enough to provide incentives for career development (Diewald and Solga, 1995).
- The 'underlife' (in the sense of Goffman, 1959) within firms, and the bargaining processes among the different levels of the firm's hierarchy, were not part of the formal occupational structure but were to some extent a quasi-institutional expression of the work ethic.
- The system of education and training in the GDR had a strong orientation towards occupational specialization, that is, to transmitting specific skills and identities, and it seemed to be quite successful in teaching competences like achievement motivation and responsibility (Lenhardt and Stock, 1997).

If one accepts especially the two last arguments, the problem in the GDR was not in the development of achievement orientation and the work ethic in its citizens, but the failure to transmit them into the formal institutions of the economy. As Bandura (1977) would argue, (former) feelings of futility may have resulted from low self-efficacy, arising from the perception of a system which was unresponsive to personal ambition. This leads us to expect that after 1989, there would have been a release of hitherto blocked subjective resources. This would especially be the case in an unstructured and chaotic transformation process where the competence to deal with institutional shortcomings, acquired in the GDR, might be helpful. The alternative view is more in line with a '*deficiency* hypothesis' concerning subjective resources and competences, i.e. that competences acquired and developed in extra-occupational contexts before 1989 would not have been transferable to the new occupational life after 1989.

Another aspect of occupational careers and positions in the GDR, largely independent of such considerations about personality influences, was the *devaluation of qualifications and occupational experiences* acquired before 1989. This is partly because of a different occupational system and partly because of different institutional embeddings for the same occupations. Such features should be especially relevant for technology-intensive occupations, where a lag between East and West existed (e.g., engineers, computer specialists), and for occupations based on specific knowledge about laws, the economy and administrative rules (e.g., economists, managers, lawyers). But most researchers claim a much more general devaluation. The reason is that the qualifications acquired, which were necessary in the state socialist economy of the GDR (whether in the processing industries, in administration, or in the service industries), were no longer useful because they were to a high degree system- and company-specific (Grünert and Lutz, 1995; Andretta and Baethge, 1995).

Compared with other societies, however, the system of training and education in the GDR and the FRG seem to be characterized by a high degree of commonality, both exhibiting a thoroughly elaborated segmentation according to various qualifications and technical fields (Diewald and Solga, 1996a). In general, this should make it easier for the GDR qualifications to serve as a resource in the transformation process and therefore ensure stable occupational careers. As Eyal, Szelenyi and Townsley (1997) have argued, cultural capital was an important source of power and privilege in communist societies and has become the dominant factor of stratification in post-communist societies.

Qualifications, however, not only accredit specific technical and professional knowledge in a narrow sense but also provide broader 'biographical portraits', including more general skills like achievement motivation, agency, responsibility, flexibility, styles of communication and the like. Such general skills are precisely the skills which were labelled as deficits of the GDR occupational system shortly after unification. On the other hand, the systems of training and education of the GDR receive quite good marks in this respect (Lenhardt and Stock, 1997).

Especially in hierarchical and authoritarian systems, indicators for individual engagement and development may be found *outside* institutional contexts like the occupational system and the economy, insofar as these formal contexts are supposed to block individual engagement and 'subjectivity' instead of integrating and developing it. For the GDR and socialist societies in general engagement in informal, practical networks, and the shadow economy, are primary examples of 'vents' for individual flexibility and creativity blocked in formal institutions. Such activities in informal networks, and the bargaining referred to earlier, within firms to improve personal working conditions and to overcome adverse conditions in the production process, were the basis of special skills for 'muddling through'.

Taken together, these arguments support the assumption that the individual life courses, incorporated competence and selves in the GDR, were not so uniform that they followed inevitably from macrosocial system imperatives, as was often the case in references to the systems of the GDR. Obviously, there was some leeway for different pathways of individual development, different strategies for coping with these system imperatives and pursuing one's own life goals, and therefore for different types of inclusion into the system (Huinink et al., 1995; Pollack, 1996; Engler, 1996; Mayer and Diewald, 1996). Such individual differences can serve as a starting point for examining successes and failures during the time after the wall came down.

The specific rules of the East German transformation as pan-German unification

The question of how these features become resources in the transformation process stems not only from interest in these individual 'heritages' stemming from the GDR period, but also from a concern with the *rules and mechanisms of the transformation* itself. I cannot deal here with all of these in detail but want to focus on two important arguments (see Mayer, Diewald and Solga, 1997 for a fuller account). The first is the legal, far-reaching acknowledgement of most vocational certification in the Unification Contract. This political decision was backed up culturally by the German tradition of a labour market segmented according to occupations (Diewald and Solga, 1996a), and should have facilitated the transfer of qualifications from the GDR labour market to that after 1989. Despite the arguments for a devaluation discussed above, failure and success with respect to inclusion and exclusion in the labour market after 1989, should therefore have been directed to a high degree by vocational qualifications, providing occupational continuity for many.

Secondly, the Unification Contract included at least one other provision presumably important for continuities and breaks in occupational careers after 1989. As a rule, people who were employed in the former state sector of the German Democratic Republic were transferred into the public service in the Federal Republic of Germany – excepting of course, the so-called 'x-sector' comprising former political functionaries and the secret service (*Staatssicherheit*). As a result, former state employees should have had higher chances of status continuity and employment compared to other employment groups.

Thirdly, non-certified capabilities should have become increasingly important in a transformation situation like the one after 1989 in East Germany. The legal framework of the Unification Contract enforced the equivalence of the GDR's educational and training qualifications with those of West Germany, providing an important prerequisite for continuity in occupation careers after 1989. Nevertheless, the necessary and sudden structural change of the East German economy led inevitably to a weakening of this principle. This is because it took time for new birth cohorts to emerge with the appropriate vocational training. Consequently, the economic change had to be managed with the cohorts already present in the labour market. Therefore, individual capabilities and orientations were more important than is the case in more stable economies, even in the later phases of careers, moving more responsibility and initiative to the individual. Pressures towards re-orientation were especially strong for the workforce in shrinking occupations. Incentives for such re-orientation combined with newly available jobs were particularly evident in the private service sectors. Personality characteristics emerging, such as *self-belief* and *control cognitions,* were probably crucial for seizing these new opportunities. It was just the type of situation where control beliefs should predict actual behaviour.

Data, operationalizations and methods

In the following analyses, I use data from the study 'Life Courses and Historic Change in the Former GDR', carried out at the Max Planck Institute for Human Development and Education. The main data collection took place between September 1991 and October 1992. Half of the interviews were completed by the end of 1991, that is, approximately two years after the historic events which together are referred to as the *Wende*. The random sample consisted of 2,323 people born in one of four birth cohorts (1929–31, 1939–41, 1951–53 and 1959–61) who, in October 1990, were living in what had up to then been the German Democratic Republic ('East Germany'). These 2,323 people were interviewed in detail about their life course. In the spring of 1993, a follow-up survey was conducted by mail in which 1,254 of the original participants took part (= 54 per cent of the original sample). The original respondents were also re-interviewed in 1996/97 for a second (or third) time using a combined (CAPI/CATI)[1] design, collecting, among other data, retrospective life histories since 1989. The present paper is based on the data on control beliefs collected in the follow-up postal survey, on working life mobility during the time of the GDR collected in the first interview, and working life mobility after 1989 collected in the follow-up postal survey (comparing the 1989 and the 1993 status positions) and in the 1996/97 panel (retrospective life histories).[1] The samples for the follow-up postal survey and the 1996/97 panel showed almost no biases compared to the original sample except for young males. For example, the unemployment rate in the follow-up sample corresponded almost perfectly to the official unemployment rates for the corresponding (national) birth cohorts.

Data on *control beliefs* were mainly collected with the help of the *CAMAQ–SV*, a shortened version of the CAMAQ (Control Agency Means–Ends in Adulthood Questionnaire, Heckhausen, 1991). The CAMAQ–SV contains a differentiated inquiry about control beliefs ('I can achieve goal X') , about means–ends beliefs ('means Y leads to goal X') and finally, about agency beliefs ('I have access to means Y, which may help me to reach goal X'). Means–ends beliefs and agency beliefs refer to the importance of, or access to, five conditional factors: effort, ability, happiness, personal relations and socio-economic conditions. The 1993 follow-up survey asked about all these beliefs as they related to working life. Additionally, two scales for *internal control* and *fatalism* were included in the first interview in 1991/92.

Although I refer to longitudinal data about life histories, data about control beliefs and control strategies are available only for one point in time, namely in spring 1993. Therefore there is no opportunity to disentangle empirically the influences of control cognitions on life course trajectories, as opposed to the impact of life course trajectories on control cognitions for working-life mobility up to 1993. Both causal directions are plausible. Therefore, the possible impact of control cognitions for employment trajectories is examined by combining the control cognitions collected in spring 1993 with the employment mobility data of the 1996/97 panel study. This ensures that control cognitions could influence only those trajectories which developed after May 1993. Up to now, 645 cases have been available with information from both the follow-up postal survey and the panel study from people who were still in the labour force. Following the same logic, the possible impact of internal control and fatalism is investigated only for employment trajectories after the date of the first wave interview: 934 such cases are available.

Results

Control cognitions in 1993 and life course during the GDR

What aspects of control cognitions carry over from the different occupational positions and mobility experiences during the time of the GDR and can therefore be seen as a legacy of the GDR? Because my main interest is limited to people who were still in the labour market after 1989, I look here only at the three younger birth cohorts of the sample. The oldest cohort had almost completely retired either by regular (women) or early (men) retirement during the first two years of the transformation process.[2] Results are not documented here in tables but will only be summarized from another article which focused on associations between the various dimensions of subjective control on the 'dependent' side of the model, and occupational status and occupational careers before and after 1989 on the 'independent' side.[3]

As for Western societies, people in higher occupational positions showed higher levels of primary control, and higher internal control beliefs, though many of the differences were quite small. It was remarkable that the highest level of tenacity was found among former managers at the middle and higher levels. They also had stronger means–ends and agency-beliefs with respect to effort and ability. In addition, they thought of themselves as having access to external conditions (socio-economic conditions and social connections). On the other side of the occupational hierarchy, people employed in unskilled positions in 1989 showed the lowest level of tenacity and slightly lower internal control beliefs than people in skilled occupations.

In summary, we find no empirical evidence that occupational careers in the GDR reflect differential subjective potential for control any more than in Western market societies. The barriers to mobility across different segments of the labour market enforced by different occupational levels may *not* have been weakened after 1989, refuting the assumption that GDR qualifications and occupational positions failed to reflect differences in subjective competences as assumed in a 'Western' occupational stratification.[4] Whether the differences are less pronounced in planned than in market economies, however, cannot be decided here.

Whereas these measures of success in occupational careers were positively linked to subjective control, indicators of informal practical network help and jobs on the side were not. This runs contrary to the expectation that informal activities and private life were the major spheres for releasing individual subjectivity and activity, and that occupational life and political participation did not provide opportunities for primary control strivings.[5] Similar associations were found with respect to occupational success *after* 1989. Upward mobility was linked with high primary control and high self-esteem; downward mobility and especially unemployment showed the opposite relationship. The control beliefs showed that the 'losers' were characterized mainly by external factors like bad luck, poor social connections, and adverse socioeconomic conditions. These were important but beyond the individual's control. The 'winners' were characterized by both external and internal factors: they believed in effort and ability as important for success (and believed that they had both). But they also said that they were lucky and had good connections.

Continuities and breaks in occupational careers after 1989

Given these results, further hypotheses concerning the impact of the former life course on continuity and discontinuity, failure and success after 1989 can be formulated as follows:

- Non-meritocratic prerequisites or advantages for occupational success in the GDR should have been comprehensively devalued. The prototypical example for such characteristics is former political loyalty as expressed by Party membership.
- Strong and permanent ties to a firm – as expressed by no or low inter-firm-mobility – should have weakened adaptability to the new

requirements and circumstances characterized, among other things, by the low stability of the former enterprises. Two factors are responsible for this. First, occupational skills linked to the needs of a specific firm are hard to sell in a labour market which is segmented primarily in terms of occupations. Second, prior experiences of moves from one firm to another might strengthen coping competences which are relevant in times of transition when the firms are unstable.
- People who, in the GDR, had pursued a lifestyle dedicated more to private, extra-occupational needs subsequently had poorer chances in the labour market and particularly high risks of unemployment.
- Old age was a disadvantage. The older people were, the more they were shaped by the now obsolete system of the GDR, the less time they had for successful coping, and the less were employers willing to invest in further education for them.
- Prior experiences of discontinuity and initiative in occupational careers should have developed competences which might be helpful in coping with new unexpected, non-routine situations like the transformation process.
- Subjective control in the form of tenacity and agency beliefs should have an impact, because such personality characteristics are especially important in turbulent times in avoiding losses and achieving gains. This impact, however, should be limited for two reasons. First, these characteristics are already partly incorporated into former occupational failure and success. Second, the Unification Contract provided strong structural forces which steered status maintenance and loss.

To give a comprehensive overview of occupational mobility in East Germany since 1989, I draw on six single logistic regression models of different labour market positions in 1993, as compared to the situation in 1989. In Table 10.1 four mutually exclusive alternatives of success and failure in the labour market are displayed: becoming unemployed, downward mobility, upward mobility, and – as a 'continuity expectation' – stability of occupational position. In Table 10.2, two further alternatives are dealt with: change of occupation, and becoming self-employed. These two are not additional or mutually exclusive alternatives to those in Table 10.3, but refer simply to other aspects of the 'continuity expectation'.

For each of these alternatives, I look at four types of explanatory factors:

- *Work-related, ascribed, and achieved assets*, which were considered to be important for occupational success as measured in 1989 before the Wall came down and which might change their significance after 1989: cohort membership and gender as ascribed characteristics, and former Party membership and network support in getting a job as achieved assets.
- *Several characteristics of occupational mobility in the GDR*. It is a little unclear what changes in occupation and shifts between firms really stand for: tenacity in goal achievement, flexibility in coping with structural opportunities and constraints, or simply experiences of discontinuity and resulting adaptation competences in working life. In any case, such experiences contradict the common presumption of immobility and a firm-related (and not career-centred) working life. Accumulation of capabilities should therefore signal capabilities which can be useful in times of societal transformation. More directly, the questions of job shifts due to private versus occupational factors and of self-initiated job shifts identify individuals who possessed or developed such orientations before 1989. They also differentiate between people who had a low versus a high job orientation, as well as people who were more active than others.

  The very detailed differentiation of different types of occupational mobility until 1989 reflects success and failure in occupational careers in the GDR. In such labour markets as East and West Germany, which are segmented along occupational lines and which rely to such a great extent on vocational qualifications, success and failure is likely to be defined in terms of the *highest* level of qualifications acquired. In addition, I distinguished between the different ways in which fits or discrepancies between level of qualification and level of occupation came about by compensating for: (a) initial employment below the level of qualification via upward mobility; (b) downward mobility after prior upward mobility and vice versa; (c) steady employment at the same level. This tells us something about the experiences of continuity and discontinuity before 1989, and whether difficulties in maintaining a job equivalent to the level of qualification acquired were being pursued against the odds.

  Whether respondents worked in 1989 in the public sector was also included, as this distinction defines at least a legal (if not a real) difference in job security after 1989 (as discussed earlier).
- Whether people were engaged in above-average levels of *informal economic activity* was included as an indicator for a possible shift of engagement and agency outside the formal economy.

- *Control cognitions*: This comprised clustering the 10-dimensional CAMAQ-items into three clusters: people who had overall comparably low values on all dimensions; people who had high ability and effort beliefs, both with respect to agency and causality, combined with much lower values for the three external dimensions of luck, personal connections, and socio-economic conditions; people with a high agency-ability belief but low causality beliefs for the three external dimensions.

In summary, the expectation is, that people who (a) had already shown self-initiative, (b) who had proven tenacity in pursuing occupational goals, (c) who did not withdraw into their private niche, (d) who did not simply stay where they were allocated, and who had already experienced instability before 1989, and (e) who believed in their abilities and efficacy were more successful after 1989 than the others. They were also better able to take advantage of the chances offered by the structural changes in the East German economy.

An initial look at successes and failures in occupational careers after 1989 reveals that roughly two thirds of the East German employees were able to keep their occupational positions during the first three-and-a-half years of the transformation process. Second, the presumed openness of the situation after 1989 was quite one-sided, at least with respect to occupational mobility. Upward mobility was considerably lower than downward mobility and even less than in West Germany (Table 10.1; see also Diewald and Solga, 1996c).[6] Downward mobility was roughly twice that of upward mobility, and the amount of unemployment even exceeded that of downward mobility, rising from zero to about 17 per cent. This points to a clear-cut polarization of opportunities in the labour market.

Which factors are responsible for belonging to one or the other group? Logistic regression was used to assess the likelihood of people in different categories succeeding or failing in the new labour market. The odds ratios displayed in Table 10.1 can be interpreted as decreases or increases of the risk in a particular category compared with the reference category. A value of 1 means no difference. For example, the odds ratio for unemployment for the cohort 1959–61 shown in Table 10.1 is .43. It means that the risk of being unemployed in 1993 was 57 per cent lower among people born between 1959 and 1961 compared to the risk of being unemployed among people born between 1939 and 1941.

Obviously, *gender* and *age* are two of the sharpest criteria for inclusion and exclusion in the labour market. Women face a higher risk of

Table 10.1 Success and failure in occupational careers after 1989[1]

1993 compared to 1989: (Percent of sample)	Unemployed (17%)	Downward mobility (13%)	Upward mobility (7%)	Stability of occupational position (63%)
Cohort (Ref. cat: 1939–41)				
1951–53	.72	**.45**	.58	**2.18**
1959–61	**.43**	.68	1.20	**2.17**
Gender: female	2.48	1.69	.40	.55
WORKING LIFE UNTIL 1989				
Occupational mobility compared to level of qualification				
Upward mobile	1.15	**9.08**	.60	.86
Upward mobile with former experiences of downward mobility	**.21**	**8.40**	**3.12**	1.23
No upward, no downward mobility	Ref. Cat.	Ref. Cat.	Ref. Cat.	Ref. Cat.
Equivalence by making up former employment below level of qualif.	**1.88**	1.50	**2.41**	.68
Equivalence by downward mobiliy following former upward mobility	1.25	.85	**4.63**	.79
Always empl. below level of qualif.	**.51**	.66	**3.60**	**.68**
Below level of qualification after downward mobility	**2.03**	**.10**	**7.56**	**.59**
Self-employed	**.26**	.90	**.17**	**2.21**
Change of occupational field	**1.95**	1.67	1.04	**.55**
Self-initiated job shifts (n)	**1.16**	.88	1.19	1.04
Job shifts between firms				
Less than average	.88	1.01	.68	.79
More than average	.80	.98	1.41	1.22

Continued on next page

Table 10.1 Continued

1993 compared to 1989: (Percent of sample)	Unemployed (17%)	Downward mobility (13%)	Upward mobility (7%)	Stability of occupational position (63%)
Job orientation: Career vs. private				
Clearly career oriented	1.01	.68	1.23	1.13
Clearly oriented to private life	**2.05**	.77	**.31**	.83
Often got a job by informal networks	1.17	.96	**1.53**	1.11
Informal economic support among colleagues above average	**1.51**	.84	1.21	1.27
Employed in public sector in 1989	**.38**	1.24	.63	**2.83**
Informal economic support among kin and non-kin outside workplace	.98	1.00	1.02	1.09
Party membership in 1989	1.04	**2.57**	.95	**.60**

[1]Figures in table are multiple logistic regression odds ratios. Bold coefficients are significant at least at 10 per cent-level.

unemployment and of downward mobility, leading to a lower chance of stability of occupational position, and they have only half the chances of upward mobility compared to men. Though women did not have equal career chances during the times of the GDR, their situation subsequently was different. Looking at the different birth cohorts, the most striking difference is between those born around 1940 and the other two cohorts. The disadvantages of age appear to have overridden the advantages of the longer investment in an occupational career. The youngest cohort in our study, i.e. those born around 1960, had the *lowest risk* of unemployment. Compared with the cohort which was eight years older, the youngest cohort had a slightly higher risk of downward mobility but much better chances of upward mobility.

An important personal asset associated with occupational success in the GDR was found to be a liability in the post-unification labour market: former *Party membership* did not lead to a higher risk of unemployment, but to it did lead to twice the risk of downward mobility. This turned out to be particularly true for the former managers but also for other occupations.

Occupational career and working life until 1989 appear to have had a strong impact on failures and successes, or continuities and discontinuities after 1989, but they are difficult to interpret in terms of personal (agency) versus structural factors. Structural forces should be responsible for the fact that the former self-employed and the public sector employees were best able to avoid the risk of unemployment. Also, coefficients for stability of occupational position before and after 1989 stress the significance of the public sector as a domain of *relative* employment security (it was still less than in West Germany; see Diewald and Solga, 1996c). It provided by far the highest stability of occupational position. On the other hand, it also offered by far the smallest window for upward mobility.

Secondly, the 'shape' of the former occupational career seems sometimes to have had contradictory impacts on the career after 1989. People who had worked in positions below their level of qualification (who were mainly people in unskilled positions) now had lower chances of status continuity. Those who had reached their position by downward mobility did not face a higher risk of downward mobility, but they were at a greater risk of unemployment. People who worked below their level of qualification from the beginning, however, had a significantly lower risk of unemployment. I will return to this distinction later.

Against initial expectations, upward and downward mobility before 1989 did not continue *after* 1989 but were 'reversed'. This could be primarily due to 'floor' and 'ceiling' effects. But why does upward mobility before 1989 imply a higher risk of downward mobility after 1989, and downward mobility before 1989 imply a higher chance of upward mobility after 1989? The explanation for this, apparently, strange result becomes quite clear after a closer look at the data. The former upwardly mobile and now downwardly mobile were driven back to the occupational level which fitted their qualifications. The same was true for the people who were downwardly mobile before 1989 and were upwardly mobile since. This latter effect, however, was primarily caused by a single group and was therefore not generalizable: people with vocational training who worked in quite well-paid unskilled level positions moved into skilled level positions after 1989. This effect *does not* reflect a general opening of formerly restricted career opportunities but rather, in German terms, a return to the level of occupation in a special segment, which fitted their qualification level.

The explanation for this result is perhaps that occupational certificates were the preferred method for reducing uncertainty in the reallocation of people to jobs after the Wall came down. This overrode doubts about the equivalence of qualifications between East and West Germany and the content and character of individual occupational training programmes. The political decision to recognize the educational system of the GDR in the Unification Contract is crucial in this respect and is culturally embedded in the East *and* West German tradition of a labour market segmented on occupational lines. This decision prevailed despite some well-known exceptions in law and business administration. Even for these professions, detailed analyses show a surprisingly high level of occupational stability. But due to the small number of cases for such specific occupational groups, this is only a preliminary impression.

The interpretation offered here is additionally supported by the fact that people who changed their occupations during the GDR had a considerably higher risk of unemployment and a lower probability of keeping their occupational positions. Shifts between firms (within the same occupation), however, had no impact on the risks or chances of subsequent success. This result is contrary to the expectation that job immobility, favouring a firm-centred career in the GDR, led to reduced chances for externalizing occupational skills in a new labour market which was no longer segmented in the same way.

The interpretations offered up to now all point to the importance of structural forces driving occupational careers after 1989. The patterns of occupational mobility also hint, however, at individual or agency factors. Relative to 'stable' careers – where in Germany the level of employment always corresponds to the qualification level without upward or downward mobility, or with upward mobility – former experience of discontinuities, disappointments, and difficulties seemed to lead to higher discontinuities after 1989 as well. This was true for opportunities as well as for risks. Cautiously, we can conclude that the individual's employment behaviour shows continuity before and after 1989. On the other hand, the 'result' of the behaviour, in terms of employment outcome, appears to have been dependent on the respective *fit* between the individual and the prevailing structural opportunities and constraints.

More directly, both the reasons for, and the initiation of, job moves before 1989 reflect individual orientations and competences. Job moves, due primarily to private motivations, can be regarded as indicators of a job orientation which was not career-oriented. 43 per cent of our respondents reported having had such job moves (81 per cent women and 19 per cent men). As might be expected, these individuals faced *double* the risk of unemployment post-1989, but not of downward mobility. They also had smaller chances for upward mobility. However, we did not find any evidence for the expected impact of personal initiative. Astonishingly, it was even (weakly) connected with a *higher* (and not lower) risk of unemployment.

Against some of the expectations discussed earlier, a higher engagement in informal practical activity inside and outside the formal work environment, in the period of the GDR, did *not* emerge as an asset. There was no sign of generalized skills or an ability to 'muddle through', which could be transferred to the work sphere or which were of help in mastering the new employment requirements after the wall came down. One exception was informal networks, which were helpful in getting a job *before* 1989. They were not generally helpful in defying the odds of failure in the transformation of the labour market, but seemed to be important in some of the relatively few cases of upward mobility that we observed.

To summarize, most of the observable labour market processes seemed to be the outcome of a few far-reaching institutional arrangements: acknowledgement of the old occupational credentials leading to status maintenance for the majority at the cost of gender discrimination and early retirement. In this perspective, the transformation process does not look like a very open or chaotic situation, in which a reassessment of individual competences led to dramatic re-locations.

The different successes and failures we have examined might not have sufficiently taken into account the significance of the various institutional contexts discussed in section 3, especially the role of structural change in the East German economy. They are therefore not very sensitive to the question of structural versus personal impacts. In Table 10.2, I draw on two types of occupational shift which represent this structural change: changes in the type of occupation and moves into self-employment. Both of these signal the need for considerable flexibility in staying in the labour force and seizing the chances offered by the new circumstances, which often means changing from a non-service to a service occupation (Diewald and Solga, 1996b). This meant a comparably higher risk of downward mobility (23 per cent compared to an average of 16 per cent among those still employed in 1993) and comparably higher chances for upward mobility (14 per cent compared to an average of 8 per cent among those still employed in 1993) as well. Both types of occupational shift should have been especially sensitive to the impact of specific individual competences because they were governed much less by formal rules than were the usual career tracks such as those in the public sector.

Apparently, both types of occupational shift predominantly affected males. Beyond this, changes of occupational field were not only simply imposed by structural forces, but seemed to be made mainly by people who had already taken this decision before 1989. More generally they were shown by people who had not followed a career exactly at their level of qualification without ups or downs before 1989. One might say that shifts between occupations after 1989 show a 'homotypic' continuity of behaviour before 1989. Experience of occupation moves in the GDR appears to have been good preparation for searching for new opportunities outside the previous occupational field. Although it cannot be decided here, it seems plausible that such experiences represent the ability to adjust flexibly to institutional failures and to muddle through outside the usual standard pathways. On the other hand, those who had oriented their occupational life more according to *private* needs during the GDR were not the people who seized the opportunities offered by the structural change after 1989.

For the second type, *moves into self-employment*, I have to be cautious in making far-reaching interpretations because it is a very heterogeneous group and consists of only 31 cases in our sample. Contradicting the findings for occupational changes, the previous shape of the occupational career seemed to be more or less unimportant, apart from the fact that former employees of the public sector rarely chose (or had to chose)

Table 10.2 Change of occupation and self-employment after 1989[1]

1993 compared to 1989:	Change of occupational field (34% of sample)	Getting self-employed (4% of sample)
Cohort (Ref. cat: 1939–41)		
1951–53	1.18	1.43
1959–61	1.17	**1.95**
Gender: female	.40	.19
WORKING LIFE UNTIL 1989		
Occupational mobility compared to level of qualification		
Upward mobile	1.54	.59
Upward mobile with former experiences of downward mobility	**2.76**	.77
No upward, no downward mobility	Ref. Cat.	Ref. Cat.
Equivalence by making up former employment below level of qualif.	**2.98**	.45
Equivalence by downward mobiliy following former upward mobility	**2.39**	1.73
Always empl. below level of qualif.	**1.98**	1.28
Below level of qualification after downward mobility	1.41	.78
Self-employed	**4.21**	–

Continued on next page

Table 10.2 Continued

1993 compared to 1989:	Change of occupational field (34% of sample)	Getting self-employed (4% of sample)
Change of occupational field	**2.19**	**.49**
Self-initiated job shifts (n)	1.04	1.16
Job shifts between firms		
Less than average	.79	.88
More than average	.92	1.05
Job orientation: Career vs. private		
Clearly career oriented	1.13	**3.15**
Clearly oriented to private life	**.53**	**2.49**
Often got a job by informal networks	1.11	**2.45**
Informal economic support among colleagues above average	1.27	**1.55**
Employed in public sector in 1989	.83	**.43**
Informal economic support among kin and non-kin outside workplace	1.02	1.01
Party membership in 1989	1.04	**2.32**

[1]Figures in table are odds ratios. Bold coefficients are significant at least at 10 per cent-level.

this means of staying in the labour force. However, this relatively small group shows a very multifaceted mix of devaluations of former resources and the use of specific personal resources as driving the change. The alternative of being self-employed attracted those who had been clearly career-oriented. Informal instrumental networks were obviously also important for taking on the risk associated with this strategy. On the other hand, it also attracted people who had been clearly oriented towards private needs outside the job, and former Party members who had lost an important career asset. In the former case, self-employment may mean seizing new chances, while in the latter case it may be perceived as a last resort for avoiding unemployment.

Control cognitions and the question of continuity in occupational careers

The focus now moves on to the question of whether inequalities in control cognitions were important for the various trajectories *in addition* to the factors already described in the previous section. In contrast with the previous section, however, we now include only trajectories which developed *after* the measurement of the control cognitions. Therefore, we cannot exclude the possibility that during the very first years of the transition period, such cognitions played another role to that played during the observation period. Due to limitations of space, only the coefficients for the control cognitions are presented. Because there were very few examples of shifts into self-employment, they were excluded from the analyses (see Table 10.3). As for the odds ratios from the logistic regressions, the coefficients displayed in Table 10.3 can be interpreted as per cent increase in rates for a given covariate (values above 1) or per cent decrease, respectively (values below 1).

We can see that control cognitions played an important role in resistance to unemployment following unification and taking up the new opportunities offered. However, they had no significant effect on upward and downward mobility. In view of the overwhelming impact of legislative and other rules following unification, the latter is what we might expect. It is more surprising that these cognitions had such an impact on unemployment and participation in the process of occupational restructuring. From the clusters of agency and causality beliefs as well as the two scales, how the individual perceived the 'responsiveness' of the social environment seemed to be particularly important. Belief in one's own abilities was insufficient. Taken together, the impact of the various control cognitions suggests that the situation in East Germany was not so closed that an individual could not play a

Table 10.3 Change, success and failure in occupational careers after 1989[1]: the impact of control cognitions

1993 compared to 1989: (Number of events)	Unemployment[2] (167)	Downward mobility[3] (53)	Upward mobility[4] (32)	Change of occupational field[5] (89)
Internal control scale (1991/92)	.87	.96	1.14	.93
Fatalism scale (1991/92)	**1.43**	.76	.89	**.71**
Work-related agency and causality beliefs (1993): Cluster				
(1) Reference: overall low values	Ref.	Ref.	Ref.	Ref.
(2) High ability-agency + high causality of luck, connections and socio-economic conditions	**2.21**	.87	1.11	.75
(3) High ability and effort beliefs, both agency and causality	.63	.97	1.44	**2.42**

[1]Figures in table are coefficients from Cox regressions on the first transition after the measurement of control cognitions, showing the effects of covarieties. Additional factors controlled for: All indicators included in Tables 10.1 and 10.2. Bold coefficients are significant at least at 10 per cent-level.
[2]The competing risks of downward and upward mobility are censored.
[3]The competing risks of unemployment and upward mobility are censored.
[4]The competing risks of unemployment and downward mobility are censored.
[5]First transition into new occupational field, competing risk of unemployment censored.

significant role in the labour market re-location after 1989. This was obviously not always the case, but only when structural change threatened the previous work place and enforced the alternatives of becoming unemployed or finding a new work place and occupation.

Conclusions

Overall, a comprehensive assessment of the transformation of the East German labour market is difficult. On the one hand, it seems to have been much more structured by rigidities in the occupational system and legal regulations than the presumption of an open situation would have us believe. The correspondences between the occupational systems of the GDR and the FRG seem to be a crucial factor in making the devaluation of former investments and qualifications selective, rather than a mass phenomenon – at least with respect to the redistribution of the work force within the new occupational system. It is not surprising, therefore, that control cognitions, which should be especially helpful in a situation of sudden change, were not decisive for status mobility. The price of that relative stability for many was a partial exclusion of women from gainful employment and an almost total exclusion of those who were older than 55 in 1990 (Mayer, Diewald and Solga, 1996). Particularly noteworthy was the high risk of *downward mobility* for former party and *nomenclatura* members: though they faced no higher risk of unemployment. This makes the East German transformation different from that of all other ex-socialist countries. In these countries, the members of the Communist Party and members of the old *nomenclatura* were much more successful in transferring their privileges into the new system. That points to the one major specific feature of the East German transformation, namely that it was and still is regulated by external (West Germany) instead of endogenous forces. Also, the transfer of elites was mainly from West to East Germany.

This conclusion should not be taken to mean that personality characteristics and individual life courses were unimportant in the processes of labour market reallocation and structural change. There were not only continuities in occupational careers, reflecting occupational segmentation, but also continuities in individual labour market behaviour. People who had left the pathway of a career within the boundaries of a single occupational field, for which they were already qualified before 1989, were much more likely to do so after 1989 as well. The criteria for getting jobs in new occupational areas and seizing the rare chances for upward mobility obviously relied on personal experiences and competencies which had been acquired and learned after leaving well-trodden pathways. On the other hand, the impact of activities outside the work sphere had little impact after 1989 compared with the overall shape of the occupational career before 1989. This leads to the conclusion that only competencies acquired within the work sphere were fruitful in forming a career after 1989. However, the similarities between the GDR and the FRG systems of training for occupations described above were probably also important factors.

Two aspects of the transformation need to be highlighted in this context. First, there was a considerable amount of within-cohort occupational mobility after 1989, irrespective of the well-known rigidities of the German systems of education and vocational training. Changes in occupation were considerably more frequent during the first three years of the transformation than in West Germany during the same time. They were also more frequent than in Poland – another country in transition (Diewald and Mach, 1998). Second, the 'need' on the part of employers for occupational flexibility could draw on a considerable wealth of personal initiatives and occupational changes during the time of the GDR. This fact is often forgotten in the macrosocial descriptions of the overall inertia in the final phase of the socialist GDR.

Compared with the low impact of subjective control on status mobility in relation to the issue of exclusion versus flexible engagement with the labour market, control cognitions come into the frame. It should not be forgotten that the part of the labour market where this flexibility applied most was not the largest. The public sector was bigger, but its existence was nevertheless crucial for the fast accommodation, not to say modernization, of the East German occupational structure to Western standards.

Notes

1. CAPI = computer aided personal interviewing; CATI = computer aided telephone interviewing.
2. For a more detailed and cohort-specific analysis of life histories, age, action control beliefs, developmental regulation, and self-esteem see Diewald, Huinink and Heckhausen, 1996.
3. Other factors included in the models for which the results are not displayed here are party membership in 1989, intergenerational mobility before 1989, whether respondents grew up with father or not, and sex (for detailed results see Diewald, Huinink and Heckhausen, 1996).

4. Similar results are reported by Kohn et al. (1990) in a comparison of the USA and Poland.
5. These results fit very well with another observation made in the context of this research. Former Party members and functionaries, when asked whether you could achieve your own goals in the GDR to a high degree, replied in the affirmative, whereas people especially engaged in informal practical networks help and activities in the shadow economy denied that you could (Diewald, 1995:234).
6. In Diewald and Solga (1996c) these results were confirmed by further analyses with the data of the GSOEP (German Socioeconomic Panel Study).

References

Adler, F. (1991) 'Soziale Umbrüche', in Rolf Reissig, Gert-Joachim Glaessner (eds) *Das Ende eines Experiments* (pp. 174–218). Berlin: Dietz.

Andretta, G. and Baethge, M. (1995) 'Zur Analyse beruflicher Transformation in den neuen Bundesländern. Bezugspunkte für eine Suchstrategie zur Interpretation empiricher Daten', paper presented at the SOFI colloquium.

Bandura, A. (1977) 'Self-efficacy: toward a unifying theory of behavioral change', *Psychological Review*, **84**: 191–215.

Diewald, M. and Mach, B. (1998) *Different Pathways to Transition? Occupational Changes and Earnings Mobility in East Germany During the First Five Years of Transition* (unpublished manuscript).

Diewald, M. and Solga, H. (1996a) 'Ordnung im Umbruch? Strukturwandel, berufliche Mobilität und Stabilität im Transformationsprozess', in Lars Clausen (ed.), *Gesellschaften im Umbruch. Verhandlungen des 27. Kongresses der Deutschen Gesellschaft für Soziologie.* Frankfurt am Main: Campus.

Diewald, M. and Solga, H. (1995) 'Soziale Ungleichkeiten in der DDR: Die feinen aber deutlichen Unterschiede am Vorabend der Wende', in J. Huinink, K. U. Mayer, M. Diewald, H. Solga and A. Sorensen (eds) *Kollectiv und Eigensium. Lebensverläufe in der DDR und danach.* Berlin: Akademie Verlag.

Diewald, M. and Solga, H. (1996b) 'Nach dem Sturm folgt zwar die Ruhe, jedoch nicht der Sonnenschein! Mobilitätsprozesse und Allokationskriterien auf dem ostdeutschen Arbeitsmarkt nach 1989', in *Final report of the Research Group II of the KSPW on Soziale Ungleichheit und Sozialpolitik.* Opladen: Leske & Budrich.

Diewald, M. and Solga, H. (1996c) 'Differenz oder Angleichung? Ein Vergleich beruflicher Mobilitätsprozesse in West- und Ostdeutschland seit 1990', paper presented to the Sektion Soziale Ungleichheit und Sozialstrukturanalyse, 28th Congress of the German Society of Sociology, Dresden.

Diewald, M., Huinink, J. and Heckhausen, J. (1996) 'Lebensverläufe und Persönlichkeitsentwicklung im gesellschaftlichen Umbruch: Kohortenschicksale und Kontrollverhalten', in *Ostdeutschland nach der Wende. Kölner Zeitschrift für Soziologie und Sozialpsychologie*, **2**: 219–48.

Elder, G. A. and Caspi, A. (1990) 'Persönliche Entwicklung und sozialer Wandel', in K. U. Mayer (ed.), *Lebensverläufe und sozialer Wandel*, special issue of the *Kölner Zeitschrift für Soziologie und Sozialpsychologie*: S22–S57 Opladen: Westdeutscher.

Elder, G. H. and O'Rand, A. M. (1995) 'Adult lives in a changing society', in K. S. Cook, G. A. Fine and J. S. House (eds), *Sociological Perspectives on Social Psychology* (pp. 452–75). Boston, MA: Allen & Bacon.
Engler, W. (1993) *Die zivilisatorische Lücke*. Frankfurt am Main: Suhrkamp.
Engler, W. (1996) '"Kommode Diktatur" oder "totalitäres System"'? in Enquete-Kommission des 12 Bundestages (ed.), 'Aufarbeitung von Geschichte und Folgen der SED-Diktatur in Deutschland', *Soziologische Revue*, **19**: 443–9.
Eyal, G., Szelenyi, I. and Townsley, E. (1997) 'The theory of post-communist managerialism', *New Left Review*, **222**: 60–92.
Gecas, V. (1982) 'The self-concept', *Annual Review of Sociology*, **8**: 1–33.
Geissler, R. (1993) 'Sozialer Umbruch als Modernisierung', in R. Geissler (ed.), *Sozialer Umbruch in Ostdeutschland* (pp. 63–91). Opladen: Leske & Budrich.
Goffman, E. (1959) *The Presentation of Self in Everyday Life*. New York: Doubleday.
Grünert, H. and Lutz, B. (1995) 'East German labour market in transition: segmentation and increasing disparity', *Industrial Relations Journal*, **26**: 19–31.
Gurin, P. and Brim, O. G. jr. (1984) 'Change in self in adulthood: the example of sense of control', *Life-Span Development and Behaviour*, **6**: 281–333.
Heckhausen, J. (1991) *CAMAQ: Control Agency Means-ends in Adulthood Questionnaire*. Berlin: Max-Planck-Institut für Bildungsforschung.
Hradil, S. (1995) 'Die Modernisierung des Denkens. Zukunftspotentiale und "Altlasten"', in *Ostdeutschland aus Politik und Zeitgeschichte*, B **20/95**: 3–15.
Huinink, J., Mayer, K. U., Diewald, M., Solga, H., Sorensen A. and Trappe, H. (eds) (1995) *Kollektiv und Eigensinn. Lebensverläufe in der DDR und danach*. Berlin: Akademie.
Inkeles, A. (1983) *Explaining Individual Modernity*. New York: Columbia Univrsity Press.
Kohli, M. (1994) 'Die DDR als Arbeitsgesellschaft? Arbeit, Lebenslauf und soziale Differenzierung', in: H.Kaelble, J. Kocka and H. Zwahr (eds.), *Sozialgeschichte der DDR*. Stuttgart: Klett-Cotta.
Kohn, M. L. (1989) 'Social structure and personality: a quintessentially sociological approach to social psychology', *Social Forces*, **68**: 26–33.
Kohn, M. L., Naoi, A., Schoenbach, C., Schooler, C. and Slomczynski, K. M. (1990) 'Position in the class structure and psychological functioning in the United States, Japan, and Poland', *American Journal of Sociology*, **95**: 964–1008.
Krampen, G. (1988) 'Toward an action-theoretical model of personality', *European Journal of Personality*, **2**: 39–55.
Lenhardt, G. and Stock, M. (1997) *Bildung, Bürger, Arbeitskraft. Schulentwicklung und Sozialstruktur in der BRD und der DDR*. Frankfurt am main: Surkamp.
Lötsch, M. (1990) *Die Hofierung der Arbeiterklasse war nicht wirkungslos. Frankfurter Rundschau*, 14.11.1990.
Mayer, K. U. and Diewald, M. (1996) 'Kollektiv und Eigensinn. Die Geschichte der DDR und die Lebensverläufe ihrer Bürger', *Aus Politik und Zeitgeschichte*, **46**, 8–17.
Mayer, K. U., Diewald, M. and Solga, H. (1996a) 'Social change and transformation – findings and lessons from the East German case', *Acta Sociologica*, 42, in press.
Meuschel, S. (1991) *Legitimation und Parteiherrschaft: Zum Paradox von Stabilität und Revolution in der DDR 1945–1989*. Frankfurt am Main: Suhrkamp.

Pollack, D. (1996) 'Sozialstruktureller Wandel, Institutionentransfer und die Langsamkeit der Individuen. Untersuchungen zu den ostdeutschen Transformationsprozessen in der Kölner Zeitschrift für Soziologie und Sozialpsychologie und der Sozialen Welt', *Soziologische Revue*, **19**: 412–29.

Rothbaum, F. M., Weisz, J. R. and Snyder, S. S. (1982) 'Changing the world and changing the self: A two-process model of perceived control', *Journal of Personality and Social Psychology*, **42**: 5–37.

Rottenburg, R. (1992) 'Welches Licht wirft die volkseigene Erfahrung auf westliche Unternehmen? Erste Überlegungen zur Strukturierung eines Problemfeldes' in M. Heidenreich (ed.), *Krisen, Kader, Kombinate* (pp. 239–72). Berlin: Sigma.

Senghaas-Knobloch, E. (1992) 'Notgemeinschaft und Improvisationsgeschick: Zwei Tugenden im Transformationsprozess', in M. Heidenreich (ed.), *Krisen, Kader, Kombinate* (pp. 295–309). Berlin: Sigma.

Skinner, E. (1985) 'Action. control judgements, and the structure of control experience', *Psychological Review*, **92**: 39–58.

Vester, M., Hofmann, M. and Zierke, I. (eds) (1995) *Soziale Milieus in Ostdeutschland.* Cologne: Bund.

Voskamp, U. and Wittke, V. (1990) '"Fordismus in einem Land": Das Produktionsmodell der DDR', *Sozialwissenschaftliche Informationen*, **19**: 170–80.

11 Changing patterns of youth transitions: vulnerable groups, welfare careers and social exclusion

Bob Coles

This chapter reviews some of the major changes affecting the three main youth transitions which have occurred in England and Germany in the last two decades and the patterns of social and economic change which have helped reshape them. In both countries the majority of young people now experience extended transitions from school to work, more complex housing careers, and longer periods of family dependency. Yet, for some groups, extended youth transitions have proved difficult to sustain or manage and, at the extreme, this has resulted in a range of different forms of social exclusion. The chapter identifies some groups who have proved 'vulnerable' to the worst effects of social and economic change. Finally, the chapter examines the potential advantages of combining two perspectives on youth research: one largely concentrating on mapping patterns of youth transitions; the other employing social psychological concepts of well-being.

In both Britain and Germany much of government policy defines youth according to chronological age. There are, however, dangers in doing this. Laws, and social policies based upon them, have proved insensitive to the extension of youth transitions during a period of significant political, social and economic transformation (Coles, 1995; Jones and Wallace, 1992; Lewis and McKenzie, 1995). This chapter uses the term 'youth' to refer to the interstitial phase in the life course between childhood and adulthood and, as such, allows the chronological ages covered by the term 'youth' to be variable according to the social and economic conditions prevailing (Elder and O'Rand, 1995). In social policy terms this is important in that it allows policy to be focused on 'needs-related' issues rather than be determined only in 'age-related' terms (Biehal et al., 1995; Coles, 1995). The transition which has received most attention in British youth research is the school-to-work transition (Ashton, Maguire and Spilsbury, 1990; Banks et al., 1992; Roberts, 1984, 1995). Yet, two other transitions are of considerable importance. The first involves attaining (relative) independence from families of origin (including beginning family formation) – the domestic transition. The second involves moving away from the parental home – the housing transition – which may or may not be associated with the school-to-work and/or the domestic transition (Jones, 1995). All three main transitions interact and, in order properly to understand the changing condition of 'youth', we need to understand the relationship between all three dimensions of youth transitions. All three have been significantly affected by social and economic change in recent decades in both England and the new Germany.

Elsewhere, it has been argued that all three transitions are best conceptualized through the concept of 'career' and through the examination of two sides of a 'careers equation' (Coles, 1995). Social science research has helped to explore how different groups of young people with different characteristics have evolved different career patterns. It has also examined how these are connected to other aspects of social, cultural and economic transformations, mainly labour market and educational change, reform of the social security system and fundamental shifts in family patterns and family relationships (O'Rand, 1996). All these institutional transformations have impacted on all three youth transitions and the ways in which they interrelate. The concept of career suggests a sequence of statuses in which each status attained has the capacity both to open up and close down further 'progression' possibilities. So, for instance, at its simplest, staying in education after the age of 16 opens up the possibility of further study after the age of 18. Leaving school at 16 makes a career in higher education less likely and the route to higher education more problematic to achieve. Leaving the parental home to live in some form of 'transitional housing' whilst developing an educational, training or employment career, can bring with it new social contacts and the opportunities and the responsibilities of independent living. Leaving home for 'negative reasons', however, is often accompanied by adverse social, material and psychological consequences, as research in the UK by Jones has illustrated (Jones, 1995). Early parenthood, both in and out of wedlock or a stable relationship, also brings with it both enhanced responsibilities and, for women, a restriction of labour market opportunities and choices (Kiernan, 1995). Together with the school-to-work transition, domestic and housing transitions are clearly important to our understanding of the re-structuration of youth in the late twentieth century (Coles, 1995).

Socio-economic change and patterns of adversity and vulnerability in youth transitions

Other chapters in this volume document changes in education, training, labour market participation, family formation and family life. As late as the mid-1970s, most young people in the UK followed 'traditional transitions'. They left school at minimum school leaving age (two thirds left school at 16) and immediately obtained employment. (Roberts, 1984). As wage earners, they formed new partnerships, became engaged, married and, upon marriage, moved away from the parental home to set up new households (Jones and Wallace, 1992; Wallace, 1987). By their mid-twenties, most young people in the UK had families of their own (Kiernan, 1995). Most young people successfully accomplished all three transitions by their late twenties. By the mid-1990s, however, this pattern had changed markedly. In most parts of the UK, fewer than 1 in 5 young people leave school at minimum school leaving age and more than one third continue into higher education between the ages of 18 and 21 (CSO, 1996). The youth labour market for 16–18-year-olds has been so radically re-structured that now nearly as many young people are involved in part-time work whilst still in full-time education as are employed as full-time workers (Sly, 1993). For the majority of young people, the school-to-work transition is now more protracted and entry into the labour market is delayed until a later age than in previous decades (Coles, 1995).

Changes in the world economy have influenced the labour market and particularly aggregate labour demand, and more especially the demand for particular types of youth labour. Political re-unification of Germany has brought together two different countries with different economies and different capacities to operate effectively in the world market (Lewis and McKenzie, 1995). In both the UK and Germany, the pattern of youth transitions has also been re-shaped by government policy, not least in the re-organization of education and training (Heinz, 1996). Partly because of changes in the global economy and partly as a result of governmental policy responses to these, the proportion of young people participating in the labour market in their teens and early twenties has fluctuated markedly, as is illustrated by Table 11.1. In many member states of the European Union (EU) the 1980s and 1990s illustrates a trend of 'extended' youth transitions, in which more young people delayed (or were forced to delay) entry to the labour market.

In the 1980s in both Britain and Germany the proportion of young men and women *not* in the labour market declined; i.e. more of these young people got jobs (even though other data indicates jobs were less likely to be obtained at minimum school leaving age). In both countries, in the 1990s there were significant *decreases* in the proportion of young people aged 15–25 participating in the labour market. On aggregate data alone, it is difficult to speculate with any certainty as to the reasons for these trends as labour market participation rates of young people are the result of many and varied factors. To be sure, one factor is labour market demand. In the UK, on the other hand, government policy intervention in education has also proved critical. In the late 1980s and 1990s reforms in the teaching and assessment of post-16 qualifications resulted in a much larger proportion of 16-year-olds achieving moderate to good qualifications, so that those 'suitably qualified' stayed on after the age of 16 to take further academic and vocational qualifications. The 1988 Education Act for England and Wales, which introduced delegated budgets for individual schools and colleges, also intensified competition between them. Schools and colleges had a financial incentive to encourage more educational participation of 16–18-year-olds and save teachers jobs. As a result there were marked increases in education participation rates in post-16 and post-18 education. The situation in Germany is similar with an extension of

Table 11.1 Proportion of young people aged 15–25 *not* in the labour market as a percentage of age and sex group

	Male				Female			
	1983	*1985*	*1990*	*1993*	*1983*	*1985*	*1990*	*1993*
UK	30.1	24.7	23.3	29.6	41.4	36.3	33.3	39.6
Germany	46.3	39.3	37.5	41.6*	52.9	44.1	41.2	46.2*
France‡	42.1	44.7	52.3	59.8	51.0	52.2	58.4	63.8
Belgium‡	54.0	56.8	63.0	63.9	58.2	58.6	65.9	67.3

*Indicates break in the series following re-unification.
‡France and Belgium given for comparison.
Source: Eurostat Yearbook 1995.

the years spent in schooling having an appreciable effect in reducing youth unemployment.

Whilst the re-shaping of the school-to-work transition has been fundamental, other aspects of youth transitions have been shaped by changes in family structure and family formation. As more and more young people delay entry to the labour market this clearly has a marked impact upon patterns of leaving home and family formation (Jones, 1993; Jones, 1995). Jones has documented how new patterns of leaving home indicate that, in the 1990s, a young person's 'housing career' is rarely a simple, one-step move. Rather, many young people leave home temporarily for education and training, only to return at a later stage (Jones, 1987). The 'housing careers' of young people are thus now dependent upon the availability of 'intermediate' and 'transitional' housing and patterns of family support, which some families may or may not be in a position to give (Jones, 1995). In Germany, too, the age of leaving home has risen considerably in recent decades, putting increased pressure on families to support their children for longer at home and support them as and when they attempt to leave.

Leaving home and participation in education, training or the labour market after minimum school leaving age is further complicated by changing patterns of family life. The vast majority of parents in both countries have children after marriage and within their first marriage or within their first cohabiting union. Yet evidence from statistical sources suggests that the proportion of young people being brought up in 'non-traditional' families in the UK is growing markedly. So, for instance, data from the Office of Population and Censuses (OPCS – now the Office for National Statistics, ONS) indicates that, in the UK, the number of lone parent families has more than doubled between 1971 and 1991 (Burghes, 1994). Since the 1960s, there has been a four-fold increase in the number of divorces and a three-fold increase in remarriages. In static, cross-sectional, terms, ONS data also indicate that three quarters of children and young people are living with their biological parents. One in six (16.6 per cent) are living in lone parent families. Around 8 per cent are living in re-constituted families, with a parent who has either re-married or is cohabiting (Haskey, 1994). Yet families may change over the period during which a child is growing up. So, for instance, a child who starts its life living with a lone parent may experience the cohabitation and later marriage of that parent (either to the child's natural parent or someone else), a partnership breakdown and/or divorce, the re-partnering of its parent and perhaps a later re-marriage. All this may take place before the child reaches adulthood. It is, therefore, important to re-interpret the static picture of family types, by projecting onto the data trends in family development, which allow us to predict what will happen to young families given the passage of time. After doing this, Haskey concluded that, by the age of 16, nearly a quarter of young people will have experienced the divorce of their parents and many of these may live in reconstituted families (Haskey, 1994). More startlingly, Kiernan and Wicks have estimated that, given current trends in divorce and lone parenthood, the percentage of young people being brought up according to the 'conventional pattern' of living, with both their married biological parents until they are grown up, will have fallen to as low as 50 per cent in the UK by the end of the century (Kiernan and Wicks, 1990).

There may be some temptation to view the decline in the 'traditional family' as a particular 'problem' of the UK. Yet patterns of family life in the new Germany may not be as immune from change as some would like to believe. Before the decline of the traditional family is dismissed as not being a potential issue for German social policy, the rapidity of changes brought about in the UK should be borne in mind. In Germany there are marked differences between the east and west as well as between south and north. In aggregate terms, divorce in the former East Germany has fluctuated by a reported 30 per cent in recent years (Eurostat, 1994). In Germany as a whole, Eurostat reports that 101,000 children are affected by the dissolution of their parents' marriage, which is a significant number but still a tiny proportion of 10.5 million children and young people under the age of majority (Eurostat, 1994).

It is important to conceptualize family formation and re-constitution as a process. All family relationships involve the negotiation and renegotiation of roles and responsibilities, freedoms and duties, and patterns of care and control (Coles, 1995; Jones and Wallace, 1992). When children and young people experience the separation and divorce of their parents, this may have wide-ranging consequences for where they live, the schools they attend, and their material and emotional circumstances. In the UK, findings from the National Child Development Study (NCDS) indicate that young people experiencing the marital breakdown of their parents in the 1960s and 1970s attempted *early* youth transitions (Kiernan, 1995). The worry remains for the 1990s, that whilst most young people now follow extended transitions, those from families which have experienced divorce and re-constitutions may leave education and their family at an early stage, with potentially perilous consequences.

The increase in the number of children born outside marriage is also markedly different between the two countries and, in Germany, by differences between East and West. In the UK live births outside of wedlock has more than doubled in the last decade. In Germany, their prevalence has remained at the level experienced by the UK at the start of the 1980s. In the former East Germany, however, births outside of wedlock accounted for over 40 per cent of live births in 1992, higher than in the UK or France and many other European countries. No disaggregation has been possible to distinguish between different types of circumstances in which births occur or identify, for instance, what proportion of these births are to cohabiting unmarried couples. Care must, therefore, be taken in interpreting these data.

Within the aggregate data on births outside wedlock, it is the growth of teenage lone parenthood which is of particular concern, especially in the UK. In Germany there seems to be less concern. Johannes Huinink, for instance, has claimed that, in the GDR, most births out of wedlock are to cohabiting, unmarried couples (because of additional social policy support) or to couples who have not *yet* lived together, because of the unavailability of suitable housing. The UK has a teenage fertility rate which is significantly higher than elsewhere in Europe; ten times that of Switzerland, four times that of Italy, three times that of France and Sweden and twice that of Germany (Kiernan, 1995). The UK has a teenage fertility rate of around 6 per cent and two-thirds of these are births outside wedlock. In Germany the teenage birthrate is around two-thirds of that in the UK with less than half of these born outside of wedlock (Eurostat, 1995). Especially in the UK, there is concern over the relatively high rates of teenage pregnancies and what this means for the quality of life of families, including: the cost of bringing up children; how young parents cope if they are economically

Table 11.2 Live births outside marriage as a percentage of all live births

	1983	1985	1990	1993
UK	15	19	28	31
Germany	15	16	15	16
France	16	20	30	33
Finland	14	16	25	30
Italy	5	5	6	7
Sweden	44	46	47	50

Source: Eurostat Yearbook, 1995.

dependent upon only one youth wage or training allowance or benefits (Bradshaw and Miller, 1991).

The analysis of NCDS data in the UK indicates a number of correlates of teenage parenting (Kiernan, 1995). First, teenage mothers (and to a lesser extent fathers) are most likely to have had mothers who also had their first births in their teens. They are also highly likely to have been brought up in families which experienced financial problems throughout their schooling years – three times more likely than those who become parents after their teens. Secondly, teenage mothers are more than twice as likely as mothers giving birth at a later age to have left school with no formal school qualifications (61 per cent compared with 26 per cent) and are twice as likely to have been ranked in the lowest quartile of educational attainment. They are also reported to have manifested much lower scores on emotional well-being.

Youth transitions, social inequalities, social exclusion and 'vulnerable' youth

So far, this chapter has sought to document major sources of change in the re-shaping of youth transitions in the UK and Germany. Yet much youth research has helped to document the ways in which 'youth' is experienced differently by different categories of young people. Sociologists, especially, have been concerned to examine 'social reproduction', including the reproduction of social inequalities, mainly concerned with class, gender and to a lesser extent ethnicity (Banks et al., 1992; Bates and Riseborough, 1993; Connolly et al., 1992). In both Britain and Germany there has also been a recognition that there are major differences between the regions both in terms of the likelihood of a young person experiencing unemployment and the economic and educational opportunity structures available to them (Ashton, Maguire and Spilsbury, 1990; Banks et al., 1992; Evans and Heinz, 1994; Heinz, 1996; Monnich and Witzel, 1994; Roberts, 1995). Clearly, one of the key factors in social exclusion is unemployment. Here the condition of the local labour market is important. Yet there is more to understanding more precisely which categories of young people become unemployed than simple aggregate unemployment rates. Within the same labour markets some categories of young people are more likely to be excluded from labour market participation than others. Roberts has argued that one of the best predictors of a young person being on the least favourable labour market 'trajectory' is the educational qualifications attained at the age of 16. He regards this as largely being determined by social class (Roberts, 1993). Yet there are other *prior*, and potentially *independent* factors which may precipitate *both* poor performance at school *and* later unemployment.

By and large, British academics have resisted using the concept of 'underclass' in describing the various processes of social exclusion affecting young people (MacDonald, 1997). Rather, they have focused on a complex range of processes through which educational disaffection, disinvolvement with training and the labour market, and drifts into homelessness occur (Blyth and Milner, 1996; Jones, 1995; Williamson, 1997). Key amongst these are the 'excluding processes' which take place around family life and the educational process. Exclusion from mainstream education can take different forms, either exclusion by school authorities or voluntary exclusion through truancy. Permanent exclusion of pupils by school authorities has increased markedly in recent years in Britain with, on one estimate, over 12,000 pupils permanently excluded in 1994–5 alone (Parsons, 1996). Whilst teachers' unions and politicians have blamed this upon unacceptable and sometimes violent behaviour, some critics have suggested that it is connected with the increased pressure of competition between schools following the 1988 Education Reform Act (Imich, 1994). On some deprived estates scores of young people under the age of 16 have had little contact with school for several years (Coles, 1996; Williamson, 1997). Exclusions from school are experienced disproportionately by different groups. A third form of exclusion from mainstream education is through the definition and classification of children and young people as having 'special educational needs'. Boys are excluded four times more than girls and Afro-Caribbean boys are more than four times more represented in the excluded population than their white counterparts (OFSTED, 1993).

Truanting (voluntary exclusion) is also known to be widespread with one national survey reporting that 10 per cent of young people had truanted once a week or more (Casey and Smith. 1995; O'Keeffe. 1993). This is also correlated with particular types of social background *and* negative outcomes in terms of school performance, training and later employment prospects. Black children truant more than other ethnic groups and children from lone parent families are more likely to truant than those living with two parents. Yet, it is too simple to write all of this off as the wilful deviance of young people or the lack of adequate family support or control from parents. Carlen has argued that much truancy is the result of the feelings of pain, hurt, suffering and humiliation young people experience at the hands of teachers and classmates (Carlen, Gleeson and Wardhaugh, 1992).

There is particular concern for children and young people who 'truant' ('run away') from families and surrogate families. There is little accurate information on the number of 'runaways', yet the trial of Frederick West for the murder of 13 young women bore testimony to that fact that many young people can simply disappear, especially when detached from family support. The research which has been conducted suggests that there are around 100,000 missing person 'incidents' (under the age of 18) in England and Scotland each year, involving around 43,000 young people (Abrahams and Mungall, 1992; Newman, 1992; Stein, Rees and Frost, 1994).

For young people under the age of 25, family support is assumed by much UK government policy, especially the 1986 Social Security Act (implemented in 1988) and benefit entitlement has been further restricted by rule changes introduced at the end of 1995 (Craig, 1991; Harris, 1989). Yet, for some young people, family support is tenuous, brittle and based upon social, psychological and economic conditions which are far from secure (Jones, 1995). Indeed, it is important to recognize that the study of youth transitions must take cognisance of the variable family support systems. Family research emphasizes that support for young people from family members is far from contractual. Indeed, it is something which is often controlled by the giver (it may be offered, but cannot be demanded), and may also have a price (the re-affirmation of the status of dependency) which a young person may not be willing to accept (Finch and Mason, 1993; Jones, 1995).

Young People 'looked after' and leaving care

So far we have examined a series of different processes of 'social exclusion' through which young people become separated from the mainstream career routes which define youth transitions. Some attempt has been made to estimate the size of each category and to outline the ways in which each process of exclusion helps to socially construct 'vulnerable youth'. Yet, one category, those 'looked after' in the public care, illustrates the degree to which the 'categories' can overlap, and the combined forces of disadvantage produce circumstances of overwhelming adversity. Young people brought up in the public care, either with foster parents or in children's homes are a tiny fraction of the population of children and young people in the UK (around 55,000 in 1991 or just over 0.5 per cent of the age cohort). Seven out of ten young people in residential care are, however, over the age of thirteen and older children and young people (over the age of 11) are twice as likely to be placed in care as younger children.

In the New Germany, there are an estimated 200,000 children and young people living apart from their families. They do so in a mixture of different residential settings from foster families, to special institutions for the handicapped, to boarding schools and homes for apprentices. In 1991, Germany had over 41,000 children and young people living in foster families, with a further 56,468 in residential care (Colton and Hellinckx, 1993). This is nearly double the number in care in the UK and a much higher proportion of the population under the age of 18. The institutional development of care in east and west Germany differ considerably although an attempt is being made to harmonise provision under a new child care law (the Child and Youth Services Act, introduced in January 1991). As with legislation in the UK, the emphasis is on attempting to rehabilitate children and young people and re-unite them with their biological parents wherever possible. Yet in both countries there is a recognition that the system has to deal with a higher than expected number of young people admitted because of various forms of addiction, runaways, para-suicides, and victims of sexual abuse. The same concerns are expressed in Britain and Germany about co-operation between different welfare services, together with shortage of suitable and supervised living accommodation for young people leaving care (Biehal et al., 1995; Colton and Hellinckx, 1993).

The impact of young people's experiences in care on later youth transitions is also a matter of serious concern (Biehal et al., 1995; Broad, 1994). Care leavers figure prominently amongst runaways and the homeless (Anderson, Kemp and Quilgars, 1993; Rees, 1993). Rees indicates that those who run away from care are much more likely to be 'chronic' runaways. They are often running from living arrangements which they find stressful, dangerous or abusive but they often find themselves running into situations in which they are also highly vulnerable. One significant difference between the legislative frameworks in the two countries is that in Germany, under the KJHG law on child care, a young person may, in exceptional cases, be looked after up to the age of 27, although it is not known to the author how likely an occurrence this is. In the UK, whilst the Children Act makes it possible for Social Services departments to offer help up to the age of 21, most young people are discharged from care soon after their 16th birthday and often lose touch with any regular or systematic social services support within two years.

The correlation between brought up in care and 'adversities' in later youth transitions is documented in a number of surveys in the UK. One study of youth homelessness conducted for the Department of Environment estimated that 1 in 4 of 'rough sleepers' were ex-residents of children's homes and a further 1 in 10 had been in foster care (Anderson et al., 1993). A survey of the prison population further reports that 38 per cent of those in prison had been in care at some stage (Walmsley, Howard and White, 1992). Some young people in care are, of course, there because of family tragedies or abuse, others because they are deemed to be beyond parental control. Young people in care, therefore, are not a homogeneous group. Yet, statistically, young people in care are much more likely to come from distinct and disadvantaged social backgrounds. One large survey compared the background characteristics of a sample of young people in care with a general population of the same age. Those in care were found to be eight times more likely to have been living with one adult than in dual parent families, three and a half times more likely to have been living in overcrowded accommodation, and three times more likely to have had a head of household in receipt of benefits (Bebbington and Miles, 1989). Yet, once young people have been removed from these various environments of material, social, physical and emotional disadvantage, care systems in the UK appear to be incapable of providing an environment in which previous disadvantage is counterbalanced. Rather, it seems, being taken into care results in the further intensification of processes of social exclusion and emotional damage. Stein and his colleagues, in the most recent study of care leavers, confirm that being received into care is likely to exacerbate a record of truancy and educational neglect (Biehal et al., 1995) This is in contrast to other care systems elsewhere in the world in which being received into care triggers an immediate programme of remedial and compensatory education (Thirupathy, 1995).

It is teenage entrants to care who are of most concern. Often such young people experience several different placements and placement breakdown. The effect of these movements in care is to be counted in confused self-identity, low self-esteem, and few, if any, educational attainments at leaving school. Three quarters of the young people studied by Garnett (1992) had no qualifications at the age of 16, compared to 11 per cent in the non-care populations in the authorities in which the research took place. The low educational attainment levels of young people in care have been explained by the fact that education itself is given low priority. The high level of non-school attendance and, more importantly, permanent exclusions among young people in care, further explains their educational under-achievement. Given this record of educational disadvantage and neglect, it is of little surprise that all recent studies of young people leaving care report that the vast majority of them are unqualified (Biehal et al., 1995; Broad, 1994; Garnett, 1992). Young people in care are thus frequently excluded from a stable living environment *and* a stable educational environment, the effects of which have considerable implications for the transitions they make to adulthood.

The low levels of formal educational achievement, at least in part, help to explain what opportunities care leavers are afforded at the age of 16. Without any qualifications they have little alternative but to leave school at the minimum school leaving age. Yet at this vital time in the life-course, they are also being required by their local authorities to consider, and for many begin, their domestic and housing transitions out of care and into 'independence'. Some young people in stable placements may, indeed, obtain reasonable 16+ qualifications. Yet even these young people have to weigh the potential benefits that post-16 education may have for their occupational careers, against the very real possibilities of having to leave their 'in care' placements, often with very little emotional, financial and social support. Being brought up in public care, therefore, not only provides a serious educational disadvantage, but being moved out of care stacks the odds against successfully completing the extended school-to-work transitions now being expected of their contemporaries. In the study by Biehal et al.(1992), 36.5 per cent of the young people leaving care were unemployed, whilst in Broad's study, half of the sample were unemployed (Broad, 1994). This compares with a national rate of unemployment amongst 16–19-year-olds of 19 per cent (CSO, 1994).

Lack of participation in the labour market is only one dimension of the after-care transitions of young people. Equally important is often highly tenuous nature of young people's relationship with the housing market. It is not unusual to find young people leaving care in the UK being placed in bed and breakfast accommodation, lodgings, and hostels often at the ages of 16/17 years. In the most recent large-scale and detailed study of care leavers by Stein and his colleagues, over half of their sample experienced more than two moves of accommodation in the two years after leaving care, and one-sixth experienced more than five moves (Biehal et al., 1995). One-fifth became homeless at some stage. Given the increasingly apparent trend for young people in the general non-care population to delay their housing transitions by remaining longer in the parental home, it is evident that for young people leaving care their enforced departure from the care system results in accelerated housing transitions. For young people leaving care one of the most important transitions they make (or are required to make) is the housing transition. Yet, far from leaving care for independence, many young people face a future of continued dependence upon the state. It is significant too that this is dependency upon age-related benefit entitlement rather than a package of support determined by an identification of their longer-term welfare needs.

As we have noted, whilst there is concern in the UK about teenage pregnancies, the vast majority of young people are delaying parenting until their late twenties (in both cases around the age of 27 for women and 29 for men). Only 4 per cent of the Economic and Social Research Council's 16–19 survey of young women had a child (Banks et al., 1992). For care leavers the story is very different. Garnett and her colleagues reported that one in seven of their female care leavers was pregnant by the time of leaving care (usually at 16) (Garnett, 1992). Nearly half of the female sample studied by Stein and his colleagues, and a third of all the sample, had become parents within two years of leaving care (Biehal et al., 1995). While over half of the pregnancies had been unplanned, over a third had been planned with their partners and three-quarters of teenage parents lived with their partners at some stage. For a large minority of care leavers, therefore, parenting is either a planned or accepted part of an (albeit early) domestic career on which they choose to embark. In their 1992 study Biehal et al. report that three-quarters of young female care leavers with children had secured tenancies, compared with only a quarter of those without children (Biehal et al., 1992). Family formation was, therefore, paralleled by a more secure housing career. Care leavers, then, represent a group of young people who, when faced with extremely poor prospects in the labour market, embark on parenting careers, and are expected to do so whilst living independently, even though this is often undertaken in severe hardship. Parenting has become the predominant transition dimension, in many ways determining the outcome of the other two – a more difficult future connection to the labour market but a more secure housing career. Furthermore, some of the after care schemes studied by Biehal et al., are reported to have switched attention to the welfare of the next generation (the babies) rather than offering support for the young parents themselves (Biehal et al., 1995).

Youth transitions and measures of welfare

Much of this chapter has described the changing patterns of youth transitions in terms of the distribution of status-sequences amongst different categories of young people. Yet, at the beginning of the chapter, 'youth' was defined not simply in terms of three major transitions, but as the interstitial status between childhood and adulthood. In some of the literature on youth there is a recognition that attaining adulthood involves various dimensions of 'citizenship' in terms of (relative) independence and responsibilities, which comes with the economic rewards of participation in the labour market and living (relatively) independently of one's family of origin and organising one's own lifestyle in accommodation apart from them. Often this is accompanied by new partnerships and family formation. Yet there are severe limitations of this 'transition model' of youth. Surely, one might ask, there is more to being adult than having a job, a partner, a home and a family? Yet the status transition model alone tells us nothing about the enhancement of well-being or welfare per se. To be sure, there is also a literature which indicates the positive social and psychological consequences of work, and a negation of these in unemployment (Jahoda, 1982; Fryer, 1992). There is also evidence that ill-health can be a consequence of both unemployment and homelessness (Bines, 1993; Burchell, 1993; Gershuny, 1993; Townsend and Davidson, 1982) But as young people negotiate their own 'welfare careers', (and as social scientists seek to understand them), what becomes clear is that some categories of young people are not simply drawn, like magnetic objects, to the status outcomes the transition model defines as 'positive outcomes'. Surely not all are sure routes to well-being and happiness? How do different combinations of outcomes combine, and how are they perceived by different people? Given difficult choices, how do young people choose between them? How do they balance different combinations of positive and negative outcomes, and how are these defined? Many young care leavers, for instance, especially young women, 'choose' early parenthood, despite this 'choice' having a potentially long-term negative effect upon their ability to gain employment or a means of providing them with the economic means of a standard of living much above the poverty line. Stein and colleagues comment that, 'for many the need to belong, to love and be loved, to have something of their own and the chance to compensate for the poor care they experienced' were decisive factors in choices to start a family (Biehal et al., 1995). Some 'choices' may be short-term, 'understandable', but hugely and unrealistically optimistic. Yet, often, within a few months of becoming mothers these young women are left on their own, with little support and little if any social contact (Biehal, et al. 1995).

Leaving home can also be the result of a mixture of motives in which some young people may make impulsive decisions they live to regret, whilst others leave only after numerous family rows, restrictions on their freedom, and in some cases, long-term abuse (Jones, 1995). Many young people leave their families, despite the fact that living independently of them often results in homelessness, poor diet, and social isolation (Kirk et al., 1991). Children and young people run away from home, or from children's homes or foster families, despite the fact that this might place them in extreme material hardship and open to exploitation and abuse.

In the UK, significant work was done as part of the ESRC 16–19 initiative to examine both the objective and subjective dimensions of youth transitions (Banks et al., 1992). Some of this explored concepts of self-efficacy, self-worth and self-esteem, as well as notions of mastery and control. A similar array of concepts has also been employed in the study of some 'vulnerable' categories of young people (Biehal, et al., 1995; Fish, 1986; Hirst and Baldwin, 1994). Where this has been done, it has been shown that, by and large, young people do manifest increases in feelings of well-being and mastery as they 'progress' through youth transitions. Those for whom employment and independent living prove difficult (if not impossible) to attain, score less well than their able-bodied, or secure and well supported, contemporaries who achieve such statuses (Biehal et al., 1995; Hirst and Baldwin, 1994). Stein and colleagues report that the majority of care leavers often have poor social networks, and that, where there was confidence and self-esteem, this was often associated with a secure sense of identity and/or positive family relationships which were, by no means, attained by all (Biehal et al., 1995).

There is a huge literature, particularly in North America, which has sought to develop and employ a range of different measures of self-esteem and well-being (Clausen, 1991; Demo, 1992; Pearlin and Schooler, 1978; McAlpine, Grindstaff and Sorenson, 1996; Rosenberg, 1979; Rosenberg, Schooler and Schonbach, 1989). Much of this also examines the relationship between different family patterns, family relationships and the social psychology of 'adolescence'. Within the UK, there is some resistance amongst youth scholars to adopting either the concept of 'adolescence' or the positivistic paraphernalia of measuring 'well-being' – and with some justification. Does 'adolescence' research adequately address the complex and extended nature of youth transitions? Is multivariate analysis capable of conveying the complexity of the career choices which exist amongst 'vulnerable youth'? Are the standard scales employed so steeped in middle-class and ethnocentric values that they are worthless in capturing the decisions that 'vulnerable youth' have to make? Surely, one of the significant advantages of qualitative approaches to youth transitions is that they help to explore the complex and changing social and economic world of young people through the meanings the young people themselves give to the world around them, rather than simply relying upon definitional and evaluative criteria imposed by the distant and uncomprehending, ubiquitous 'professional youth researchers'? Even within the literature, there is some recognition that a reliance on standardized scales, largely developed in the US, runs the risk of naively imposing a white, middle-class, privileged and distinctively American, view of family life, family relationships and 'adolescence' upon inappropriate groups (Barber, Chadwick and Oeter, 1992). Yet it is hard to resist the argument that, despite these methodological reservations, youth researchers would do well to explore more systematically some of the conceptual thinking which lies behind measures of self-esteem, efficacy, control, and well-being, and to explore these further, even within research projects which are primarily qualitative or ethnographic.

Conclusions

This chapter has reviewed a number of major changes to have occurred in the patterning of youth transitions in the UK and Germany in the last two decades. It has emphasized the importance of considering all three youth transitions together, rather than studying any one in isolation from the others and illustrated how changes in the private worlds of families and households are as important to consider as changes in public institutions such as work, employment, training and education. The chapter has focused attention on 'vulnerable' categories of young people and argued that much of this vulnerability is socially constructed through a diverse and complex set of processes of social exclusion covering the family and home as well as schools and labour markets. It has shown how these processes make later youth transitions particularly problematic – hence the definition of 'vulnerability'. In the case of care leavers, it is often the management of the care which leaves them educationally disadvantaged, and the management of their leaving care at such an early age. This sets them adrift from support, uncompetitive and under-resourced, and required to stand alone, at the very age at which the state expects their non-care peers still to be dependent upon family support. This suggests that, until the state is willing to transform the care and leaving care systems, the most vulnerable and disadvantaged young people are being abandoned by the state *in loci parentis*, in a way which would bring moral condemnation were a natural parent to behave in a like manner. Other processes of social exclusion can also be seen to be as much determined by those in positions of authority and power (in schools or in families) as by those who are excluded, who are relatively powerless, and uncomprehending, of the long term consequences of the decisions they make, or about decisions made about them.

In reviewing the relationship between patterns of family formation and later youth transitions, this chapter has suggested that there are trends well underway in which the routes to youth homelessness, long-term youth unemployment, poverty, and youth crime, will become well-trodden highways, if we do not heed the lessons of policy failures in the 1980s. Yet the policy agenda still seems to be one which punishes those pushed (or enticed) down such routes rather than helping divert them from following them. It is to be hoped that policy errors made in the UK are not replicated in the rest of Europe.

References

Abrahams, C. and Mungall, R. (1992) *Runaways: Exploding the Myths*. London, NHC Action for Children.

Anderson, I., Kemp, P. and Quilgars, D. (1993) *Single Homeless People*, London: HMSO.

Ashton, D. N., Maguire, M. and Spilsbury, M. (1990) *Restructuring the Labour Market: The Implications for Youth*, London: Macmillan.

Banks, M., Bates, I., Breakwell, G., Bynner, J., Emler, N., Jamieson, L. and Roberts, K. (1992) *Careers and Identities*, Buckingham: Open University Press.

Barber, B. K., Chadwick, B. A. and Oeter, R. (1992) 'Parental behaviours and adolescent self-esteem in the United States and Germany', *Journal of Marriage and the Family*, **54**: 128–41.

Bates, I. and Riseborough, G. (1993) *Youth and Inequality*, Buckingham: Open University Press.

Bebbington, A. and Miles, J. (1989) 'The background of children who enter local authority care', *British Journal of Social Work*, **19**: 349–68

Biehal, N., Clayton, J., Stein, M. C. and Wade, J. (1992) *Prepared for Living*, London: National Children's Bureau.

Biehal, N., Clayton, J., Stein, M. C., and Wade, J. (1995) *Moving On: Young People and Leaving Care Schemes*, London: HMSO.

Bines, W. (1993) *Homelessness and Health.* MA dissertation, Department of Social Policy and Social Work, University of York.

Blyth, E. and Milner, J. (1993) 'Exclusions from school: A first step to exclusion from society', *Children and Society*, **7**(1): 255–68.

Blyth, E. and Milner, J. (eds) (1996) *Exclusions from School,* London: Routledge.

Bradshaw, J. and Miller, J. (1991) *Lone Parent Families,* Department of Social Security Research Report No 6. London: HMSO.

Broad, B. (1994) *Leaving Care in the 1990s,* London: Royal Philanthropic Society.

Burchell, B. (1993) 'The effect of labour market position, job security and unemployment on psychological health', in D. Gallie, C. Marsh and C. Vogler (eds), *Social Change and the Experience of Unemployment.* Oxford: Oxford University Press.

Burghes, L. (1994) *Lone parenthood and Family Disruption: The Outcomes for Children.* London: Family Policy Studies Centre.

Carlen, P., Gleeson, D. and Wardhaugh, J. (1992) *Truancy: The Politics of Compulsory Schooling.* Buckingham: Open University Press.

Casey, B. and Smith D. (1995) *Truancy and Youth Transitions.* England and Wales Youth Cohort Study, Research Series Youth Cohort Report No. 34. London: DfEE.

Clausen, J. A. A. (1991) 'Adolescent competence and the shaping of the life course', *American Journal of Sociology,* **96:4**, 805–42.

Coles, B. (1996) *Youth and Social Policy: Youth Citizenship and Young Careers.* London: UCL Press.

Coles, B. et al. (1998) *Meeting the Needs of Young People on Social Housing Estates*: Coventry: Chartered Institute of Housing.

Colton, M. J. and Hellinckx, W. (1993) *Childcare in the EC.* Aldershot: Gower

Connolly, M., Roberts, K., Ben-Tovim, G. and Torkington, P. (1992) *Black Youth in Liverpool.* Culemborg: Italy, Giordano Bruno.

Craig, G. (1991) *Fit for Nothing? Young People, Benefits and Youth Training.* London: The Children's Society.

CSO (Central Statistical Office) (1996) *Social Trends.* London: HMSO.

Demo, D. H. (1992) 'The self concept over time: research issues and directions', *Annual Review of Sociology.* **18**: 303–26

Elder, G. and O'Rand, A. (1995) 'Adult lives in a changing society', in K. Cook, S. Fine, A. Gary and J. House (eds), *Sociological Perspectives on Social Psychology.* Boston: Allyn & Bacon.

Emich, A. (1994) 'Exclusions from school: current trends and isuues', *Educational Research,* **36**(1), pp. 3–11.

Evans, K. and Heinz, W. (eds) (1994) *Becoming Adult in England and Germany.* London, Anglo-German Foundation.

Eurostat (1994) *Demographic Statistics.* Luxembourg: Office for Official Publications of the European Community.

Eurostat (1995) *Eurostat Yearbook 1995.* Luxembourg: Office for Official Publications of the European Community.

Finch, J. and Mason, J. (1993) *Negotiating Family Responsibility.* London: Routledge.

Fish, J. (1986) *Young People with Handicaps: The Road to Adulthood.* Paris: Centre for Education Research and Innovation (OECD).

Fryer, D. (1992) 'Psychological or material deprivation: why does unemployment have mental health consequences?' in E. McLaughlin (ed.), *Understanding Unemployment*. London: Routledge.

Garnett, L. (1992) *Leaving Care and After*. London: National Children's Bureau.

Gershuny, J. (1993) 'The psychological consequences of unemployment: an assessment of Jahoda's thesis', in D. Gallie, C. Marsh and C. Vogler (eds), *Social Change and the Experience of Unemployment*. Oxford: Oxford University Press.

Haskey, J. (1994) 'Stepfamilies and stepchildren in Great Britain', *Population Trends*. **76**: 17–28.

Harris, N. S. (1989) *Social Security for Young People*. Aldershot, England: Avebury.

Heinz, W. (1996) 'Youth in transition in cross-cultural perspective', in B. Galaway and J. Hudson (eds), *Youth In Transition: Perspectives on Research and Policy*. Toronto: Thompson Education Publishing.

Hirst, M. and Baldwin, S. (1994) *Unequal Opportunities: Growing Up Disabled*. London: HMSO.

Huinink, J. and Wagner, M. (1995) 'Partnerschaft, Ehe und Familie in der DDR', in J. Huinink, K. U. Mayer, M. Diewald, H. Solga and A. Sorensen (eds), *Kollerktiv und Eigensinn. Lebensverläufe in der DDR und danach*. Berlin: Akademie.

Imich, A. (1994) 'Exclusions from school: current trends and issues', *Educational Research*, **36**: 3–11.

Inkeles, A. (1983) *Exploring Individual Modernity*. New York: Columbia University Press.

Jahoda, M. (1982) *Employment and Unemployment: A Socio-psychological Analysis*. Cambridge: Cambridge University Press.

Jones, G. (1987) 'Leaving the parental home; an analysis of early housing careers', *Journal of Social Policy*, **16**: 49–74.

Jones, G. (1993) 'On the margins of the housing market: housing and homelessness in youth', in *Young People In and Out of the Housing Market*. Edinburgh: University of Edinburgh, Centre for Educational Sociology.

Jones, G. (1995) *Family Support for Young People*. London: Family Policy Studies Centre.

Jones, G. and Wallace, C. (1992) *Youth Family and Citizenship*. Milton Keynes, England: Open University Press.

Kiernan, K. (1995) *Transitions to Parenthood: Young Mothers, Young Fathers – Associated Factors and Later Life Experiences*. Unpublished paper.

Kiernan, K. and Wicks, M. (1990) *Family Change and Future Policy*. York: Joseph Rowntree Memorial Trust, Family Policy Studies Centre.

Kirk, D., Nelson, S., Sinfield, A. and Sinfield, D. (1991) *Excluding Youth: Poverty among Young People Living Away from Home*. Edinburgh: University of Edinburgh, Department of Social Policy and Social Work.

Lewis, D. and McKenzie, J. P. R. (1995) *The New Germany: Social, Political and Cultural Challenges of Unification*. Exeter: University of Exeter Press.

McAlpine, D. D., Grindstaff, C. F. and Sorenson, A. M. (1996) 'Competence and control in the transition from adolescence to adulthood: a longitudinal study of teenage mothers', in B. Galaway and J. Hudson (eds), *Youth in Transition: Perspectives on Research and Policy*. Toronto: Thompson Education Publishing.

MacDonald, R. (ed.) (1997) *Youth, the 'Underclass' and Social Exclusion*. London: Routledge.

Monnich, I. and Witzel, A. (1994) 'Arbeitsmarkt und Berufsverlaufe Junger Erwachsener', *Zeitschrift fur Sozialisationsforschung und Erziehungssoziologie*, **14**: 262–77.

Newman, C. (1992) *Young Runaways: Finding from Britain's First Safe House.* London: The Children's Society.

OFSTED (1993) *Achieving Good Behaviour in Schools.* London: HMSO.

OFSTED/SSI (1995) *The Education of Young People Who Are Looked After.* London: HMSO.

O'Keefe, D. (1993) *Truancy in English Secondary Schools* (A report prepared for the DFE). London: HMSO.

O'Rand, A. (1996) 'Structuration and individualisation: the life course as a continuous, multi-level process', in A. C. Kerckhoff (ed.) *Generating Social Stratification.* Boulder: Westview Press.

Parsons, Carl. (1996) 'Permanent exclusions from school in England in the 1990s: trends, causes and responses', *Children and Society.* **10**(3).

Pearlin, L. I. and Schooler, C. (1978) 'The structure of coping', *Journal of Health and Social behaviour,* **22**, 337–56.

Phillips, T. (1996) 'Schools sxclusion of black "caused Brixton Riot"', *Guardian,* 5 June 1996.

Rees, G. (1993) *Hidden Truths: Young People's Experiences of Running Away.* London: The Children's Society.

Roberts, K. (1984) *School Leavers and their Prospects: Youth and the Labour Market in the 1980s.* Milton Keynes: Open University Press.

Roberts, K. (1993) 'Career trajectories and the mirage of increased social mobility', in I. Bates and G. Riseborough (eds), *Youth and Inequality.* Buckingham: Open University Press.

Roberts, K. (1995) *Youth and Employment in Modern Britain.* Oxford: Oxford University Press.

Rosenberg, M. (1979) *Conceiving the Self.* New York: Basic Books

Rosenberg, M., Schooler, C. and Schoenbach, C. (1989) 'Self-esteem and adolescent problems: modelling reciprocal effects', *American Sociological Review,* **54**: 1004–18.

Sly, F. (1993) 'Economic activity of 16- and 17-year-olds', *Employment Gazette,* July.

Stein, M., Rees, G. and Frost, N. (1994) *Running the Risk: Young People on the Streets of Britain Today.* London: The Children's Society

Thirupathy, P. (1995) 'Care systems and leaving care in England and Singapore', MA dissertation, Department of Social Policy and Social Work, University of York.

Townsend, P. and Davidson, N. (eds) (1982) *Inequalities of Health.* Harmondsworth: Penguin Books.

Wallace, C. (1987) *For Richer, For Poorer: Growing Up In and Out of Work.* London: Tavistock.

Walmsley, R., Howard, L. and White, S. (1992) *The National Prison Survey 1991: Main Findings,* Home Office Study No. 128. London: HMSO.

Williamson, H. (1993) 'Youth policy in the United Kingdom and the marginalization of young people', *Youth and Policy,* **40**: 33–48.

Williamson, H. (1997) 'Status Zero, youth and the "underclass": some considerations', in R. MacDonald (ed.), *Youth, the 'Underclass' and Social Exclusion.* London: Routledge.

Postscript

12

Meeting challenges in the new Germany and in England: new directions for theory and data collection

Fred W. Vondracek

Attending the workshop on 'Adversity and Challenge in the Life Course in the New Germany and England' as an observer from the other side of the Atlantic, my slightly detached perspective allowed me to appreciate the enormity of the task the participants set for themselves. Clearly, the disintegration of the Soviet Union and the political, economic and social consequences of this event deservedly represent the focus of much of the work that is done by social scientists in Germany. Although Britain has not been affected directly, many of the indirect consequences of the fall of communism are felt there, as well. In spite of the almost cataclysmic nature of this watershed event, it is also clear, especially perhaps from a transatlantic perspective, that other circumstances have contributed in important ways to the adversities and challenges faced by Germans and Britons at the close of the twentieth century and into the next millennium.

The most important of these has been likened to the industrial revolution which, first in England, and later in the United States and Germany, fundamentally changed the political, economic and social structure of society. Variously referred to as the technological revolution, the dawn of the information age or, somewhat more specifically, the globalization of national and regional economies, its impact cannot be fully appreciated at this time. After all, revolutions cannot be evaluated while they are occurring; only history adequately judges their impact, and that happens often after the fervour of the revolution has been forgotten and the consequences can be ascertained by cool and rational minds. What we do know is that the massive restructuring of industry, which has been ongoing in the United States and Britain since the early 1980s, and which has only recently begun in Germany, is part and parcel of the technological revolution. What we know also is that the globalization of the labour market, for better and for worse, is also a direct consequence of the same developments. Ultimately, the changing pattern of lives, of careers, and of transitions can be traced to the joint consequences of the end of the cold war and the fall of communism, on the one hand, and the technological revolution, on the other.

All of the papers presented in this volume deal with various aspects of the challenges that have arisen in response to the complex changes mentioned above. In looking at the various topics addressed, however, it is clear that two specific emphases emerged: the first is a focus on young people and the second is a focus on career development. Although these emphases may have emerged spontaneously, they certainly appear reasonable in any effort to understand adversity and challenge in the life course as they relate to the dramatic institutional and structural changes in the new Germany and England. Clausen (1991, 1993) and Vaillant and Vaillant (1981) have documented the fact that the choices made by men and women early in their lives have consequences for success or failure, stability or change, for the rest of their lives. Young people, especially adolescents, are therefore the logical subjects of research that attempts to understand the impact of change on the life course of individuals. A further incentive for studying adolescents is the well-recognized need to develop longitudinal data bases to enable social scientists to elucidate the relationship between institutional/ structural change and individual development. Frequently, these behavioural outcomes are cast in terms of success or failure and, in Western societies, successful lives have most often been defined in terms of occupational success (Clausen, 1993). Thus, the emphasis on the career development of young people also appears well-founded.

One additional issue becomes apparent in reviewing the collective contributions to the workshop. That issue is related to the different disciplinary backgrounds of the researchers and appears to have resulted in a predominant (although by no means exclusive) focus on analysing and comparing institutional and structural changes in society and their impact on certain groups or classes of individuals. Traditionally, sociologists and economists have been much more interested in structural change and its impact on various groups of individuals, while psychologists have tended to pay more attention to personality factors that enable particular individuals to function effectively across a variety of contexts. Perhaps because of the dramatic nature of the institutional/structural changes considered by the contributors to this volume, there appears to have been a special emphasis on these changes, but a corresponding neglect of the role of individual characteristics in accommodating those changes. The psychologist Martin Ford has stressed the necessity to conceptualize the entire person-in-context, not simply one particular aspect, attribute, or process (M. Ford, 1992). John Clausen, a prominent sociologist, expressed similar sentiments in the following way: 'At the very least, we need to identify the [personality] components that ought to be considered if we want to approximate the most important features of the functioning person at any given time, and we need to relate these components to role performance within the social structure. Then we can address the dynamic processes that produce those features through various types of socialization and social selection' (Clausen, 1991:5).

What these statements suggest is something that has become increasingly evident to me and to my collaborators over the past decade: there is a remarkable convergence, across disciplinary boundaries, regarding the desirability of embracing more comprehensive, more complex, more interdisciplinary conceptual and theoretical perspectives. Why, one might ask, is this happening now? I believe that the answer is before our eyes: the relative order and stability that prevailed in most of the industrialized societies prior to the 'information age' and prior to the end of the cold war are gone. In virtually every area of life, change is dramatic and profound, and instability and volatility appear everywhere. In this new environment, many of the models, theories and methods of the social and behavioural sciences that were based on assumptions of relative stability or gradual change over time are no longer adequate. What is needed is a comprehensive and dynamic framework that reduces or eliminates the boundaries between person and environment, is sensitive to change, and is not confined by rigid disciplinary boundaries.

Toward a comprehensive and dynamic framework for the study of person-in-context

Working in the area of life-span career development, my colleagues and I have spent more than a decade searching for a conceptual framework that focuses neither predominantly on person attributes nor on environmental conditions as the primary determinants of behaviour. Although our substantive focus has been career development, it has been our conviction that, at least in Western industrialized societies, career development is as central as any developmental process in the human life course. Consequently, it should be clear that any conceptual framework for understanding and studying career development or work must be sufficiently general to apply to human development, regardless of the specific substantive area that is the focus of study. Thus, our initial efforts led us to adapt Lerner's (1978) developmental-contextual framework to the study of career development across the lifespan (Vondracek, Lerner and Schulenberg, 1986). This represented a very deliberate effort to move the field beyond the dominant organismic models with their emphasis on normative stages that were becoming increasingly irrelevant in a world in which dramatic change had become the norm and stability the exception. The developmental–contextual framework has been influential in the field of career development (cf. Borgen, 1991) because it introduced more dynamic conceptualizations of person and environment than those offered by simple person–environment matching models (e.g., Holland, 1985). Although it has been useful as a metamodel that has influenced the way scientists and practitioners think about career development, it has been criticized as being too broad, too inclusive, and too general to promote the formulation of specific hypotheses.

Three major conceptual advances in our understanding of human behaviour and development 'in-context' represent the foundation of a new approach to career development that was introduced in 1995 as a 'comprehensive model' of career development (Vondracek and Kawasaki, 1995). They are the Living Systems Framework (LSF; D. Ford, 1987), Developmental Systems Theory (DST; D. Ford and Lerner, 1992) and Motivational Systems Theory (MST; M. Ford, 1992). Because key features of these new models explicitly deal with variables and processes that are central in individuals' efforts to deal with challenge and adversity in the life course, I will attempt to summarize them briefly.

In introducing his Living Systems Framework (LSF) for understanding humans as self- constructing living systems, D. Ford (1987) stated that his aim was to develop a conceptual framework for understanding individuals as complex, functional entities. In order to accomplish this, he conceptualized three basic phenomena that collectively account for human development: (1) the unitary functioning of the whole person-in-context; (2) the functioning of the component parts of the person; and (3) stability and change in the functioning of the component parts of the person and the person-as-a-whole. Clearly, this approach attempts to be a unifying framework because it eliminates the arbitrary boundaries between person and context. Moreover, it explicitly incorporates nomothetic knowledge (i.e., knowledge about characteristic features of development in particular populations) and ideographic knowledge (i.e., information about particular individuals) (Nesselroade and D. Ford, 1987). Although it is clear that 'a person's functioning and development cannot be understood separate from the environments in which his or her life is embedded' (Ford and Lerner, 1992:111), in this framework the person's environment does not cause the person's behavioural patterns. Instead, the features and characteristics of the individual's environment selectively facilitate or constrain possible developmental pathways. Any particular environment may be quite supportive of some pathways and obstruct others. Consequently, it makes little sense to isolate one specific behaviour from others that may be occurring at the same time.

When researchers attempt to simplify their models (for example, to facilitate hypothesis testing) they may end up forcing complex human behaviour into a simple linear cause and effect conceptual model. In fact, when examining complex, ongoing behaviour-environment patterns, it becomes apparent that they differ from one person to another and from one occasion to another 'because people vary in what they want, how they decide to go about producing the desired consequences, what they actually do, the ways they anticipate and evaluate their progress, the emotions that are aroused in relationship to the activity, the conditions of their biological functioning, the kinds of environment in which they interact, and the attributes of those environments upon which they selectively focus their transactions' (D. Ford, 1987:145). The standard response of behavioural and social scientists, when confronted with such complexity, has been to insist that neither the theory nor the methodology exist for dealing with such complexities in their research. However, this is no longer true.

In order to deal with this seemingly overwhelming complexity and to represent the unitary functioning of the whole person-in-context, the LSF proposes the concepts of behaviour episode (D. Ford, 1987:143–52) and behaviour episode schemata (D. Ford, 1987:352–8). The former represents a time-limited pattern of behaviour that occurs in a specific context and has several defining attributes. Specifically, it is guided by some form of intention or personal goal, it includes a variable pattern of activities that are selectively organized in order for the individual to accomplish the goal, and it occurs within a specific set of environmental conditions that organize the behaviour pattern in such a way as to facilitate or constrain progress toward the goal. These defining attributes require some elaboration. They include the person's goals, intentions, and hence his motivations for behaving in a certain way. They include patterns of activities, preferably skills, that help the person to accomplish the goal. Finally, they include always a specific set of contextual circumstances that either promote or inhibit progress toward the goal. Clearly, the whole person-in-context is represented in the behaviour episode. The behaviour episode is terminated when the desired goal is achieved, when some internal or external event pre-empts continued attention and directs behaviours toward a different goal, or when the evaluation of progress leads to the conclusion that the intended goal cannot be achieved on that occasion (D. Ford and Lerner, 1992). It is clear from this description that 'goals and contexts are the anchors that organize and provide coherence for the activities within a behaviour episode' (M. Ford, 1992:24).

Behaviour episodes are temporary phenomena that nevertheless collectively represent a person's past experiences. Thus, it may be assumed that people construct a repertoire of relatively enduring generalized behavioural patterns which, in the LSF, are conceptualized as behaviour episode schemata. These behaviour episode schemata represent the 'functioning of the whole person-in-context because that is what is involved in any given behaviour episode' (Ford, 1992:26). The person's total accumulation of these relatively enduring behaviour patterns may be conceptualized as personality. Viewed from this perspective, individuals' efforts to deal with the challenges and adversities of life are determined as much by their personality as by the particular life circumstances in which they may find themselves at any given point in time.

Achievement and competence

Our interest in adversities and challenges in the life course leads us to be especially interested in particular kinds of behaviour episodes and behaviour episode schemata, namely, those that represent effective functioning, i.e., those that facilitate or accomplish the person's underlying goals. In Motivational Systems Theory, effective functioning must be related to goals and contexts because they represent the anchors of behaviour episodes. At the situational, or behaviour episode level of analysis, the concept of achievement is invoked to represent effective behaviour, and it is defined as 'the attainment of a personally or socially valued goal in a particular context' (M. Ford, 1992:66). At the personality, or behaviour episode schemata level of analysis, effective functioning is defined as competence, i.e., 'the attainment of relevant goals in specified environments, using appropriate means and resulting in positive developmental outcomes' (M. Ford, 1992:67). Note that the definitions of both achievement and competence are stated in such a way that the behaviours cannot be considered apart from the contexts within which they are occurring. Because of this, generalized (trait-like) competence and achievement are rejected in favor of a more differentiated set of descriptions that are 'anchored in particular contexts and value systems that specify what goals are "relevant", what means are "appropriate", and what developmental outcomes are "positive"' (M. Ford, 1992:67).

In view of the foregoing it should be clear that competence and achievement, as conceptualized here, are quite different from the 'impoverished concepts of competence' discussed by Evans (this volume) in relation to the unsuccessful efforts of the Manpower Services Commission to promulgate policies for the preparation of adolescents for entering the work force. In the language of Motivational Systems Theory (MST), those concepts of competence were 'impoverished' because they failed to be linked to relevant personal goals, appropriate means and positive developmental outcomes. What, then, are the prerequisites for behaving effectively, i.e., for achievement to occur and for competence to be acquired? M. Ford (1992) has specified four requirements for behaviours and behaviour patterns that accomplish or facilitate progress toward the person's goal(s). The first of these is that the person must be motivated to persist in working toward the goal until it is achieved. Second, the person must have the necessary skill to produce the desired results, and third, the person's biological systems must be capable of supporting the motivation and skill aspects of the behaviour episode. Fourth, and finally, the person must be operating in a responsive environment, which is one that permits successful conclusion of the behaviour episode. It is important to note that if any one of these four ingredients of effective functioning is missing, effective functioning will not occur.

It is immediately apparent that among the contributors to this volume, some of these prerequisites have received more attention than others. One obvious focus has been the examination and comparison of institutional and social contexts, with an eye toward whether they have been more or less responsive, particularly to the needs of young people with regard to opportunity for employment and occupational success. Another focus has been the evaluation of the educational and vocational training system with regard to whether it produces individuals who have the skills necessary to be successful in the modern workplace. The issue of whether the person's biological structure and functioning support the motivation and skills components of effective functioning has rarely been addressed explicitly, because it is usually assumed that if the person achieves a certain level of skill (which can be assessed relatively easily), the person's underlying biological structures and processes are adequate. The aspect of effective functioning that has perhaps received the least attention has been the motivational component, probably because it is difficult to define, and its relationships to other aspects of behaviour are complex.

In MST, motivation is viewed as residing within the person, as future-oriented (i.e., anticipatory and preparatory in nature), and as evaluative rather than instrumental (M. Ford, 1992). What this means is that motivation cannot be imposed from outside (although circumstances that are favourable for the development of motivation can be created). It also means that motivation helps people to imagine future outcomes that may be meaningful or important to them, thereby preparing them to act in ways that produce desired futures for them. Finally, it means that motivational processes 'identify and "size up" problems and opportunities' (M. Ford, 1992:73). The importance of these processes in the efforts of individuals to deal with the adversities and challenges presented by the new political, technological, economic and social realities of the twenty-first century cannot be overstated. Consequently, it would seem to be reasonable to focus increased efforts in research and intervention on gaining a better understanding of the specific processes involved in human motivation.

There are three basic motivational components in the Living Systems Framework (D. Ford, 1987), which are described in M. Ford's (1992) MST as 'the organized patterning of an individuals' personal goals, emotions, and personal agency beliefs' (p. 78). This statement requires some elaboration and clarification. Personal goals are viewed as representing directive cognitive processes. In effect, their content represents future desired consequences (or undesired consequences that are to be avoided) and their basic process is to direct the other components of the person to engage in activities designed to produce these consequences. It is important to understand in this context that goals assigned by parents, teachers, or employers, or culturally defined goals, can have a motivational impact only if they are accepted as personal goals. Clearly, further research is needed to enhance our understanding of interventions that may be used in helping people to incorporate socially, economically, and morally desirable goals without compromising the basic freedoms of democratic society.

Personal agency beliefs represent the second component of motivation. M. Ford (1992) prefers the term personal agency beliefs to other, related concepts such as control beliefs (Skinner, Chapman and Baltes, 1988), expectancy (Atkinson, 1964; McClelland, 1985), and self-efficacy (Bandura, 1982; Betz and Hackett, 1986) because personal agency beliefs include both beliefs about one's own personal capabilities and beliefs related to the context in which one is attempting to realize one's goals. In other words, capability beliefs refer to the person's assessment about whether he or she has the capabilities (e.g., skills, knowledge, energy) to achieve a particular goal, while context beliefs refer to the person's expectation of whether his or her context will facilitate or support the achievement of the goal. Considering the two independently misses the important observation that it is the patterning of these two processes that ultimately determines whether the person will pursue a personal goal or decide not to do so (M. Ford, 1992). The third and final component of motivation according to MST involves the person's emotional arousal processes. Because emotions arouse the person to deal with problems and opportunities, they represent an important source of motivational energy. In a sense, they provide the person with additional evaluative information that is anticipatory in nature and may prepare the person to proceed toward a goal or to abandon it.

In summary, M. Ford's (1992) MST proposes that personal goals, emotions, and personal agency beliefs operate in complex, non-linear patterns in every behaviour episode. All three of these components are necessary for success in achieving a particular goal. For example, even if a person has well-defined goals, is emotionally activated, and believes that the requisite skills are in place, little will be accomplished if the person has extremely negative context beliefs and thus feels that the context will not facilitate or be supportive of his or her efforts. The person is likely to feel discouraged or hopeless. When something like this happens, the behaviour episode is usually abandoned because the goal may seem unattainable, or because another, presumably less difficult, goal is substituted. On the other hand, if context beliefs are positive and capability beliefs are strong, a robust personal agency belief pattern prevails and effective functioning is a likely outcome.

Conclusions

If science is to play an important role in helping individuals to deal successfully with the adversities and challenges of life, questions regarding achievement and the development of competence have to be moved to the forefront of the research agenda. Given the intimate link between motivation and the development of competence, researchers should heed the statement that 'motivation is at the heart of many of society's most pervasive and enduring problems, both as a developmental outcome of demotivating social environments and as a developmental influence on behaviour and personality' (M. Ford, 1992:201). From this perspective, motivation represents the psychological foundation for dealing with adversities and challenges, and for developing competence in everyday life.

For social and behavioural scientists the consequences of accepting this perspective are far-reaching. First and foremost, the adoption of a broader, more comprehensive, conceptual framework that cuts across disciplinary boundaries and addresses the whole person-in-context should be a priority. D. Ford's (1987) Living Systems Framework represents such a model, but because of its complexity and sheer volume (almost 800 pages) it has not been utilized widely. One exception is M. Ford's (1992) Motivational Systems Theory, which has succeeded in showing the utility of comprehensive theoretical frameworks in guiding research and in developing applications that are useful in dealing with adversities and challenges in the real world.

When scientists adopt conceptual models that represent all of the component processes of the person, and that show how these processes are organized in complex patterns of unitary functioning in the variety of human environments, the collection of research data that portrays both people and their environments is critical. Obviously, it is still necessary to be selective in data collection. One of the advantages of having an explicit and comprehensive theoretical framework, however, is that it can guide the selection of variables to be assessed and therefore of data to be collected. For example, MST offers a detailed framework for classifying and examining personal goals. It also offers guidance for the assessment of personal agency beliefs and for examining how specific patterns of personal agency beliefs influence how people go about pursuing their goals. The unit of analysis in the LSF and in MST is always the person-in- context. Consequently, the LSF and MST offer guidance on classification and assessment of environments.

Clearly, the use of the conceptual models that have been introduced above will not solve many of the significant problems facing scientists and practitioners who deal with the dramatically altered realities of a rapidly changing world. Advances in information technology will only further accelerate the change processes currently underway. One of the by-products of the age of information technology is to overwhelm the capacity of people of all walks of life to organize and use information effectively. Reinventing the wheel is one symptom of being overwhelmed with information. Scientists are not immune to this error. Consequently, there may be a tendency to propose new models and new methods without, however, giving proper attention to extant theories and models that are being superseded not by better ones but by newer ones. I hope that my comments will prevent that error and result in the thoughtful evaluation and use of some of the innovative work that I have described, however, inadequately, in the preceding pages.

References

Atkinson, J. W. (1964) *An Introduction to Motivation*. Princeton, NJ: Van Nostrand.

Bandura, A. (1982) 'Self-efficacy mechanism and human agency', *American Psychologist*, **7**: 122–47.

Betz, N. E. and Hackett, G. (1986) 'Applications of self-efficacy theory to understanding career choice behaviour', *Journal of Social and Clinical Psychology*, **4**: 279–89.

Borgen, F. H. (1991) 'Megatrends and milestones in vocational behaviour: a 20-year counseling psychology retrospective', *Journal of Vocational Behaviour*, **39**: 263–90.

Clausen, J. A. (1991) 'Adolescent competence and the shaping of the life course', *American Journal of Sociology*, **96**: 805–42.

Clausen, J. A. (ed.) (1993) *American Lives: Looking Back at the Children of the Great Depression*. Berkeley, CA: University of California Press.

Ford, D. H. (1987) *Humans as Self-constructing Living Systems: A Developmental Perspective on Behaviour and Personality*. Hillsdale, NJ: Lawrence Erlbaum.

Ford, D. H. and Lerner, R. M. (1992) *Developmental Systems Theory: An Integrative Approach*. Newbury Park, CA: Sage.

Ford, M. E (1992) *Motivating Humans: Goals, Emotions, and Personal Agency Beliefs*. Newbury Park, CA: Sage.

Holland, J. L. (1985) *Making Vocational Choices: A Theory of Vocational Personalities and Work Environments* (2nd edn). Englewood Cliffs, NJ: Prentice-Hall.

Lerner, R. M. (1978) 'Nature, nurture, and dynamic interactionism', *Human Development*, **21**: 1–20.

McClelland, D. C. (1985) *Human Motivation*. Glenview, IL: Scott, Foresman.

Nesselroade, J. R. and Ford, D. H. (1987) 'Methodological considerations in modeling living systems', in M. E. Ford and D. H. Ford (eds), *Humans as Self-constructing Living Systems: Putting the Framework to Work* (pp. 47–79). Hillsdale, NJ: Lawrence Erlbaum.

Skinner, E. A., Chapman, M. and Baltes, P. B. (1988) 'Control, means–ends, and agency beliefs: a new conceptualization and its measurement during childhood', *Journal of Personality and Social Psychology*, **54**: 117–33.

Vaillant, G. E. and Vaillant, C. O. (1981) 'Natural history of male psychological health, X: work as a predictor of positive mental health', *American Journal of Psychiatry*, **138**: 1433–41.

Vondracek, F. W. and Kawasaki, T. (1995) 'Toward a comprehensive framework for adult career development theory and intervention', in W. B.Walsh and S. H. Osipow (eds), *Handbook of Vocational Psychology: Theory, Research, and Practice* (pp. 111–41). Hillsdale, NJ: Lawrence Erlbaum.

Vondracek, F. W., Lerner, R. M. and Schulenberg, J. E. (1986) *Career Development: A Life-span Developmental Approach*. Hillsdale, NJ: Lawrence Erlbaum.

Index